GERMAN LABOR COURTS

GERMAN LABOR COURTS

BY

FRIEDA WUNDERLICH

WITH A CHAPTER ON THE LABOR COURTS
IN THE GERMAN JUDICIAL SYSTEM

BY ERNST FRAENKEL

CHAPEL HILL
THE UNIVERSITY OF NORTH CAROLINA PRESS
1946

COPYRIGHT, 1946, BY THE

UNIVERSITY OF NORTH CAROLINA PRESS

PRINTED IN THE UNITED STATES OF AMERICA

PREFACE

I AM DEEPLY INDEBTED to Ernst Fraenkel, outstanding attorney for the German trade unions under the Republic. Dr. Fraenkel went over the entire manuscript in detail, making valuable additions, interpreting the German system to the American reader, and contributing from his own rich experience. I further record my indebtedness to Ulrich Katz and George M. Wunderlich, who read the manuscript and contributed suggestions. Dr. Katz has painstakingly checked and rechecked data with unfailing patience. Herbert Solow has done the final laborious editing. To Alvin Johnson every page, every word, represents a debt of unending gratitude.

For permission to quote from Ernst Fraenkel's *The Dual State* and Gregor Ziemer's *Education for Death* I wish to thank the authors and the Oxford University Press.

GLOSSARY OF ABBREVIATIONS

The following abbreviations are commonly used in the German literature referring to the statutes, organizations, and publications in question; full titles are rarely, if ever, cited.

- **ADGB** Allgemeiner Deutscher Gewerkschaftsbund, General Federation of Free Trade Unions (Socialistic)
- **Afa** Allgemeiner Freier Angestelltenbund, General League of Free Trade Unions of Salaried Employees (Socialistic)
- **AGG** Arbeitsgerichtsgesetz, Labor Court Act
- **AOG** Gesetz zur Ordnung der nationalen Arbeit, National Socialist Labor Act
- **ARS** *Arbeitsrechtssammlung*, Continuation of *RAG*, Collection of Court Decisions. Roman numerals refer to volume; Arabic numerals to page; and unless otherwise indicated all references are to Part I
- **BRG** Betriebsrätegesetz, Works Council Act
- **DAF** Deutsche Arbeitsfront, German Labor Front
- **DGB** Deutscher Gewerkschaftsbund, German Confederation of Trade Unions (Christian workmen and salaried employees)
- **DHV** Deutschnationaler Handlungsgehilfenverband, German National Trade Union of Commercial Employees (Christian, affiliated to Gedag)
- **DJ** *Deutsche Justiz*, German Official Law Gazette
- **GDA** Gewerkschaftsbund Der Angestellten, Trade Union League of Salaried Employees (Liberal, affiliated to the Ring)
- **Gedag** Gesamtverband Deutscher Angestelltengewerkschaften, Christian Salaried Employees' Federation (affiliated to DGB)
- **GGG** Gewerbegerichtsgesetz, Industrial Court Act
- **GO** Gewerbeordnung, Industrial Code
- **JW** *Juristische Wochenschrift*, Periodical published by the German Bar Association (Deutscher Anwaltsverein).

GLOSSARY OF ABBREVIATIONS

KGG Kaufmannsgerichtsgesetz, Commercial Court Act
NSBO Nationalsozialistische Betriebszellenorganisation, National Socialist Shop Cell Organization
NSDAP Nationalsozialistische Deutsche Arbeiter Partei, German National Socialist Workers Party
PrG *Preussische Gesetzsammlung*, Collection of Prussian Laws
RABl *Reichsarbeitsblatt*, Government Labor Gazette. Roman numerals refer to parts. Unless otherwise indicated section one, official part, is referred to. Arabic numerals refer to years and pages.
RAG *Entscheidungen des Reichsarbeitsgerichts und der Landesarbeitsgerichte*, ed. by Hermann Dersch and others. Labor Court Decisions quoted with volume of this collection. ARS is a continuation. Roman numerals refer to volume; Arabic numerals to pages; and unless otherwise indicated all references are to Part I.
RGBl *Reichsgesetzblatt*, Official Law Gazette. Since 1922 it has been published in two parts. The Roman numerals refer to the parts. The Arabic numerals refer to years and pages.
RGZ *Entscheidungen des Reichsgerichts in Zivilsachen*, Official collection of Civil Law Decisions of the Federal Supreme Court
Ring Gewerkschaftsring Deutscher Arbeiter-, Angestellten- und Beamtenverbände, Confederation of Workers, Salaried Employees and Civil Servants (liberal)
RTA Reichstreuhänder der Arbeit, Federal Trustee of Labor
RVO Reichsversicherungsordnung, Social Insurance Code
RWR Vorläufiger Reichswirtschaftsrat, Provisional National Economic Council
SA Schutzabteilung, Storm Troops
SS Schutzstaffel, Elite Guard
SP *Soziale Praxis*, Periodical
VH *Vierteljahrshefte zur Statistik des Deutschen Reichs*, Official Statistical Quarterly
Vela Vereinigung Leitender Angestellter, Federation of Executive Employees
ZdA Zentralverband der Angestellten, Union of Salaried Employees (affiliated to Afa)
ZPO Zivilprozessordnung, Code of Civil Procedure

CONTENTS

	PAGE
Preface	v
Glossary of Abbreviations	vii

INTRODUCTION: THE LABOR COURTS IN THE GERMAN
    JUDICIAL SYSTEM   3

HISTORICAL SURVEY OF GERMAN LABOR COURTS

1. Developments up to 1891 21
2. The System from 1891 to 1927 25
    Industrial Courts
        Organization—Jurisdiction—Procedure—Conciliation—Functions—Administrative Functions
    Other Special Courts 29
    The Period of the First World War 31
    1901-1918 in the Light of Statistics 33
    An Appraisal of Industrial and Commercial Courts 34
    The Post-War Period: 1918-1927 40
        Background—Amendments and Emergency Solutions—Survey—Reform Discussions

THE DEVELOPED SYSTEM (1927-1933)

3. Legal Regulations 59
    The Constitution of Labor Judicial Authorities . 60
        Labor Courts—District Labor Courts—Federal Labor Court
    Jurisdiction 65
    Procedure 71
    Summary Procedure 78
    Exclusion of Labor Court Jurisdiction . . . 79

CONTENTS—Continued

	PAGE
4. The System in Action	83
Territory of Courts and Chambers	83
Chairmen and Assessors	86
The Work of the Courts in the Light of Statistics	92
5. Appraisal	106
Structure and Performance	107
Technical Structure and Every-day Litigation—Interpretation of the New Labor Law	
Trade Unions and the Labor Courts	120
Representation in Courts—Appointment of Assessors—Agreed Arbitral Bodies	
Summary	133

THE PERIOD OF NATIONAL SOCIALISM

6. The Change in Labor Relations	137
7. Labor Courts in the Judicial System	151
Introduction	151
Justice and Labor Law Jurisdiction	153
Political Justice	163
Dispersal of Jurisdiction	172
Summary	185
Appendices	187
Labor Law before 1918	189
Labor Law under the Weimar Republic	191
Trade Unions	200
Notes	205
Bibliography	237
Index	241

INTRODUCTION

THE LABOR COURTS
IN THE GERMAN JUDICIAL SYSTEM*

By ERNST FRAENKEL

THE UNDERSTANDING of special problems of foreign law, such as the German Labor Court statute, is possible only if the reader is familiar with some general underlying legal principles. Students of special problems of foreign law run definite dangers. They tend to take it for granted that fundamental institutions existing in their own time and country also control legal systems in general. Hence, at the very beginning of this treatise, it is essential to stress the fact that every special legal provision within the German legal system is understandable only within the framework of that system. This holds especially true for rules of procedure and evidence, the topic of this study. In order to avoid grave misunderstandings of the frequently-used terms of the German law of procedure and evidence, a few general remarks concerning the basic difference between German and Anglo-American law of procedure and evidence seem advisable.

Although, to be sure, the translation of the English word "court" as "Gericht" is absolutely correct, one must recognize the fact that German law knows nothing comparable to the Anglo-Saxon legal institution called "the court," characterized basically by its universal jurisdiction. German law is characterized by the co-existence of a variety of *kinds* of courts, a variety originating in the basic distinction between private and

*This introduction is primarily concerned with the German court system as it existed before 1933.

public law. The court, in the narrower German sense, has jurisdiction only in conflicts involving questions of private and criminal law. In Germany, legal problems concerning public law have long been decided by special *administrative* courts, bodies quite distinct from courts in the narrower sense. It would be misleading to call these institutions "administrative tribunals," since they meet completely the definition of a "court" in the German law. Their members are independent with respect to the decisions they render in particular cases. The test of whether a state agency is to be called a "court" in accordance with German law is relatively simple. Unlike administrative agencies, which are subject to instructions from superior officials in each individual case, a state agency is a court if its members are subject to the law and only the law. The role played by German courts within the system of German law is characterized by the antagonism between legally independent judicial bodies and a hierarchical, centralized bureaucracy entrusted with the state administrative functions.

Each—courts in the narrower sense and administrative courts—represents an independent system with its own courts of appeal and review instances. No ordinary court can exercise judicial review of a decision of an administrative court or vice versa. German law long recognized co-existent "highest" courts but no universal Supreme Court in the American sense.

These general remarks have definite significance for the understanding of the special problems to be studied here. In social insurance, compulsory in Germany during some sixty years for old age, invalidity, sickness, and industrial accidents, and in unemployment insurance, compulsory since 1927, legal relations between the insured and a social insurance institution have been regarded as part of public law. Cases arising out of the application of social insurance statutes belonged, therefore, to the jurisdiction of special federal administrative courts. Labor courts had nothing to do with such problems. It should be noted that all problems of workman's compensation are beyond the jurisdiction of the labor courts, since every German worker is insured against industrial accidents. Claims of workers in case of industrial accidents are directed not against an employer but rather against a social insurance institution.

A similar situation has existed with regard to civil service law. As soon as a person was appointed to civil service by the Reich, by a state, by a municipality, or by any other institution of public law, his legal relations with the legal entity which appointed him formed part of public law. Civil servants enjoy special protection in German law. They are appointed for life and can be dismissed only for special causes enumerated by statute. The question of whether a civil servant is subject to dismissal or any disciplinary punishment is in the jurisdiction of special federal and state administrative courts; neither the ordinary courts nor the labor courts can interfere with the procedure of these special courts. The decisions of the latter are not subject to judicial review. The Reich, the states, and other institutions of public law are, however, subject to the rules of private law in any case in which they do not exercise governmental functions, but in which rather, like private persons, they participate in the ordinary processes of economic and social life. As soon as the Reich or a state acts in the realm of private law, it is called "Fiscus" and may be sued both in contract and tort in ordinary courts. It should be noted, furthermore, that not every person who renders services to an institution of public law enjoys the special privileges granted by public law to civil servants. By far the greater part of those who render services to the Reich, the states, etc., are considered private law employees. They stand in contractual relations with the "Fiscus" and may sue their employer both in contract and tort in the labor courts in accordance with the labor court statute. It may be noted that, although the National Socialist German Workers Party (Nationalsozialistische Deutsche Arbeiterpartei, henceforth referred to as NSDAP), has the character of an institution of public law, because of a special statute of December 1, 1933,[1] employees of the NSDAP may sue it in the labor courts, provided that they do not exercise functions considered to be governmental.

Since the German administrative courts are true courts in the proper meaning of that term, their decisions are recognized as *res judicata* by ordinary courts and vice versa. Acts of administrative agencies are, however, to a large extent subject to judicial review. Where no decision has been rendered by an administrative court in a particular case, a court may decide the validity of an administrative act as a collateral issue if the decision depends upon the question of whether or not the administrative act was legal. This holds true both for ordinary courts and labor courts. The most famous German labor case, for instance, was concerned with the question whether a collective agreement brought about by means of compulsory arbitration was valid; the decision depended upon the question of whether the arbitration authority had acted within its jurisdiction. The real issue of the case was the problem of the extent to which the labor court was entitled to subject acts of the state arbitration authority to judicial review. The principle that questions of discretion cannot be reviewed by courts whereas questions of law may be, led in Germany to the same theoretical and practical difficulties as exist here.

On account of the fact that several independent court systems exist within Germany, each court is compelled first to determine whether it has jurisdiction in any particular case. Preexamination as to the functional jurisdiction of the court implies an ex-officio decision as to whether the issue belongs to private or public law and, furthermore, whether a particular case in private law comes within the jurisdiction of an ordinary court or of a special court, such as the labor court. The problems of functional jurisdiction belong to the most difficult problems of German law. Very nice distinctions of substantive law control this basic question. The problem is the more significant inasmuch as the decision of a court lacking functional jurisdiction is considered null and void. These considerations may explain why so much of this treatise is concerned with the problem of the jurisdictional scope of labor courts. The problem is extremely knotty since the general rule that both ordinary and labor courts have jurisdiction only over suits in private law is subject to very significant exceptions. Both political considerations and convenience influenced the legislator to give, by special statute, jurisdiction to ordinary courts in some matters of public law and to deprive ordinary courts of their jurisdiction in other matters involving private law. No general "due process" clause prevents the German legislator from shifting jurisdiction. This problem is particularly acute in the field of labor law. The history of the German labor court statute, which will be dealt with in this essay, is to a considerable extent a struggle between private law and public law, veiled under a mask of disputes over jurisdictional and procedural problems.

But this distinction between the single court system of Anglo-American law and the plural court system of German law is not sufficient to explain the danger involved in the uncritical application of the term "court" to all institutions called "Gericht" in German. The translation of legal terms is by no means exclusively or primarily a problem of philology but rather belongs to the field of comparative law. A German scholar, for example, would at first tend to translate the term "commission," used so frequently in American administration, as "Verwaltungsgericht," since its members function independently. But as soon as he learns that the decisions rendered by these commissions are subject to court review, he would probably lean toward "Verwaltungsbehörden" as a better translation. In the end he is likely to abandon all attempts at translation and to speak of "Kommissionen," thus applying the rule that often the best translation is no translation whatsoever. Since, however, the use of foreign terms is stylistically disagreeable, an author dealing with problems of foreign law must ask his reader from the very beginning to imagine all legal terms of the foreign legal system as bearing invisible quotation marks.

The application of English terms to institutions of German law leads to results which are at best approximately correct. This statement may be proved with respect to the German legal institution "Gericht," i. e., "court." An American will look in vain for a jury in any German court. For centuries German law knew no juries in private law cases; in criminal cases jury trial was abolished in 1923 by a simple emergency decree. The fact that the abolition of trial by jury after seventy-five years of the use of this procedure was scarcely opposed or criticized, is ample proof that the institution was never deeply rooted in German life or legal thought. Public opinion did not notice the disappearance of juries. But the absence of juries does not mean that laymen are excluded from a role in the judicial process in Germany. The German court system is rather characterized by close collaboration between trained judges and laymen. The latter serve as associate judges on the bench beside a presiding judge, always a trained jurisprudent, and sometimes beside one or more trained associate judges. The learned and lay judges together form "the court" and decide by majority vote questions both of facts and of law on the basis of common deliberations. Learned and lay judges have the same voting power. This system exists both in criminal and administrative law and in all first instance cases of the law merchant.

This treatise will deal with the application of this principle, so typical of German law, to labor cases. It may be noted, however, that ordinary private law cases, such as property, contracts, tort, and family relation cases, are decided by courts in which no laymen serve as judges.

The absence of trial by jury implies that there is in the German legal system nothing comparable to the American law of evidence. Instead of the complicated rules of American law of evidence, German law provides that the court, and to a considerable extent the presiding judge, decides in its own discretion whether or not evidence shall be excluded or admitted. The significance of this statement is understandable only if one takes into consideration the contrasting roles which judge and counsel play in American and German law. Contrary to American law, the witnesses in German courts are examined by the presiding judge and not by counsel of the parties. The German code of procedure provides that in exceptional cases counsel may examine witnesses directly and on cross. But this provision has no significance whatsoever. I can recall no case in which this provision was applied nor can several other former members of the German bar whom I have consulted. The attempt to introduce the Anglo-Saxon system of examination and cross-examination into German law was a failure, for both the German bar and bench regarded the German system as satisfactory. It may even be doubted whether the majority of German judges and attorneys were familiar with the fact that there existed a legal possibility of substituting examination and cross-examination by counsel for examination by the presiding judge.

In Germany the judge decides (a) which witnesses shall be examined and (b) what questions shall be put to them. His decisions on both points are based on briefs and oral pleas by the parties. A German brief sets forth not only the facts but also the names of the witnesses and descriptions of other means of evidence which the parties desire to be examined by the court. Whether or not they deal in their briefs also with legal problems is up to the parties.

As compared with American law, the German law of pleading is very informal. An American lawyer visiting a German court and reading the files may even get the impression that no law of pleading exists. The briefs constitute primarily a mere preparation for trial.

In the trial courts, counsels (or the parties) make statements with respect to facts and means of evidence suggested in the preparatory briefs. If the German lawyer uses the term "plead" (plädieren), he has in mind any *oral* statement of counsel concerned with questions of fact, law, evidence, or procedure. Even in this stage, the presiding judge plays a significant role. It is his duty to discuss the case with counsel both from the point of view of fact and of law. He may make suggestions and raise questions in order to clarify the issues as much as possible. The associate judges, whether learned or lay, have the same function. Because of the relatively insignificant role played by counsel in the German court system, it is not up to the parties to "take issue." The court decides which facts are relevant and must be proved by one or the other party in accordance with legal rules which fix the problem of burden of proof. A court order regulating all questions of evidence for the particular case (Beweisbeschluss) enumerates in detail those facts on which witnesses will be examined by the court. Witnesses, according to German legal theory, are not witnesses of the parties but witnesses of the court. As a rule, German lawyers are not permitted to pre-examine witnesses before they testify in court. What is called in Anglo-American law "the preparation of a case," is considered in Germany a violation of legal ethics. Acts of counsel during the decisive stage of the case, i.e., the examination of witnesses, are very much restricted in German law: they may merely, after the presiding judge has examined a witness, raise some additional questions as permitted by presiding judge in his own discretion. The American reader may be astonished to learn that neither statements by counsel nor the testimony of witnesses is recorded verbatim in shorthand. The German code of procedure gives the presiding judge the task of summarizing the testimony by dictating its essence to a clerk in the presence of counsel. The judge makes the record of the trial. No report of a German law suit contains the questions and answers so characteristic of American case reports.

Lest this statement create a false impression with respect to the finding of fact in German courts, the reader must take into consideration the character of German courts of appeal. In civil as well as in criminal cases, parties may introduce new evidence in courts of appeal and ask the court to re-examine witnesses examined in the court of first instance. Although in a restricted sense, the court of appeals functions as a second trial court. There is a strong tendency in German law to bar from appellate courts evidence which they failed to produce in the first instance. The German labor court system particularly is characterized by an attempt to concentrate the examination of witnesses in the labor court proper, i. e., in the first instance. These problems will be discussed below.

The fact that laymen serve as associate judges not only in the labor courts but also in the labor appellate courts, may partly be explained by the fact that labor appellate courts are also fact-finding tribunals. The labor appellate courts, like ordinary appellate courts, decide, on the basis of trial record and the briefs of the parties, whether witnesses shall be re-examined or further evidence introduced. It should be emphasized that examination of witnesses by the appellate courts is by no means exceptional.

Contrary to the appellate courts, the highest courts are restricted to questions of law. Both questions of procedure and substantive law are subject to review in the highest courts, but questions of evidence are open only in a very restricted sense. This treatise will deal with the particular fact that, in labor cases, even in the highest court, laymen serve as associate judges, a legal rule unparalleled in the German court system. This provision may be explained by the ubiquity of "mixed questions of law and fact" in labor cases. Mixed questions of law and fact are the proper domain of lay judges. Since the lay judge is familiar with the mores of every day life, he is frequently far better equipped to decide these nice questions than is the learned judge. The basic idea of the German court system can be found in the consideration that a sound decision may result from the collaboration of learned and lay judges jointly discussing an individual case from different angles. It is taken for granted that the learned judge will underline the legal aspect, whereas the lay judge will emphasize experience and common sense.

Aside from factors deeply rooted in history, the fact that German law knows nothing comparable to jury trial may suffice to explain that the distinction between "law" and "equity" is foreign to German law. This does not mean, however, that "equitable" considerations are insignificant in the German legal system. Quite the contrary. All German law is overshadowed by a few very broad provisions similar to the estoppel doctrine of Anglo-American law. It is up to the court to decide in an individual case whether to apply the precise provisions of statute or these broad provisions which are, as a matter of principle, also laid down in statutes. In fact, however, these very broad provisions lack precision to an extent that they can be understood only as a sort of delegation to the court to decide individual cases in accordance with its own belief as to what is just and in accord with precedent. The whole German law of labor conflicts, for instance, was based on three basic provisions of the Civil Code (Bürgerliches Gesetzbuch), Sections 157, 242, 826,[2] which have meaning only in the light of precedent. As a consequence of the ever-increasing significance of these broad statutory provisions, a very definite tendency existed in German law which may be characterized by the phrase "from statute to precedent." There is no longer any validity in the frequently elaborated theory that the basic distinction between civil law countries and common law countries may be found in the emphasis laid on statute in civil law countries and on precedent in common law countries. The growing significance of statutory law in the Anglo-American legal system matches the growing significance of precedents in Germany. Starting from opposite poles, the two systems have been marching toward each other until they are, at least in this respect, no longer very far from each other. Under these circumstances, it is obvious that the appointment of laymen as associate judges in the highest court in labor cases has a great significance for the development of substantive labor law.

It is the theory, set forth in these introductory remarks, that the basic distinction between American and German law must be found far more in procedure and evidence than in substantive law.

The American student of the German labor court system should familiarize himself with the roles of judge and counsel in ordinary German court proceedings in order to understand the most significant problem of this study, namely, the exclusion of members of the bar from labor courts of first instance and the admission of officers of bona fide trade unions and employer organizations as counsel of parties to a suit. The pros and cons of this rule will be discussed below. But here it must be emphasized that this step is by no means as revolutionary in the German legal system as might appear to the American reader. The central figure in all German trial court proceedings is not the attorney but the judge. One must not overlook the oft-repeated statement that Common Law is a judge-made law; no less significant is the fact that in the German legal system the judge has a power in many respects more important than he has in common law countries. A realistic analysis of the court acts in all countries will lead to the conclusion that the overwhelming majority of all cases depends not on the decision of legal but rather on factual questions. When one combines the legal with a sociological approach and turns one's attention from "the law" as laid down in statute books and court decisions, to the law as a force in everyday life, one may conclude that court decisions in common law countries are based on "attorney-made facts," in civil law countries on "judge-made facts." From a sociological point of view, American law must be characterized as "attorney law," German law as "judge law."

The exclusion of members of the bar as counsel in first instance labor courts implies a tremendous increase of the power of the presiding judge. It is one of the foremost tasks of this study to analyze in detail the position of the German judge in a sort of procedure which is, perhaps, less formal than any other court procedure under modern conditions of life.

The advocates of the German labor court system have praised this lack of formality. Labor and other progressive forces within the Weimar Republic looked on the labor court statute as one of the proudest achievements of German democracy. It is, therefore, prima facie the more astonishing that the Hitler regime did not substantially alter the German labor court statute of 1926 but rather borrowed some of its most characteristic provisions for his general law of civil procedure. This fact may serve as an excuse for some general remarks with respect to the historical significance of the German law of procedure and evidence which found its climax in the Labor Court Act.

The organization and function of the courts within a given system of law is primarily a problem of constitutional law. Like all other constitutional questions, this one is understandable only from the historical point of view. Students of comparative law who are familiar with common law and who seek to deal with civil law (or vice versa), should not overlook the crucial significance of the early seventeenth century for the understanding of the basic distinctions between the two systems of law. Civil law countries witnessed, in that period, the rise of absolutism, a revolutionary interruption of the organic historical development which, thanks to the Puritan and Glorious revolutions was avoided in England. On the Continent, the tendencies usually labelled in English constitutional history as Tudor and Stuart absolutism were successful; neither German nor French history knows a historic figure comparable to Lord Coke. In both countries common law courts were swept away. The absolute state created by Richelieu (1585-1642) in France and copied on German territory first by Friedrich Wilhelm the Grand Elector of Brandenburg (1640-1688) was based on a hierarchical centralized bureaucracy. Administration was the nucleus of the absolute state. In Prussia the courts were nothing but sections of this universal bureaucracy.

The bureaucratic character of the German courts is deeply rooted in the absolutism which was characteristic of the formative period of modern German history. German judges remain today primarily civil servants within a specific, bureaucratic hierarchy. The judge is appointed by the Minister of Justice. The idea of elected judges has always been completely foreign to German law. The bench is wholly separated from the bar. Only in very exceptional cases are former attorneys appointed as judges. As a rule, the young jurist, after having passed his examinations, decides whether he will become a member of the bench or a member of the bar. Once appointed a noncommissioned judge, he is on the lowest level of a career in many respects similar to the career of an officer in the army or of a civil servant in the administrative hierarchy. Although he has enjoyed independence with respect to decisions in individual cases, the judge has always been supervised by superior officials. The chief justice of a given court is not only the presiding judge; he is also the representative of the Minister of Justice. Reports written by associate judges are of the greatest significance for their professional career. Neither public opinion nor members of the bar have much opportunity to check the abilities of an individual judge. The decisions rendered by the German courts are characterized by their anonymity, and "dissenting opinions" are not published. Frequently in German courts an associate judge must write the opinion of the court although he voted against it in the secret executive meeting of the court. The secrecy of the meeting is considered vital to the maintenance of the authority of the court. German law looks on the judge not as an individual, but rather as an instrument of an agency of the state. Removed from the control of public opinion, the individual judge depends completely, as far as his career is concerned, on the opinion of his superiors. To reach a higher level in the judicial hierarchy is not only a financial object but also a question of social prestige. For the individual judge, the latter point of view is particularly significant in Germany since, as a heritage from bureaucratic absolutism, the German nation remains divided into social castes whose members have little social contact with each other. If one takes into consideration the fact that the chief of the judicial agencies also controls the career of state attorneys, sheriffs, recording officers, clerks of the courts, etc., one may imagine how significant are the problems handled by the "administration of the judiciary" (Justizverwaltung).

The various hierarchical bureaucracies within the individual states and the German Reich have a peculiar character due to a centuries-old tradition. The question of whether a given state agency forms a part of this or that bureaucratic hierarchy is, therefore, of decisive significance for the spirit prevailing in this agency. This problem became acute with respect to labor courts. This treatise will discuss at considerable length the organizational question of whether the labor courts were to be regarded as part of the judicial machinery or to be incorporated into the administration and supervised by the Minister for Social Affairs. In studying these problems, the American reader should keep in mind that in all periods of modern history administrative agencies have played a far more significant role in the thinking of the average German than have courts. Educated in the traditions of mercantilism, the German bureaucracy and the German masses always looked on economic liberalism as an alien theory. Reliance on the state, rather than protection from the state has characterized the attitude of the man on the street.

The struggle over these organizational questions raged for many years and was finally settled by a compromise. Although *de jure* "courts" in the German meaning of this word, the labor courts acquired to a large extent the character of social agencies. The judge in the labor court looks on most of the cases which he has to decide as on questions to be settled from the point of view of *social justice* rather than as problems which have to be decided in accordance with *statutes* and *precedents*. The judge in the labor court is, in very truth, primarily an administrator.

In no stage of procedure is the judge more powerful than in his unceasing efforts to persuade the parties to settle by voluntary agreement. In reality voluntary agreements are nothing else but the acceptance of the proposals of the presiding judge, who often makes outright threats of an adverse verdict to force such an agreement, threats necessarily successful wherever no appeal is possible. Both the German Code of Civil Procedure[3] and the statute concerning labor courts provide that the trial judge should regard it as his primary duty to bring parties together rather than to render a decision. There are even no legal objections to voluntary agreements settling problems at least partly beyond the issue of the case or the jurisdiction of the court. Stimulated by his superiors to settle as many cases as possible by means of voluntary agreements, the individual judge is quite familiar with the fact that those responsible for his future career may consider those judges the best whose records indicate the highest percentage of voluntary agreements. From a sociological point of view it is misleading to call the German labor courts "trial courts": primarily they must be regarded as institutions entrusted with the task of settling conflicts on the basis of considerations of social expediency.

The statistics discussed in this treatise as to the number of cases settled by means of voluntary agreements do not completely reveal the significance of the problem involved. Even in exceptional cases in which voluntary agreements could not be achieved by the presiding judge, the latter's attempts to reach one may have had a definite significance for the final decision. The statutes provide that, at the very beginning of the trial—even before formal statements have been made by the parties or witnesses have been examined—the presiding judge is obliged to make an effort at a settlement. In this stage of procedure, even the most gifted judge is unable to suggest a solution which takes merits into consideration. The settlement advocated by the presiding judge is, therefore, necessarily based primarily on his instinctive feelings. Once having expressed an opinion as to what solution might seem reasonable from the point of view of social expediency, he is biased for the remainder of the proceedings.

The position of the judge within a given legal system is fully understandable only if two different points of view are taken into consideration. The power entrusted to the judge in relation to the individual parties is one side of the picture; his power in relation to the legislator and the executive is the other. Although far more powerful in his relation to the individual parties than is his American colleague, the German judge has never enjoyed a position comparable to that of a common law judge in relation to the legislator and the executive.

The separation of the administration and the judiciary, after both had been merged in the period of early absolutism was, particularly in Prussia, an achievement of enlightened despotism, i.e., of Natural Law. Natural Law provided that the judge be independent insofar as the decision of individual cases is concerned. Within the German legal system, the independence of the judge was always restricted to judicial functions in a narrower sense. In common law countries, the jurisdiction of the judiciary is based on acts traditionally exercised by the courts; in Germany, the courts have been entrusted with those powers which correspond to an idea of the judiciary in accordance with Montesquieu's maxims concerning the separation of powers. An analysis of the role played by the judiciary in the two systems of law must, even today, take into consideration the real situation of the judiciary in eighteenth-century England, and the misunderstanding of this situation embodied in Montesquieu's famous essay.

The German courts have never had the power to regulate questions of evidence and procedure by means of general "rules." The proclamation of general rules is, according to German constitutional principles, the domain of the legislator. The legislator may delegate these powers to administrative agencies. But the idea that this power might be delegated to courts is as foreign to German legal thinking as is the theory that the regulation of all questions of procedure and evidence is basically a function of the judiciary. The jurisdiction of the judiciary with respect to procedure and evidence is exactly the same as with respect to substantive law. The judge applies to an individual case rules of evidence and procedure laid down in statutes. It is only by means of the interpretation of statutes that the judge may exercise a "creative" function. Since the provisions of the German Code of Civil Procedure are, as a rule, more detailed than those in the most important parts of the German Civil Code (e.g., contract and tort), the significance of judge-made law is even greater in the substantive than in the field of procedure and evidence.

A treatise dealing with the organization and functions of the German labor courts must be based completely on the statutes which regulate these problems. According to German legal theory, the whole law has been codified in statutes. Provided that a problem has not been regulated in a special statute, the answer must be found in broader provisions of a statute of a more general type. The American reader must keep in mind the fact that the labor court statute mentioned so frequently in this treatise is nothing but a special statute designed to adapt the general provisions of the German Code of Civil Procedure to the particular situation of labor cases. Behind all the provisions of the Labor Court Act, the general rules of the Code of Civil Procedure retain force provided that they are not replaced explicitly by the labor court statute. Although not legally bound to follow the precedents of higher courts, the German labor courts in actuality interpreted the provisions of the Code of Civil Procedure in accordance with the precedents set forth in the decisions of ordinary courts. On the other hand, the decisions of the labor courts served to a certain extent as precedents in ordinary courts. Thus, labor law has exercised in the twentieth century a certain pioneering function, similar to the role which the law merchant played in an earlier period of German legal history.

HISTORICAL SURVEY

Chapter I

DEVELOPMENTS UP TO 1891

THE LEGAL SYSTEM created after the founding of the German Reich neglected the labor contract.[1] In Roman law, on which the German Law was based in many respects, the labor contract appeared as a special form of rent contract, corresponding to the conditions of a slave economy. This modest character of the labor contract persisted although labor's importance grew constantly. In the Civil Code, which came into force in 1900, only twenty of the 568 sections relating to contracts dealt with the labor contract, although this very type was of major significance for millions of citizens. Labor law was supposedly regulated by special annexes to corporation law as found in the Commercial Code, the Industrial Code, state laws such as the mining laws, and special statutes relating to domestic servants.

Lack of understanding of the labor contract was general in the judiciary. Justice was slow, expensive, and inaccessible. The worker could sue only under poor law or if able to pay fees in advance. Even when he could pay fees, the worker could not match the skillful lawyer whom he had to oppose. Judges, aloof from economic life, were primarily interested in jurisprudence and without understanding of the workman's social situation. The latter always had to wait a long time before the court decided and in the event of an adverse decision he had to pay ruinous costs, including the fees of the employer's lawyer, in accordance with a general German rule. Thus, there arose and spread the idea that courts help only the well-to-do and that workers had better avoid them.

Gradually there arose an understanding that the labor contract is of a special character, and that a poor, insecure working class had no time or money to protect its legal rights. France showed the way in handling litigation between employers and employees in line with the special needs of the labor contract. In 1806 probivirial courts (*conseils de prud'hommes*), composed of representatives of employers and labor, with a chairman chosen alternately from each group, were formed in Lyon, expressing by their name the idea that common sense is more essential than legal knowledge in litigation between employers and employees. These courts rapidly spread to other parts of France. Set up in the Rhenish provinces during the French occupation, they were maintained when the provinces were incorporated in Prussia in 1815. Experience was so satisfactory, that eight similar courts, varying only in detail, were formed in other parts of Germany. Their members were elected by employers, master mechanics, and independent artisans paying above a minimum in taxes. Employers had a majority of one, and the chairman was elected by the group. Parties to controversies appeared personally and proceedings were divided into two parts, one before a board of conciliation, the other before a board of judgment. The courts decided disputes between manufacturers and all employees, including home workers.[2]

Factory courts formed in other parts of the country, especially Berlin and Westphalia, as a kind of small claim courts, do not seem to have been very successful. A Prussian decree of 1833 concerning mandatory, summary, and small claim cases, introduced a summary procedure for wage claims of journeymen and laborers and provided for special divisions of the ordinary courts to decide on all small claims by accelerated procedure.[3]

The Prussian Industrial Code of January 17, 1845,[4] left existing courts undisturbed and provided that labor disputes arising between guild members and journeymen or apprentices should be settled by special authorities or, where such did not exist, by guild officers under the chairmanship of a communal official. Industrial disputes involving non-guild members were to be settled by the police, a very unpopular authority. In conflicts between agricultural workers and their masters the police authorities had jurisdiction. In all cases, appeal was to the ordinary courts.

Agitation to copy the Rhenish courts induced the Prussian government to provide, by a law of February 9, 1849,[5] that industrial courts composed of employers and workers be established throughout Prussia. The plan failed, however. Only eleven courts were created, and by 1855 all had disappeared.[6] Their failure may be attributed mainly to unequally distributed high costs and to a lack of common sense which resulted in delivering verdicts instead of seeking settlements.[7] Saxony passed a law (October 15, 1861)[8] making the establishment of courts optional, but only one was set up.

A similar course was pursued in the Industrial Code (Gewerbeordnung) of June 21, 1869, of the North German Confederation, the first law in this field destined to cover the entire Reich two years later.[9] Section 108 provided that "disputes between independent industrial employers and their workmen respecting the commencement, continuation or termination of a labor contract, their mutual obligations under it, and the granting or content of letters of reference, shall be submitted to specially appointed authorities, insofar as such exist. Where nonexistent, the matter shall come before the regular communal authorities, against whose decision appeal may be made to the courts. Communal authorities may institute arbitration courts by local statute for the settlement of such disputes, members being chosen from among employers and employed in equal numbers." Comparatively few towns made use of these powers. By the end of 1889, only seventy-four such courts had been formed, some on paper. They varied in composition, procedure, and jurisdiction; their judgments were not enforceable unless appealed to the ordinary courts. With few exceptions they failed to meet the need.[10]

By a law of 1881, the guilds (Innungen) were empowered to decide disputes with apprentices and to set up arbitral courts composed of a chairman and an equal number of guild members and journeymen to decide disputes with journeymen. An amendment of 1887 extended jurisdiction in some cases to nonmembers.

An unsatisfactory variety of courts existed in the eighties:

seventy-four communal courts established under the provision of the Federal Industrial Code with rules varying from one locality to another, others on the French model, guild courts, five mining courts in Saxony, special courts in Hamburg and Bremen, and ordinary courts to decide cases not covered by other courts. Communal authorities were not up to the task of settling disputes and did not employ special officials for this function.

Agitation for unified regulation began with the founding of the Reich and was intensified by industrialization. Bills were introduced in the Reichstag in 1873, 1874, and 1878. After the mid-eighties, the Reichstag was favorable to the idea of industrial courts, and discussions and resolutions led to legal unification. Following the great Westphalian miners' strike (1889), the government introduced a bill for the establishment of industrial courts (Gewerbegerichte) on a voluntary basis (i.e., leaving it to the municipalities to decide whether to establish them). The bill was passed before the labor protection law which it was supposed to guarantee, and went into effect on April 1, 1891.[11] The law left guild courts undisturbed. All other industrial courts were obliged to accept the essential provisions of the new law (i.e., equal representation of employers and employees and exclusion of lawyers.) The Rhenish courts were allowed to continue and to retain some peculiar features, e.g., the choice of a president from among the court members.

Chapter II

THE SYSTEM FROM 1891 TO 1927

INDUSTRIAL COURTS

Organization

THE NEW courts were set up within the municipal administrations of larger communities. Since many municipal authorities were disinclined to assume the financial burden or were afraid that such courts might have a socialistic character, establishment was, by amendment of July 30, 1901, made compulsory for cities of over 20,000 inhabitants.[1] Should these fail to act, the central government might set up courts. Jurisdiction might cover a group of communities, or be limited to a particular industry[2] or district. Employers and workers of the principal industries had to be consulted by the municipality before establishment of a court. The courts administered both federal and state law in accordance with the general principles prevailing in Germany.[3] They could be divided into chambers according to groups of industries or occupations.[4] Each court had a chairman, one or more vice-chairmen, and at least four assessors, one-half of them belonging to the working class, one-half to the employers. Where several chambers were set up, each had a chairman. The number of vice-presidents and assessors was fixed by local statute according to the amount of work and other conditions.[5] Membership was open to persons over thirty years of age and of good standing who had not received poor relief during the year preceding election.

Chairmen, appointed by the municipal authority for at least one year, could not, unlike the French practice, be employers or workers. They were usually public officials. Complete legal training was not required by law, but most chairmen had this qualification. Their term of office was fixed by local statute. Reappointment or life appointment was permitted.

Assessors must have resided in or been economically connected with their district for at least two years preceding election. Officials of trade unions were ineligible if not working in their trades. Assessors were elected by direct, secret, and equal suffrage for terms of from one to six years. The amendment of 1901 provided for proportional representation. Voters had to be at least twenty-five years of age and to reside or work in the district. Women were barred from voting. When an assessor elected as a worker became an employer (or vice versa), he had to resign. Assessors received no salary but were compensated for time lost and travelling expenses. The law forbade refusal of compensation for lost time. Expenses not covered by court fees were borne by the municipality.[6]

Arbitration agreements could deny jurisdiction to industrial courts; such agreements could provide for boards formed of an equal number of workers and employers, with a chairman belonging to neither group.

Jurisdiction

The jurisdiction of the person of the industrial courts covered employers and employees, the latter term including workmen, journeymen, apprentices (to whom the Industrial Code applied), and home workers to whom employers furnished materials; and even managers, foremen, and higher technical employees with annual earnings not exceeding 2,000 marks were included. Those with higher salaries were catalogued arbitrarily as employers. The extension of jurisdiction to home workers who procured their own materials, and classification of such as employers or employees, were matters for local statute. Assistants and apprentices in pharmacies and commerce, and, because of the special discipline needed, workers employed in industries under military and naval authorities were excluded. Employees of public works other than military and naval were included.

After the amendment of 1901 broadened jurisdiction, the

courts were competent to decide disputes concerning the commencement, continuation, or dissolution of labor relations, including the return of letters of reference, tools, etc., the execution of labor contracts, claims for damages arising out of any of the foregoing, and claims against fellow-workers arising out of joint work.[7] In short, jurisdiction covered merely disputes resulting from individual employment relations with an employer or fellow-worker. The courts had no jurisdiction over disputes arising out of collective agreements.[8] The most frequent causes of disputes were demands for arrears of wages and for compensation for discharge without notice.[9]

Procedure

In principle, procedure was the same as that for civil disputes in ordinary courts. Complaints could be filed orally and recorded by the court's secretary. Divergences from ordinary civil procedure aimed at simplification and acceleration. Procedure was informal. Most complaints were made by workers.[10] Within twenty-four hours, the chairman had to set a day for hearing and summon the parties. As the primary object of the courts was to reconcile the parties, proceedings were divided into two stages. At preliminary hearings, the chairman tried to settle cases alone. If no agreement could be reached, at least two assessors—more if so ordered by local statute—were summoned[11] and all arguments were repeated at a formal, public hearing. Personal appearance of the parties could be required. Attempts at conciliation were obligatory at all stages, and a final effort had to be made at the end of the proceedings. Lawyers were not admitted. Workers could be represented by relatives or fellow-workers. For workers unable to appear personally, some courts appointed representatives from among the worker-assessors. Others allowed members of nonprofit legal advisory agencies to appear. Representation by trade union officials, although not expressly recognized by law, was gradually admitted although it continued to be contested. Trade union officials were not allowed to make a profession of representing members, even without charge. After statements had been made, proofs examined, and witnesses or experts heard, decisions were made by the courts. Agreements and final judgments could be enforced.

The statute provided that both decisions regardless of whether or not appealed, and agreements concluded before the court and entered in the record, could be executed. Often the presiding judge drafted an agreement later adopted by both parties. The sheriff could execute an agreement concluded before the court as soon as a copy of the record was sent him by one party.

Appeals to the ordinary district courts (Landgerichte) could be made if the amount involved in the dispute exceeded 100 marks. The amount was determined by court judgment. Less than 10 per cent of cases brought before all courts were appealable.[12] With improved working conditions, the number increased slightly, e.g., in Berlin from 4 per cent in 1895 to 7.5 per cent in 1904. In general appeals were made by employers.

Conciliation Functions

Entirely apart from their main judicial functions, the industrial courts had conciliation functions concerning collective disputes, i.e., disputes of interest, not individual disputes of right. At first, the industrial courts could set up boards of conciliation only by request of both parties. This restriction, in combination with the fact that neither employers nor employees were much inclined to use the institution, made it rather ineffective during the first years. Failure to settle a few important disputes revealed its inadequacy.[13] The amendment of 1901 provided that if neither or only one party to a dispute acted the chairman should induce both to call on the court. He might invite them to appear and levy a fine for failure to respond. When a board was formed, arbitrators in equal number were appointed by each side to assist the chairman.[14] When no agreement was reached, the chairman could decline to cast the deciding vote and declare the case unsettled, or he could effect a majority decision which was not legally binding. The increase in his authority led to wider board activity.[15]

Collective agreements were frequently deposited with the industrial courts, and often the chairman assisted informally in eliminating obscure or illegal clauses.

Administrative Functions

The administrative functions were quite separate from the judicial. The courts acted as advisors of local authorities on industrial questions. Officials could ask advice concerning the value of dwellings provided by employers, the necessity of a rural sickness fund, construction safety rules, Sunday rest, etc. Such work never became important, but some influence was exercised over urban labor conditions. Moreover, the industrial courts could make proposals to legislative bodies concerning continuation schools, public employment offices, and other labor matters.[16] Some courts set up legal information bureaus.

For the exercise of such functions, the courts formed committees on which employers and workers were equally represented whenever their interests were involved.

OTHER SPECIAL COURTS

In addition to the industrial courts, there were other courts. In disputes between handicraft masters and journeymen, the industrial courts could be replaced by guild arbitral courts (Innungsschiedsgerichte),[17] constituted in practically the same way, i.e., equal employers and journeymen representation with an impartial chairman. The jurisdiction of a guild arbitral court was superior to that of an industrial court. Appeal to the ordinary courts was possible. The guild courts were unpopular since labor considered them partial. By refusing to elect representatives, labor frequently prevented their establishment,[18] in which cases the industrial courts had jurisdiction.

The guilds proper had exclusive jurisdiction in disputes between masters and apprentices; apprentice contracts were considered educational, not labor contracts. For this purpose the guilds could establish committees (Innungsausschüsse) composed equally of employers and employees. Only a few guilds—432 out of 11,399 in 1904[19]—exercised this right.

Since some mines extended over several communities, and since as a rule municipalities were not well informed about mining conditions, special mining industrial courts (Berggewerbegerichte) were established by several state authorities.[20] Costs were borne by the states. These courts did not become popular.

The number of assessors was fixed by the state, not by the community. Prussia provided for only two assessors and since the employers' was usually a lawyer while representation by trade union officials was denied to labor, the labor assessor was at a disadvantage. The chairmen did not win labor's confidence. Only after the World War did the Prussian Minister of Commerce authorize four assessors. The abolition of mining courts demanded by trade unions was achieved only with the enactment of the Labor Court Act in 1927.[21]

Disputes involving crews of seagoing vessels were decided by marine offices (Seemannsämter)[22] in home ports or attached to consulates abroad. As a rule, the parties had recourse to ordinary legal procedure. Only in exceptional cases were decisions of the special bureaus final.

The great success of the industrial courts led, in 1904, to the establishment of similar courts known as commercial courts (Kaufmannsgerichte), for the settlement of labor conflicts between merchants and employees.[23] The Social Democrats had sought to place such litigations under the industrial courts. The commercial employees' trade unions, however, with the exception of a small socialist wing, felt themselves a separate social group and demanded separate courts. Modeled on the industrial courts, the commercial courts were frequently linked with them through a common chairman, vice-chairman, and office staff.

The law did not define the term commercial employee, but it excluded all with incomes above 5,000 marks. Jurisdiction as to subject matter corresponded to that of the industrial courts but covered disputes arising from agreements whereby the employee had promised not to compete with his employer after the end of an employment relationship.[24] The courts had the same conciliation and administrative functions as the industrial courts.

In distinction to the industrial courts, the chairman of a commercial court had to be a judge or higher administrative official. No arbitration agreements could set up a special committee to replace the commercial court. Appeal was possible in litigation involving a sum in excess of 300 marks.[25]

In districts where no special courts existed, the ordinary

courts had jurisdiction in cases which would normally have fallen to the industrial courts or commercial courts. In such districts, industrial and commercial disputes could be brought before local officials (Gemeindevorsteher) comparable to justices of the peace. Their decisions could be appealed to the ordinary courts and had legal force, but the central state authority could displace such officials by special state bodies. In Prussia, for instance, official arbitrators were nominated. The material competence of communal officials was restricted.

THE PERIOD OF THE FIRST WORLD WAR

During the First World War, the industrial and commercial courts lost in importance, although their number increased by four and two respectively.[26] The guild arbitral courts were reduced in number from 420 to 350. Litigation decreased during the war by nearly two-thirds for industrial courts and by nearly three-fourths for commercial courts. This was a result of the industrial truce concluded between employers' organizations and trade unions in 1914, the shortage of labor, and the willingness of employers to grant labor demands. Currency inflation, followed or preceded by salary increases, removed some employees from jurisdiction. From 1915 on, committees were established to settle grievances and disputes in industries having military contracts. The Auxiliary Service Law of December 5, 1916,[27] provided for the establishment of workers' committees in industrial undertakings having more than fifty workers. These were to settle grievances against the management. The statute furthermore provided for the establishment of conciliation committees to settle disputes about leaving certificates[28] for all workers and which could be called in collective disputes, like the conciliation boards of the industrial and commercial courts. Although supposed to settle collective disputes only, their competence was sometimes wider. They handled individual disputes of farm workers in special chambers.

A law of November 7, 1917, provided that substitutes for drafted assessors should be elected by the communal legislature with consideration for organizations which had won seats in the last previous election.[29]

TABLE 1
Number of Cases Handled[30]

YEAR	By Industrial Courts				By Commercial Courts		TOTAL
	Between employers and workers		Between workers	Total	Cases of employees	Cases of employers	
	Cases of workers	Cases of employers					
1901	70,227		274	70,501	......	......	......
1902	82,166	5,559	425	88,150	......	......	......
1903	89,907	7,192	462	97,561	......	......	......
1904	96,295	6,660	359	103,314	......	......	......
1905	102,240	7,980	384	110,604	13,500	785	14,285
1906	106,260	10,774	351	117,385	18,131	2,156	20,287
1907	105,585	9,598	403	115,586	20,177	1,817	21,994
1908	109,850	5,878	358	116,086	21,869	1,543	23,412
1909	105,557	6,338	372	112,267	22,585	1,586	24,171
1910	109,731	7,976	308	118,015	23,379	1,806	25,185
1911	114,455	8,199	362	123,016	25,127	1,823	26,950
1912	115,624	7,724	384	123,732	26,083	2,000	28,083
1913	114,106	6,848	239	121,193	27,494	1,975	29,469
1914	96,020	4,378	170	100,568	26,977	1,358	28,335
1915	59,785	4,156	83	64,024	14,022	882	14,904
1916	44,105	3,379	58	47,542	10,387	738	11,125
1917	39,016	3,976	40	43,032	7,340	768	8,108
1918	36,801	2,192	62	39,055	6,518	496	7,014

1901–1918 IN THE LIGHT OF STATISTICS

In 1913 there were 949 courts in Germany, as compared to 791 in 1902. Eight were mining courts, two were restricted to special industries; 420 were guild arbitral courts, 25 were state courts.³¹ Of the 296 commercial courts, 253 were connected with the industrial courts.³²

TABLE 2

TERMINATION OF CASES

(In Percentages)³³

YEAR	BY INDUSTRIAL COURTS		BY COMMERCIAL COURTS	
	By agreement	By judgment of full court	By agreement	By judgment of full court
1901	41.8	....	....	....
1902	45	18.1	....	....
1905	43.5	16.1	44	18.5
1910	41.9	15.7	40.6	13.3
1913	39.3	15.8	40.1*	17.2
1918	38.3	11.8	44.5	12.2

*Commercial chambers of ordinary courts achieved only 8–8.2 per cent of agreements.

TABLE 3

DURATION OF SUITS ENDED BY JUDGMENT OF FULL COURTS

YEAR	LESS THAN ONE WEEK	1–2 WEEKS	2 WEEKS– ONE MONTH	1–3 MONTHS	3 MONTHS OR LONGER
	INDUSTRIAL COURTS (in percentages)				
1902	29.7	31.6	23.4	11.1	1.1
1913	23.2	29.2	28.4	16.4	2.8
1918	13.8	26.1	31.0	21.6	7.5
	COMMERCIAL COURTS (in percentages)				
1905	20.6	26.8	26.7	21.2	4.7
1918	9.7	19.7	29.8	32.7	8.1

TABLE 4
VALUE OF CLAIMS, 1914–1918
(In Percentages)

	INDUSTRIAL COURTS	COMMERCIAL COURTS
Under 20 marks	36.8	6.1
20–49 marks	27.4	11.4
50–99 marks	17.5	17.7
100–300 marks		35.7
More than 300 marks	13.0	21.0
Undetermined	5.3	8.1
	100.0	100.0

TABLE 5
CONCILIATION ACTIVITIES OF INDUSTRIAL COURTS IN COLLECTIVE DISPUTES

	1905	1913	1918
NUMBER OF APPLICATIONS			
By both parties	165	204	44
By employers alone	10	18	7
By workers alone	175	140	105
Ended by agreement	128	167	93
Ended by award	25	75	29
Neither agreement nor award	164	75	28
Unfinished	...	...	6
Award accepted by both parties	14	58	26
By employers alone	3	10	...
By workers alone	6	7	3
By neither	2	1	...

AN APPRAISAL OF INDUSTRIAL AND COMMERCIAL COURTS

The industrial and commercial courts were among the most successful and popular experiments in social policy before 1914. To be sure, they were not popular at once. First distrusted by the trade unions, they soon came to be appreciated by them. The confidence of employers was won more slowly. The latter were not accustomed to co-operating with workers, and many felt that to do so was to make a great concession. They were accustomed to preference being given their views over those of workers. Parity aroused no enthusiasm among the privileged. To employers, the office of assessor was a burden, to the worker, a prize. At first, some factory inspectors reported that workers did not dare file complaints except when already dismissed.

Many technical shortcomings of the early period were corrected by the amendment of 1901. Up to that time, much of the dissatisfaction was ascribed to electoral complications which in some communities reduced participation by the requirement of advance registration.[34] Employers disliked the excitement aroused in elections by socialist campaigns for votes. Some communities were afraid of strengthening Social Democratic influence through an industrial court. This fear was aggravated when in the first elections the Social Democratic Party in many cases won a majority of employer votes, showing that there were left sympathies among independent artisans and a lack of interest among others. In Frankfurt a.M., at one time, all assessors were Social Democrats because nonsocialist employers refused to vote.

Majority rule gave small artisans the same voting power as employers of 500 workers and, on the workers' side, favored the socialist unions.[35] Large industry claimed that, since 75 per cent of all employers were in small businesses, employer assessors were all small businessmen,[36] close in their views to workers and unable to do justice to large interests. Majority rule brought instability and a quick turnover of assessors. It would have been wiser to have made assessors and judges more permanent until labor judicial principles had been established.

Some communities tried to correct the injustice of majority rule by occupational group voting. In one election in Cologne, the socialists received 51 per cent of all votes, the Christian Socialists 49 per cent.[37] Under majority rule the socialists would have received all twelve seats, under the proportional system, seven. Under the vocational group system they received eight. The system was, however, awkward and artificial. Proportional representation was established by the amendment of 1901 and by many local statutes. Greater justice was achieved and objections declined.

The fact that the establishment of the courts brought an increase of litigation was a shock to the public and to employers. In Stuttgart, for instance, where a comparatively capable court had functioned earlier, litigation rose from 23 per cent of the industrial population in 1888-90 to 43 per cent in 1892.[38] Suits by commercial employees in Leipzig increased from 140 in 1903 to 719 in 1905, one year after the establishment of the commercial court. The increase did not, however, mean an intensification of conflict. It was merely a proof that the ordinary courts had been too expensive and slow. Many workers now had their first opportunity to advance claims. The increase of litigation showed how great had been the need for quick, cheap, and informal adjudication.

Employers' distrust of the industrial and commercial courts during the first period manifested itself in a proposal to make all cases appealable to the ordinary courts. Occasionally a large industrialist, in order to make appealable a case which he had no chance of winning in an industrial court, answered a workers' complaint with a counteraction involving more than 100 marks.[39]

The objection raised in the first years that the courts gave preference to workers' claims, is refuted by statistics.[40] A handicap which the industrial courts had to overcome in this period was the low compensation granted chairmen; it was impossible to employ any but young men just out of training. The post apparently was considered relatively unimportant. Berlin at first employed chairmen on part-time only; after four years the capital created seven full-time positions.[41]

The chairmen, however, grew into the new tasks and helped develop labor law, which had been retarded because of the lack of ordinary court decisions. Since all labor courts were of the first instance and there was no co-ordinating higher court, the only way to avoid contradictory decisions was through mutual criticism. For this purpose and for the exchange of experiences, a private association of industrial and commercial courts[42] (Vereinigung der Gewerbe- und Kaufmannsgerichte) was formed. An association of courts was a new phenomenon in Germany. It published a periodical, the Gewerbe- und Kaufmannsgericht.[43] The association kept a file of reports, decisions, and collective agreements. At its annual meetings, questions of principle, technical organization, and important decisions were discussed.

Not all shortcomings could be overcome or all demands met. Labor considered the age limits on voting and eligibility for assessorship too high. They protested against women's disenfranchisement, which had been achieved under the slogan of the sanctity of the family. Labor disliked the continuance of the guild arbitral courts and the exclusion of agricultural workers, and resented the fact that appeals were to ordinary courts. Conciliation and advisory functions did not acquire great importance. The latter had been given to the courts merely because there was no other institution which could submit workers' demands and inform the government of labor's views. Since, however, these opinions of the courts were always compromises between the two groups, they were not especially illuminating as to labor's views. Only where a compromise was important (e.g., exception from Sunday rest rules, inclusion of workers in flower shops in the industrial code, etc.), were the authorities interested in consulting the courts. Activity in this field remained slight (cf. n. 16). Employers did not favor this sort of activity. As late as 1911, the employers' assessors of the Frankfurt Industrial Court refused to attend a committee meeting to formulate for the state government an opinion concerning the maximum number of apprentices to be trained by each master craftsman. Having notified the chairman that they considered the discussion unproductive, they were disagreeably surprised when a fine was imposed for non-appearance.[44]

In 1914, the employers' assessors of the commercial courts petitioned the Reichstag for the abolition of the courts' rights to initiate proposals. The employees' assessors argued that such proposals were the only way for employees to make their demands officially known, while employers also had chambers of commerce.

The great advantages of the industrial and commercial courts as compared with ordinary courts were cheapness, rapidity of action, a chance to sue for small sums, a good possibility of settlement without formal hearing, and the co-operation of workers and employers well acquainted with industrial and labor conditions and able to appreciate the facts. The fee charged depended upon the amount involved in the dispute, one to three marks being usual. There were, in general, no other costs but the fee borne by the losing party. This did not have to be paid in advance.

A conspicuous advantage was speed. In 1908 only about 2.3 per cent of suits carried to a final judgment lasted over three months.[45] While in ordinary courts decision was the rule and amicable settlement the exception, the trend was reversed in the industrial and commercial courts. Here, in a large part of all cases, agreements were achieved without convocation of the full court.[46]

TABLE 6

SETTLEMENT OF CASES

	BERLIN* (1895-1904)
Number of cases handled (per year)	10,702–12,872
Settled by agreement......	52.3 per cent
Withdrawal of complaint...	22.8 " "
Admission of the claim.....	0.4 " "
Renunciation.............	0.1 " "
Judgment by default.......	10.5 " "
Final judgment...........	13.9 " "

*SP, Dec. 7, 1905, pp. 265–66.

A great proportion of the time of the industrial court was taken up with small industries, especially building, clothing, restaurants, and food.[47] The courts were used less by large industry. The impartial character of the courts was generally recognized. In the beginning, some judges showed in the phrasing of judgments ("however" and "although") that they had been outvoted by laymen—a method contrary to the German attitude that the opinion of the individual judge should not be disclosed. Attempts were made by central associations to influence assessors or to call them to account for their votes. But even those at first inclined to be partisans of one group, later stressed the importance of compromise and of decisions made according to law. All reports of factory inspectors agreed on the impartiality of worker assessors. Unanimous decisions were frequent. Nor did judges come under the political influence of the municipal council as had been feared.

Although the courts considerably limited the autonomous rule of the employer in his shop, the employer came to recognize their value. When, in 1912, the chambers of handicraft and of commerce, composed of employers, were asked for an opinion on the labor court system, they answered approvingly.[48]

The working class hailed the courts as a great step forward. Before the creation of the industrial courts, only property owners had been elected or appointed to the various state and municipal administrative and advisory boards. The same was true of appointment as jurors and associate judges (Schöffen) in petty commercial cases. It was in the industrial and commercial courts that, for the first time, the less privileged could take part. Jastrow[49] said that there was no state institution to which the worker clung more than to 'the industrial courts. Especially appreciated was the fact that no dispute was too small for these courts. Thus the industrial and commercial courts succeeded in winning full recognition from all groups.

The one fundamental objection was to the very idea of special courts. It was argued that the government, instead of splitting the court structure, should have reformed the ordinary courts and their procedure. It would have been necessary to make the whole judicial system less expensive, formal, and slow. Those who favored a unified judicial system protested the threatening atomization of the judiciary.

THE POST-WAR PERIOD: 1918-1927
Background

With the great extension of labor law after the war, the industrial courts and other labor courts proved insufficient. Mining and guild arbitral courts had been unsuccessful. A dual system for workmen and commercial employees was no longer necessary since the distinction between the two had tended to diminish to a certain extent and a great part of the commercial employees no longer regarded themselves as future entrepreneurs but recognized their solidarity with the working class.[50] Only some commercial courts were fully occupied.[51]

Although courts were distributed through all parts of the country, they did not cover it. Many areas of large or small size, especially rural districts and those with little industry, were within the jurisdiction of no court. Nor did the courts cover all workers' groups. The system had resulted in unjustifiable inequalities. Agricultural and domestic workers, employees of the Reich, the states and municipalities, railroad workers on the roads, technical employees with salaries of more than 2,000 marks, commercial employees with salaries of more than 5,000 marks a year, and employees of non-commercial and non-industrial enterprises, had no recourse but to ordinary courts. A typist working for a commercial enterprise had to resort to the commercial courts; if she shifted to a lawyer's office, she had to go to the ordinary courts.[52] For these groups, law suits were expensive, time-consuming, and often irrelevant, since many judges in the ordinary courts had slight contact with the workers' lives. Labor felt the need of special labor courts of appeal.

The revolution which broke out at the end of the war brought recognition of the special character of labor law[53] and a desire to unify and supplement the scattered and inadequate regulations. With the formation of a Committee for the Creation of a Unified Labor Law, in connection with the Federal Ministry of Labor, the question of a unified judicial system became urgent.

Amendments and Emergency Solutions

Since complete reform could not be effected rapidly, several amendments during the years 1920-23 sought to adapt the laws to new conditions,[54] e.g., in adjusting to the depreciated money value the income limits which defined competence, right of appeal and compensation.[55] The franchise age was lowered, women and recipients of public relief were enfranchised, proportional representation was made compulsory, officials and members of trade unions and employers' associations were generally admitted to represent parties in the courts. New elections of assessors were ordered. These were overdue, since the term of office of the sitting assessors had been prolonged by decree of July 12, 1917, until six months after the end of the war. When elections were held in 1920, some of the assessors had been in office for about ten years, while the groups which had nominated them had undergone fundamental changes.

The amendment of January 14, 1922,[56] enlarged the court's jurisdiction by including actions for damages caused by improper references given by an employer as to a worker's record (actions which in German, unlike the American, law, lie in contract rather than in tort) and those based on violations of agreement restricting competitive activities of an employee after termination of the employment relationship (cf. n. 24).

Special administrative agencies, the conciliation committees,[57] were entrusted with litigations arising out of the new laws which did not differentiate between industrial, commercial, or other employees. The establishment and popularity of these administrative agencies can be explained only if one takes into consideration the changes produced by the revolution of 1918. The workers controlled the war administration, but they had only a very restricted influence on the courts on account of the independence of the judges. This may explain why unions preferred the conciliation committees as administrative agencies to the courts and objected to judicial review of these "quasi-judicial" agencies. In detail, the type of litigation handled by conciliation committees was concerned with the following:

(1) Disputes arising out of the Works Council Act (Be-

triebsrätegesetz)⁵⁸ e.g., concerning dismissal,⁵⁹ departure from agreed principles, hiring, and other differences of opinion between employers and representative shop bodies. The BRG provided that conflicts concerning composition, competence, procedure, expenditures, right of franchise, and elections should be decided by district or state economic councils or, when an enterprise extended beyond a single state or came under the supervision of the federal government with respect to labor conditions or employment, by the Provisional National Economic Council (Vorläufiger Reichswirtschaftsrat, henceforth referred to as RWR). Since the district councils were never established, their functions were transferred to the conciliation committees. The RWR retained its functions. In disputes arising out of the BRG, the works councils were entitled to file suit in favor of the worker and to plead before the courts; no costs were charged when they lost. Two distinct methods of procedure were provided for works council disputes. Normal judgment procedure ending with a final decision was applicable to dismissal conflicts, while a special summary procedure of administrative nature, ending with a resolution (Beschluss), was applicable to all others.

(2) Disputes arising out of the Provisional Agricultural Labor Decree of January 24, 1919,⁶⁰ especially as to the cash value of wage payments in kind and the wages and work of disabled veterans.

(3) Disputes arising out of the Federal War Pension Act⁶¹ over alleged violation of the rule that pensions of war veterans and of their widows and orphans must not be taken into account in calculating wages.

The conciliation committees were unfit to fulfill all these new tasks. They were inadequately equipped for legal decisions; their decisions conflicted, they had no power of enforcement. The chief objections of employers to the conciliation committees was the lack of judicial review. The conciliation committees were federal agencies. Contrary to the state laws, the federal law had established administrative courts only in a very few cases. The statute concerning conciliation committees had not provided for a special administrative court entrusted with the review jurisdiction over decisions of the conciliation committees.

On the other hand, the decisions of the conciliation committees were unenforceable. A party who recovered in such a committee, had to apply to a court for a writ of enforcement. When deciding on writ, the court was entitled only to examine whether the conciliation committee had acted within its general "jurisdiction." In applying the crucial "jurisdiction" test, courts differed frequently in interpretation and annulled conciliation committees' judgments because of legal considerations affecting the merits of the case rather than the authority of the committee.

A great simplification in the conciliation but not in the court system was the Arbitration Decree of October 30, 1923,[62] relieving conciliation authorities of duties in legal disputes.

Pending a comprehensive plan of labor courts, jurisdiction was given to the industrial and commercial courts, which thereby acquired the character of provisional labor courts for such cases. Where no industrial or commercial courts existed, labor court chambers were established as departments of the conciliation committees.

Under the new regulation, the commercial courts covered commercial employees, the industrial courts all manual workers.[63] In order to fit the courts for their new work, an administrative decree[64] provided that, at new elections of assessors, the newly included groups be given consideration and that those industrial courts which would have an increase in types of cases should add new types of assessors. Special chambers were to be established in the industrial courts for railroad labor cases.

The chambers were composed of an impartial chairman and one representative each of employers and workers. Decisions of the labor courts and chambers were to be final.

The Arbitration Decree of October 30, 1923, relieved the industrial and commercial courts of arbitration functions which they had to some extent continued to exercise in competition with the conciliation committees. The reform embodied the idea of separating conflicts of right from those of interest. The judicial system thereby became definitely distinguished from conciliation and arbitration. Under the former were to come chiefly individual disputes[65] and such collective disputes as were disputes of right (i.e., concerning the existence of collective agreements and their interpretation, contract actions because of violations of collective agreements, and tort actions in labor conflicts). Under the conciliation-arbitration system were to come disputes concerning future employment conditions. Henceforth, the *application* of law was to be by judicial authorities and separate from the *creation* of law which was to be by conciliation and arbitration bodies. This separation of functions became characteristic of the German system.[66]

The regulation of 1923, supposed to abolish maladjustments and confusion, created new inequalities and insecurity. Competence was not the same for all employee groups. As far as non-industrial and non-commercial workers were concerned, the industrial and commercial courts had jurisdiction only in cases based on the Works Council Law, and not in cases based on the labor contract. Industrial and commercial courts now functioned in two ways. Their decisions, if based on the GGG and KGG, could be appealed only if the object were above a certain value. If a dismissed industrial worker were to sue for wages and reinstatement, the industrial court could decide the wage claim subject to appeal, the reinstatement claim definitively. Farm workers had to resort first to an ordinary local court. Thus the system remained complex and hence lost some public sympathy. A uniform, nationwide, comprehensive system was urgently needed.

Survey [67]

The following list shows the multitude of agencies among which labor jurisdiction was distributed at the beginning of 1927:

The industrial courts } appeal to ordinary courts
The commercial courts

Mining courts

FROM 1891 TO 1927

Ordinary local courts (Amtsgerichte) for all other workers, when the sum in dispute was below 500 marks; appeal to Landgericht

Ordinary district courts (Landgerichte) for the same, when the sum was above 500 marks

Guild committees for apprentices in handicraft
Guild arbitral courts for journeymen in handicraft } appeal to ordinary courts

Arbitral bodies established by collective agreements

Provisional labor courts for agricultural workers, cases of dismissal covered by the *BRG*, war veterans; no appeal

Provisional National Economic Council (*RWR*), litigation concerning the executive function of works representation in plants of the Reich or those located in two or more states (summary procedure)

In 1927[68] there were:
- 558 industrial courts
- 12 mining courts
- 12 state courts

582

in 1919[69]:
- 462 industrial courts
- 13 mining courts
- 14 state courts

489

339 (in 1919, 274) commercial courts, 259 (in 1919, 217) affiliated with industrial courts

260 labor court chambers, of which
- 67 were affiliated with industrial courts
- 11 were affiliated with commercial courts
- 11 were affiliated with industrial and commercial courts
- 64 were affiliated with ordinary courts
- 83 were arbitration committees
- 3 were chambers of arbitration committees
- 21 were other authorities

There were 37 special chambers, divided as follows:
- agricultural and forestry, 23
- trade, industry, public enterprises, 14
- railways, 30
- guild arbitral courts, 691 (in 1925, 790; in 1919, 292)

Of the 558 industrial courts, 316 covered single communities, 103 several communities or parts of communities, 139 larger areas. Fourteen were restricted in material competence.

TABLE 7

Year	All Complaints	Percentage Initiated by Workers	Percentage Initiated by Employers	Percentage of Cases Between Workers	Conciliation Cases	Opinions and Proposals
Industrial Courts Exclusive of Guild Arbitral Courts						
1919	59,820	94.9	5.0	0.1	588	7
1920	84,325	93.5	6.4	0.1	626	9
1921	97,319	93.0	6.9	0.1	334	11
1922	110,095	93.6	6.3	0.1	..	..
1923	131,970	94.6	5.3	0.1	809	3
1924	124,242	95.1	4.9	..	..	10
1925	146,305	94.6	3.3	2.1	..	6
1926	147,425	97.8	2.1	0.1	..	2
1927*	64,079	97.3	2.6	0.1	..	..
Commercial Courts						
1919	11,235	96.1	3.9	..	66	14
1920	17,300	95.3	4.7	..	54	15
1921	23,185	95.4	4.6	..	10	2
1922	23,787	94.8	5.2	..	..	..
1923	28,682	97.5	2.5	..	3	2
1924	40,657	97.8	2.2	..	..	6
1925	48,446	97.9	2.1	..	..	32
1926	45,759	98.1	1.9	..	..	23
1927*	18,102	97.1	2.9	..	..	..

*One-half year.

The labor court chambers handled 49,721 cases in 1924; 26,342 in 1926 (of which 24,350 were judgment and 1,992 summary cases).

TABLE 8

SETTLEMENTS OF CASES, FIRST HALF OF 1927[70]
(In Percentages)

METHOD OF SETTLEMENT	INDUSTRIAL COURTS	COMMERCIAL COURTS	PROVISIONAL LABOR COURTS*	
			Judgment procedure	Summary procedure
Compromise......	37.6	37.1	18.5	....
Abandonment.....	1.3	3.5	1.3	....
Admission........	2.6	3.	0.8	....
Withdrawal.......	19.6	15.9	30.3	....
Default..........	12.8	12.6	1.3	....
Formal judgment..	15.8	15.7	24.6	51.4
Other methods....	10.3	12.2	13.9	38.0
Unsettled.........	....	....	9.3	10.6

*Provisional labor courts were labor court chambers and industrial and commerical courts as far as their jurisdiction was based on the Arbitration Order of Oct. 30, 1923.

Of 5,068 appealable cases in the industrial courts, 1,733 were actually appealed; of 4,797 in the commercial courts, 930 were appealed.

In 1926 all provisional labor courts handled 26,342 cases in judgment and summary procedure.

The industrial courts handled 16,761 cases=63.6 per cent of the total.
The commercial courts handled 5,499 cases=20.9 per cent.
The chambers handled 4,082 cases=15.5 per cent.[71]

Reform Discussions

It was inadvisable to wait for a unification of labor law before regulating the court system. A complete labor court system was a crying need. Since collective agreements had normative effect, their interpretation was of equal significance to that of law. Reorganization of the courts was warmly discussed. There was unity of opinion as to the necessity of creat-

HISTORICAL SURVEY

TABLE 9

LITIGATION IN 1927
(In Percentages)

	INDUS-TRIAL COURTS	COM-MERCIAL COURTS	CHAMBERS Judgment	Summary
DURATION				
1 week or less...........	11.5	9.9	6.7	9.9
1–2 weeks..............	24.2	23.6	26.2	25.3
2 weeks–1 month........	35.1	35.5	40.3	27.8
1–3 months.............	22.9	24.1	22.1	32.2
More than 3 months.....	6.3	6.9	4.7	4.8
VALUE				
20 marks or less.........	21.0	3.9	15.7	....
21–50 marks............	24.6	9.7	10.1	....
51–100 marks...........	21.4	15.3	12.6	....
101–300 marks..........	17.1	33.8	10.1	....
More than 300 marks....	7.9	26.5	10.1	....
Value undetermined.....	8.0	10.8	41.4	....
CASES				
Worker against employer.	97.3	....	....	....
Employer against worker.	2.6	....	....	....
Worker against worker...	0.1	....	....	....

TABLE 10

OBJECTS OF COMPLAINTS IN COMMERCIAL COURTS
(In Percentages)

	1919	1920	1921
Cases concerning beginning, continuation, termination of labor contracts; delivery of letters of reference.......................	11.5	12.1	11.4
Disputes concerning contractural relations....	65.0	69.5	71.8
Returning of letters of reference.............	2.0	1.5	1.5
Damage claims, non-fulfillment of obligations, incorrect registration in certificates........	21.4	16.7	15.2
Competition clause.......................	0.1	0.2	0.1
	100.0	100.0	100.0

ing a complete network of labor courts with its own Supreme Court to guarantee uniformity of law. Lay members were to serve in all instances and jurisdiction was to cover all employees. Opinions, however, were divided concerning the relation of labor courts to the regular judiciary and the admittance of lawyers to practice. The chief point of contention was as to whether labor courts should be special agencies or part of the judicial system. There seemed to be three possibilities. Those

TABLE 11

CASES IN THE LABOR COURT CHAMBERS
(In Percentages)

JUDGMENT PROCEDURE	1924	1925	1926	1927*
Dismissals BRG..................	90.7	87.7	90.3	89.0
Wage disputes of agricultural workers	1.0	2.1	1.3	1.5
Disputes on hiring of workers.......	0.9	0.8	0.5	0.7
Complaints concerning accounting of war veterans' pensions...........	0.3	0.3	0.4	0.3
SUMMARY PROCEDURE				
Works representation.............	0.8	3.4	2.6	4.4
Substituted agreements to dismissals.	0.2	3.1	3.2	2.1
Dissolution......................	0.2	2.0	1.2	1.5
Imposition of fines................	2.0	0.4	0.4	0.4
Calling of a provisional works council, etc...........................	3.9	0.2	0.1	0.1
	100.0	100.0	100.0	100.0

*Jan. 1.—June 30.

TABLE 12

CASES PENDING BEFORE THE THIRTY RAILWAY CHAMBERS

DATE	TOTAL CASES	JUDGMENT PROCEDURE	SUMMARY PROCEDURE
1925.............	1,070	934	136
1926.............	1,215	1,132	83
1927*............	356	337	19

*Jan. 1.—June 30.

who advocated preservation of the existing arrangement, i.e., affiliation of the courts to communal authorities,[72] argued that the courts had been particularly successful in maintaining close and intimate contact with the people. The communities were opposed, however, because of the financial burden. Attachment to the communities did not seem consistent with the extension of courts to agricultural districts. It was feared that communal courts, after the cities' democratization, might be at the mercy of local political factors. Moreover, insuperable difficulties would have been created in the matter of appeals. Hence, this solution won little support. The two practical possibilities were complete independence or organic union with the ordinary courts. The legal profession[73] and employers[74] advocated the integration of labor courts with the ordinary courts. The socialist trade unions demanded a complete set of special courts.

Labor argued that ordinary courts could not provide a procedure as informal, simple, quick, and inexpensive as that of special courts. Dislike of the ordinary courts was widespread in the unions. "The professional legal organism (Zünftige Justiz) with its antiquated ideal of a state aloof from and disdainful of the people (veraltetes volksfeindliches Staatsideal), has brought the state to the abyss," [75] wrote the free trade union organ. Experienced labor court judges cannot become educators of reactionary jurists if the latter are concerned with labor cases only on a part-time basis; the roles of educators and educated are reversed under such circumstances, they argued. Socialist workers believed the judges would not protect the constitution. They could not forget the unsocial decisions of pre-war courts, their bias toward unorganized workers and strikebreakers.[76] The free trade unions fought, although with less vigor, "the judges' monopoly of the post of chairman," [77] as an Afa League[78] resolution formulated it in 1925; they believed that judges were influenced by the interests and ideology of the ruling class.[79]

Because of the independence of the judiciary and the life tenure of judges, jurisprudence had not become adapted to the new democracy or the popular power. There was tension in the first years after the revolution when some judges showed hostility toward the Republic.[80] Judges were regarded by organized labor as unfamiliar with the industrial issues involved in labor disputes and frequently biased. Universities did not deal with labor law as a special field of law.[81] There were complaints that judges decided from a narrow legalistic point of view. They were accustomed to taking a strictly juristic view without considering the humanitarian aspect involved. In spite of their tradition of integrity, it was argued they had been so long part of the bureaucratic machine and had moved in so much the same circles as the employers that they would not have been able to treat labor fairly. Among those who recommended independence of the labor courts was one group, such as Kaskel,[82] Sinzheimer,[83] Umbreit,[84] Potthoff,[85] Luppe,[86] and others who proposed the creation of comprehensive labor law authorities, including placement service, vocational guidance, conciliation, social insurance, factory inspection, etc., thus uniting administration, jurisprudence, and arbitration in one office.[87]

The Deutscher Gewerkschaftsbund, German Confederation of Trade Unions, the DGB (Christian workmen and salaried employees) was in favor of incorporating labor courts within the regular judicial system.

The jurists argued that independent labor courts would destroy the unity of the judicial system. In their opinion, the setting up of special courts, e.g. the Federal Economic Court, the Cartel Court, and tenant protection courts (Pachteinigungsämter), was an unsound development. If continued, the ordinary courts, cut off from the social life-stream, would dry up. Even the Social Democratic Minister of Justice, Gustav Radbruch, diverging from his party, declared in the Reichstag on February 22, 1922, that separation from the ordinary courts "would mean a death sentence to ordinary justice and thereby for the first time create real class justice." The ordinary courts would become "heaps of ruins."[88] The legal profession's lack of understanding of workers could be attributed only to its lack of familiarity with their problems. The impact of concrete experience would be strong enough to overcome the narrowness of the legal mind (Paragraphengeist), said Sinzheimer, who was close to Radbruch. The deplorable lack of confidence in the ordinary courts could be abolished only by bringing the judge into contact with labor law, not by separating him from it. Universities could give training in labor law, thus far neglected.[89] The judicial system should be imbued with a social spirit, not artificially alienated from the life of the people. In fact, it had already been influenced by the industrial and commercial courts. Labor chambers in ordinary courts could satisfy specialization requirements.

From the point of view of organization and expenses, an independent system would be inexpedient. Some labor courts would be under-occupied. Labor contracts, combined with other contracts (for instance rent) would then have to be dealt with in two courts. In Hamburg and Bremen industrial and commercial courts had been successfully incorporated in the ordinary courts.

The Federation of Employers' Associations saw in the cooperation of the social administration in the establishment and supervision of courts an unsound combination of judicial and administrative functions.[90] It fought alleged politization of justice.

Not less hotly debated than the question of the incorporation of labor courts, was that of the admittance or exclusion of attorneys, especially in the lower courts. Those who demanded incorporation also favored admittance (with the exception of the Christian trade unions who in this question shared the views of the Socialist unions). Labor was solid in demanding exclusion. It argued the continued validity of the reasons which led to barring attorneys from the industrial and commercial courts, i.e., speed, cheapness, equalization of forces, and the factual rather than legal character of cases.[91] The unions were, furthermore, convinced that the exclusion of lawyers would guarantee the lack of formality which they regarded as so desirable. Organized labor viewed representation by members and officials of economic associations of employers and employees, a custom authorized by law in 1922, as successful. Such representation—according to organized labor—was the only kind in accord with the spirit of Article 165 of the Constitution.[92] The trade unions argued that labor, unable to afford skilled counsel, would be at a disadvantage. They feared that the will to amicable settlement would be weakened if lawyers fortified the parties' arguments and if an eventual compromise must cover a lawyer's fee.[93] Accustomed to civil law procedure, lawyers would protract matters unnecessarily. Cases in labor courts should be handled without delay, but lawyers would have to break off to go to other courts, especially in large cities, and thus cause delays by demanding adjournments. They might be induced by an employer client to impede a quick decision. What was needed was not logical deduction but an understanding of economic interests and professional problems, which men engaged in the practice of law would lack. Lawyers, far from being better experts, would have no time to prepare trifling cases. The representatives of unions were checked by their organizations. "The trade unions must defend the rights of the people against professional interests." [94] All lawyers in rural areas—the trade unions argued—were socially close to employers and would hardly care to represent workers. Lawyers are usually employers themselves, whose professional organizations dislike collective agreements. Therefore, it was argued, the majority of lawyers seem hostile to collective agreements, the basis of labor law,[95] and would be unable to serve them. The unions, furthermore, were opposed to the idea that one lawyer might represent—although in different cases—both employers and employees. Such procedure could lead to hypocrisy. "One can be employer-social-minded, or employee-social-minded, but not supernaturally objective-social," wrote Clemens Nörpel, labor law expert of the Free Trade Unions.[96] The main argument against lawyers, not much emphasized in the discussion, was frankly formulated by Kahn Freund when, in December, 1932, the profession again demanded admittance. He said that the law applied in courts was created mainly by a trade union fight and so the unions should enjoy a privilege over those who had held aloof. Workers could avoid suffering from union monopoly of representation by joining a union. A compulsion to organize, exercised by the

AGG, was a sound idea.[97] Representation by trade unions was expected to strengthen the latter's influence since it meant supervision of workers' assessors and thereby influence on the courts.

The bill of 1923, backed by the Reichsrat, had stipulated admittance of lawyers for cases in which the amount in dispute exceeded 300 marks, and for cases specified in the BRG. In order to protect the defeated party from overcharges by lawyers, the latter's compensation from a winning party was to be fixed by the court, within reason and according to circumstances. Labor rejected this solution arguing that not the sum but the difficulty of the problems involved should be the criterion. The defeated party would have to pay the bill of two lawyers and, even in successful cases, the employer would have to pay the lawyer of the works council, since the council was financed by him.

The whole legal profession (including many socialist jurists) and all employers demanded admittance of lawyers to courts of all instances.[98] They saw in exclusion a denial of full legal protection. Since the enactment of the GGG, the situation had fundamentally changed. In 1890, labor law was as good as nonexistent and most decisions had to be made in the spirit of common sense. In 1927, labor law had developed into a well-established system. It was not distrust that excluded lawyers in 1890, said Jastrow,[99] the pioneer of the industrial court, but a desire to give courts the benefit of a "closed season," because at that time labor organizations were weak and workers too poor to consult lawyers. Lawyers of big manufacturers could easily have dominated procedure.

Even in case of admittance of lawyers, the presiding judge could compel the parties to appear and could speak face to face with them, jurists argued. He could prevent delays. Equality would be better guaranteed by general lawyer representation, because in any case the large employers' organization, which employed a full-time lawyer as an official, could be represented by him. An employer accustomed to treating workers conciliatorily, might have to be represented by a militant official of an association if the organizations got a monopoly. An employer might have more confidence in his own lawyer than in an official of an association.

The argument of equality of weapons, it was said, was an admittance of better representation by lawyers. It should be the aim of the law to provide the best possible representation. Equality should be established by limiting lawyers' fees and putting at the disposal of the poorer party the services of poor law counsel, a device which had worked well in the past. (It could be objected that workers did not like to accept poor law.) The argument that the well-to-do party would be privileged could be applied to ordinary courts as well, university professors of civil and labor law pointed out in a memorandum in which they advocated admittance of lawyers.[100]

The legal profession declared itself interested in aiding the development of labor law by influencing judicial interpretation. It rejected the insinuation that a money interest determined its attitude—fees in cases concerning small sums would be trifling —but declared that the prestige of the profession was at stake. No "proletarian sense of justice" existed; it was artificially created.

Monopoly of representation by organizations was demanded by trade union officials, it was argued, in order to protect their jobs. One view had it that they were not always able to help in difficult questions of law. The unorganized worker would be unprotected, since not even employees of nonprofit legal advisory agencies would be admitted.

With 179 against 169 votes, the Reichstag rejected admittance of lawyers in the primary instance but adopted it for the higher instances (cf. pp. 71-73).

Beginning in 1920, some twenty or thirty drafts of a Labor Court Act were prepared,[101] five of official character. The Committee on Labor Legislation draft[102] provided in two instances independent courts outside the framework of the ordinary court system in the third courts related to the Federal Supreme Court. A draft of the Federal Minister of Labor provided for incorporation into the regular system. Responding to the protests of the free trade unions, the government in 1923[103] brought forward a draft which, despite higher costs, provided a compromise on the question of incorporation. It had to be withdrawn when currency inflation seemed to bar all reforms. In June, 1925, a new government draft was submitted which took into account all previous expert suggestions as well as the reform of ordinary court procedure effected in 1924. The organization it proposed was the same as in the draft of 1923.

Discussion was very passionate; no agreement could be achieved in the Provisional National Economic Council, which issued two opinions. In the Reichstag, differences of opinion concerned mainly organization, admittance of lawyers and jurisdiction. Only the Communist Party entirely opposed setting up of labor courts, characterizing them as a sample of class justice. After many changes, the bill was passed in the Reichstag on December 13, 1926,[104] with 210 votes against 140 and seven abstentions.[105] Voting did not strictly follow party lines.

THE DEVELOPED SYSTEM (1927-1933)

Chapter III

LEGAL REGULATIONS

THE AGG ENDED THE LIFE of industrial and commercial courts, guild arbitral courts, mining courts, and labor court chambers. The guilds wanted to retain their arbitration courts, but the trade unions argued that many existed on paper only and had impeded the industrial court which was under compulsion to find out whether a guild court existed before it could act. The opposition of trade unions had resulted in the abolition of these courts for journeymen. Guild jurisdiction over apprentice litigation was upheld, but with possibility of appeal to the labor courts. Special methods were kept for seamen alone. Unification had been achieved.

The law provided a "continuous net" of labor adjudication covering all employees, provided for practically all types of dispute both in contract and tort between employers and employees, regardless of the amount at issue or the income level of the parties, and provided for the enforcement and interpretation of collective agreements. With few exceptions, labor cases formerly within the jurisdiction of ordinary civil courts were transferred to the labor court system.

The act set up a complete structure of authorities with comprehensive jurisdiction and their own rules of procedure. While the ordinary system had four types of courts (two types of the first instance), the AGG set up three stages, Arbeitsgerichte or labor courts, Landesarbeitsgerichte or district labor courts, and the Reichsarbeitsgericht or Federal Labor Court.

The question of incorporation was solved by a compromise: courts of the first instance were autonomous, completely independent of ordinary courts although in close contact with them by virtue of the fact that the chairman was, in nearly all cases, an ordinary judge. The fact that some attorneys were permitted to serve as chairmen is not without interest. The experience, however, was not encouraging. Courts of the second instance were part of the ordinary district courts, the Federal Labor Court of the Federal Supreme Court. While ordinary courts were under the supervision of the department of justice insofar as administration was concerned, labor courts at all levels were established and supervised by the justice administration in co-operation with the social administration (in the Reich the Federal Ministry of Labor, in Prussia the Ministry of Commerce and Industry, in Saxony the Ministry of Labor and Public Welfare, etc.). Courts of first and second instance were under state administration and their expenses were paid by the states. The Federal Labor Court was under federal administration and its expenses were borne by the Reich. Labor courts at all levels had both professional and lay judges. Consultation of employers' organizations and trade unions was provided for in many cases, as for instance, in the establishment of courts and chambers and the issuance of general instructions concerning administration and service supervision.

THE CONSTITUTION OF LABOR JUDICIAL AUTHORITIES

Labor Courts

Labor courts were, as a rule, to cover the area of an ordinary local court (Amtsgericht). By exception they could be set up for a larger or smaller area, especially one constituting an economic unit. Like all German courts, they were divided into chambers. Each consisted of an impartial chairman, a vice-chairman, and two assessors, one from the ranks of labor, one from the ranks of the employers. In conflicts involving associations, the number of assessors was doubled (since several organizations usually participated on the workers' side). Separate chambers for wage earners, salaried employees, and handicraft workers were compulsory. Where two groups of employees were involved, the chamber for the class constituting a majority was competent. After hearing the employers' associations and trade unions on the matter, the authorities might combine the chambers for wage earners and salaried employees. Special chambers could be established for specified vocations, industries, or groups of workers. The competence of a special chamber could be extended to the districts of other labor courts. Special chamber assessors had to belong to the special vocation, industry, or group.

Chairmen and vice-chairmen, appointed by the state administration of justice in agreement with the supreme state authority for social administration, generally had to be professional judges. Other persons who were neither employers nor employees might be appointed if qualified for judicial office.

Chairmen and vice-chairmen had to possess knowledge and experience in labor legislation and social problems. Preference was to be given to former chairmen of arbitration bodies. As judges by vocation, chairmen of labor courts had life tenure, but as chairmen of labor courts they were appointed for a specified time of from one to nine years. After three years, life tenure might be granted for the special task as chairman of the labor court. This modification had been considered necessary in order to facilitate the elimination of persons unfit for the special obligations of labor authorities. Fear that insecurity of tenure might restrict independence and eliminate persons politically undesirable to one group, was not well founded. Since chiefly civil servants (former judges) were nominated, they could, on the expiration of their terms, be reinstated in a position equivalent to that previously held. During their period of office in the labor courts, they had the same rights and duties as other state judicial officers.

Employer and employee assessors were not elected by their respective groups as for the industrial and commercial courts but were appointed for a term of three years[1] by the superior administrative authority in agreement with the president of the ordinary district court, from lists presented by employers' associations and bona fide trade unions. The law prescribed that proper care be taken to give representation to minorities. In appointing assessors, the social administration rather than the judicial dominated. Separate nominations had to be made for wage earners and salaried employees unless the authorities authorized merging of the chambers.

Assessors had to be German citizens in good standing, at least twenty-five years of age, with at least one year's background as employer or employee in the area. Nobody could refuse to serve except on well-defined grounds. No officials of a labor judicial authority could be assessors. Nobody could be both an employers' and a workers' assessor. The term employer was broadly defined so as to include even those who might temporarily have no employees.

The following were eligible as employers' assessors: (1) statutory representatives and members of the supervisory board of private corporations, with the exception of delegates appointed thereto by the works councils; (2) public officials as representatives of public enterprises; (3) business managers empowered to hire employees or holding a proxy or general power of attorney; (4) members and officials of employers' associations, if empowered to represent them.

Members or officials of bona fide trade unions could be workers' assessors. Unemployed persons could be assessors. The office was honorary, but compensation was provided for loss of earnings and expenses.[2] Employers who discriminated against workers that had been appointed assessors or because of their discharge of assessorial duties were liable to fine. Complete protection against dismissal, analogous to that for members of works councils, had been demanded by trade unions but was rejected in the Reichstag as unjustified.[3] Assessors could be removed from office for gross breach of official duties.

In order to increase their prestige, assessors were given the title of labor judge. Their influence on court administrative policies was to be increased by formation of an assessors' committee in each labor court having more than one chamber. The committee was to consist of employers' and employees' assessors in equal number (at least three), elected separately by the two groups of assessors. They were to be consulted on, among other matters, the formation of chambers, allocation of business, and assignment of assessors to chambers, and could communicate their wishes to the labor court chairman. Business, chairmen, and assessors were assigned to chambers by the chairman. Assessors were summoned in sequence according to a list prepared by the chairman at the beginning of each business year and after hearing the assessors' committee. No deviation was permitted.

The trade unions had demanded that there be four assessors, but financial considerations made this impossible. Many communal statutes had provided for four, but the number was reduced to two because assessors appointed from trade union lists were better prepared than workers had been in the beginning.

Workers assessors felt less helpless after the revolution of 1918 than in the nineties. This may be explained by increased self-respect among workers and by the training which assessors received from their unions. Large unions had special schools to train officers, assessors for labor courts and administrative agencies, and works council members. Labor law classes were important in these schools.[4] The same holds true with respect to adult education, which flourished under the Weimar Republic as never before.

District Labor Courts

District labor courts were connected with ordinary district courts[5] and were composed of similar chambers. The chambers consisted of a chairman, a vice-chairman appointed from among the higher ranks of the district judiciary, and one or two assessors of employers and employees, appointed in a manner similar to that of labor courts. Chairmen had to be experienced in labor questions. Their appointment was valid as long as their membership in the ordinary district courts, i.e., usually for life. Assessors were called district labor judges. Their qualifications were the same as in the labor courts, except that they had to be at least thirty years of age and had to have had not less than three years' experience as assessors of a labor judicial authority. An assessors' committee was formed in every district labor court. Business, chairmen, vice-chairmen, and assessors were assigned to chambers by the presiding officers of the ordinary district court, with the assistance of the chairmen of the district labor court. Assessors were summoned in sequence, according to a list prepared by the chairman. The district labor court acted as court of appeal from the labor court.

Federal Labor Court

The Federal Labor Court was part of the Federal Supreme Court in Leipzig, i.e., one "senate" of the Supreme Court, somewhat differently composed from the other senates, but equivalent to them. Its judicial members were judges of the Federal Supreme Court. The number of labor senates was fixed by the Federal Minister of Justice in agreement with the Federal Minister of Labor. Only one was established. In distinction to the other supreme court senates, only three of the five members of the labor senate, the chairman and two associate judges, were professional judges. One each was appointed from the ranks of employers and employees. All professional judges had to have training and experience in labor legislation and social questions. The practice of the two lower courts, of giving lay members a majority, was abandoned since the Federal Labor Court was no fact-finding tribunal but decided only questions of law on which professional judges had to have decisive influence. Only the lay judges had to have had industrial experience.[6] The non-judicial assessors, known as Federal Labor Judges, had to be at least thirty-five years of age and to have had considerable experience as employers or employees. They were appointed for three years by the Federal Minister of Labor in agreement with the Federal Minister of Justice, from lists provided by the central federations of the employers associations and the trade unions. Regulations were similar to those for assessors in lower courts. No assessors' committee was set up.[7] Assessors were assigned work as in the lower courts.

JURISDICTION

Jurisdiction of person covered employers, wage earners, salaried employees and apprentices of all income levels. The old limit of 2,000 marks for technical and 5,000 for commercial employees was dropped. Associations of employers and employees and works councils were competent to sue or be sued. Persons who performed work for others without standing in what might be considered a labor relation in a narrower sense (e.g., homeworkers, or contractors deriving the greater part of their earnings from their own piecework) were considered analogous to employees and were included. The industrial court distinction between homeworkers who provided material and others was dropped. The term "persons similar to employees" was much disputed as to whether it covered such persons as commercial agents, contractors, newspaper reporters, and others. In general, the courts considered as decisive the degree of personal and economic dependence on an employer, as well as as the possibility of making profits.[8] Except in summary procedure, the courts were competent even when action was brought by a legal successor, e.g., the legal representative of a deceased worker.

One of the greatest achievements of the new regulation was that federal, state, and municipal workers could sue in contract or tort in the labor court, provided that the claim was based on the labor relationship. This provision corresponded to the general German rule that courts are open for suits against the Reich or a state, provided that the rights claimed against the sovereign are in "private law."

As mentioned above (p. 5), the relationship between civil servants and the government is in "public law." As an exception to the rule that the ordinary courts have jurisdiction only in private law matters, the code of civil procedure had entrusted them with jurisdiction in cases brought by civil servants against the government, provided that nothing but salary was at issue. The labor law does not fix rules concerning civil servants. The labor courts have no jurisdiction in civil service cases. A suggestion of the eminent labor lawyer, Heinz

Potthoff, to extend jurisdiction to civil servants was generally rejected.

Outside the competence of the labor courts were crews of sea-going vessels,[9] members of the armed forces, and, as a rule, legal representatives of corporations and public and private associations. Handicraft guilds kept jurisdiction over apprentices working for a member because master craftsmen had argued that public hearings in the courts would be detrimental to the master's authority. Guilds could regulate their own procedure. A committee of employers and employees in equal number, usually with an impartial chairman, issued an award. Accepted awards could be executed by order of a labor court chairman. If one party failed to accept, action could be instituted in the competent labor court within a fortnight. If no committees were established, the labor courts had jurisdiction.

Local jurisdiction was, in general, dependent on the defendant's residence or place of business. For employment or apprenticeship governed by a collective agreement, the contracting parties could select jointly a labor court without local jurisdiction. Parties to an individual contract could do the same. In summary procedure, the labor court in the area of the workers' representative body was competent.

Jurisdiction was manifold. In some matters it was exclusive, in others, concurrent with that of ordinary courts. Some matters could be excluded by collective agreement.[10]

Jurisdiction with regard to subject matter covered four types of conflicts to the exclusion of the ordinary courts and irrespective of the sum involved: 1) those between employers and employees arising out of the labor relationship; 2) conflicts between fellow-workers; 3) conflicts between parties to collective agreements; and 4) conflicts arising out of the works council relation.

1. Litigation between employers and employees (including apprentices) covered civil actions arising out of employment, regardless of whether in contract or tort. Declaratory judgments as to the existence or absence of a contract of employment (or articles of apprenticeship) were explicitly mentioned in the statute. The court had, furthermore, jurisdiction in actions arising out of inconclusive negotiations toward labor

contracts and damage suits based on information given concerning a dismissed worker after expiration of a labor contract. The test was not the existence of a contract but rather the employer-employee relationship. Only disputes concerning inventions were excluded unless they concerned compensation. The act foresaw that labor courts would not be expert enough to judge the technical implications of patent litigation. The inclusion of compensation for inventions created difficult legal problems, since in many cases compensation was disputed because it was not clear whether an invention existed or to which type it belonged. In such cases, ordinary courts were also competent in the compensation question. Unlawful acts giving rise to tort actions were such things as damage done by an employee to property of an employer or failure of an employer to comply with protective health legislation.[11]

2. The labor courts were competent to decide disputes between fellow workers arising out of common employment (e.g. distribution of the proceeds of collective piecework) and out of unlawful acts connected with employment (e.g. bodily injury in a brawl which arose in connection with work).

3. The courts had competence in litigation between parties to a collective agreement or between such parties and third parties. Before 1927 such disputes went before the ordinary courts. They covered various types of conflicts:

a. Litigation in declaratory judgment procedure concerning the existence or nonexistence of a collective agreement, e.g., the question of whether the associations met all the legal requirements of eligibility to conclude collective agreements.

b. Litigation concerning the fulfillment of obligations[12] stipulated for the contracting parties by agreement. Instances of such disputes were those arising from an alleged violation of the duty to preserve the peace, or concerning the maximum employment figure of apprentices, or non-use of an agreed employment office. Another instance was a declaratory judgment which established clearly the content of a collective agreement. This could be demanded by anyone with a legal interest in the facts of a collective agreement. Such judicial declarations could prevent lawsuits.

Declaratory judgments in cases between employers' organizations and unions concerning the meaning of a doubtful provision in a collective agreement were *res judicata* not only between the parties but also for all labor contracts controlled by the collective agreement involved.

Since collective agreements were also construed as third party beneficiary contracts, workers were, in exceptional cases, entitled to sue an employer's organization for breach of contract concluded between the organization and the union. This question was significant when, after a strike, the parties agreed that all workers be reinstated but an individual employer refused to rehire one worker. In this case, the latter could sue the employer's organization in the labor court. Procedure in such cases was both complicated and unsatisfactory. No direct claim was recognized by most courts against the former employer because the labor contract was dissolved and a tort action did not lie.

Injunctions asked by private persons were not very powerful weapons as compared to the contempt-of-court rules of Anglo-American Law because a defendant disobeying such an injunction could only be fined or imprisoned for six weeks at most. It was usually considered more convenient in labor cases to sue for damages immediately rather than to seek an injunction. The basic question of whether or not particular union activities were considered illegal by the court was settled implicitly in the damage verdict.

Temporary injunctions in labor conflicts, although legally possible, were not common. In temporary injunction procedures special rules of evidence prevailed involving a risk for the plaintiff. After an injunction was granted, a defendant could seek its review through a procedure in which ordinary rules of evidence were applied. If in this second procedure, the court decided that the injunction granted was unjustified, the plaintiff had to pay damages regardless of whether or not he was guilty of an illegal act when seeking the injunction.

Injunctions such as that *In re Debs* are impossible in German law. An action based on *public* nuisance would be characterized as belonging to *public* law. The labor courts have no jurisdiction in public law cases.

c. Tort actions based on unlawful measures adopted in the

course of labor disputes and questions concerning freedom of association (e.g., claims of nonstriking workers against a striking trade union claiming damages) were in the jurisdiction of the courts. Another instance would be compulsion used by a trade union to obtain dismissal of workers organized in another union. Tort actions played a small role compared to contract actions. This is primarily due to German agency law, which provides that, as far as contractual claims are concerned, the principal is liable for the activities of his agent within the scope of his contractual duties. But in tort actions the principal could seek to prove that he had not been negligent in choosing and supervising his agent, and might thus disclaim liability. The courts were quite liberal in interpreting this rule. Unions could introduce evidence that a picket was known as a reliable person and had been instructed to abstain from illegal acts. If such evidence was convincing, the plaintiff could not recover.

It should not be overlooked that contractual liability, especially in cases of collective agreement, was very strict in German law.

Injunctions were not only possible in labor conflicts but were asked in several cases. The whole problem was considered so irrelevant, however, that the labor court statute did not deal with it at all. Labor injunctions were not even mentioned in the years-long discussions leading up to enactment.

Disputes between associations and members were not in the jurisdiction of labor courts (e.g., payment of dues, penalties, expulsion). Inclusion was proposed by the Reichsrat with the government's agreement but was dropped because there was no desire to have employers participate in decisions on trade union conflicts or vice versa. The German labor movement was divided into competing groups, and none was eager to have the other look into internal quarrels. Moreover, the organized employer or worker suing his association would thereby have been deprived of his advocate.[13]

4. By way of a special summary procedure (Beschlussverfahren, cf. pp. 78-79), the courts had jurisdiction in a number of disputes connected with the Works Council Act, e.g., concerning the setting-up, composition, and activities of works councils

and elections thereto. The procedure also included cases in which a labor court decision was substituted for the consent of works councils to dismissal or transfer of one of its members, or concerning the termination of membership of works representation, the dissolution of representative bodies, the convening of provisional bodies, or concerning the imposition of fines for infraction of works rules or infringement of principles agreed on between works councils and employers for hiring.

Under certain conditions, jurisdiction could be extended to complaints made by third parties against employers and employees or vice versa. Such cases usually belonging to the ordinary courts could be taken over when a legal or direct economic connection existed between the claim and a civil action pending in a labor court or shortly to come before one. Thus, for instance, an employer could connect a breach of contract suit against a former employee with a suit against another employer who had hired with knowledge of the breach, although the latter case would ordinarily fall in the jurisdiction of the ordinary courts. Or, when a dismissed employee sued for arrears of wages, the employer could file a counter plea because of the employee's debt for goods delivered by the employer's shop. No labor court had jurisdiction in such cases, however, if another court was exclusively competent for the establishment of the claim, e.g., certain cases reserved to the landlord and tenant courts. Jurisdiction could not be extended to matters concerning inventions.

As an exception to the rule that labor court jurisdiction could not be established by agreement, civil actions between private corporations and legal representatives not considered employees could be brought in a labor court by agreement.

Although jurisdiction was widened, some labor matters still were excluded. Ordinary civil courts had jurisdiction in cases not set forth in the AGG, in suits concerning inventions, and, after a Marine Office decision as first instance, in cases concerning crews of sea-going vessels. The labor courts were obliged in all cases to examine their competence ex officio, regardless of whether or not the defendant pleaded lack of jurisdiction.

Criminal cases could not come before labor courts. The ordinary criminal courts had jurisdiction over offenses against labor laws enforceable by penal sanctions, such as matters of hours of work and safety provisions. The demand of the Reichsrat and the RWR to include criminal cases involving violation of protective laws was rejected by the Reichstag because it seemed uncertain that labor judges would be fit to administer criminal justice and because it was feared that the inclusion of criminal cases might prejudice confidence in the courts. At the Congress of the ADGB in 1931, Nörpel[14] advocated inclusion of penal violations of protective laws because of the slow and inefficient enforcement of ordinary criminal courts. Such cases would be handled more quickly and receive more publicity in labor courts. In fact, factory inspectors' reports frequently complained of the inadequacy of penalties and enforcement. Prosecutors of murder cases have little understanding of the importance of violations of hours of work legislation, Nörpel argued.

Nor were administrative disputes in the labor field in the jurisdiction of labor courts. Even the administrative function of the industrial and commercial courts concerning opinions and proposals was dropped. Administration adjudication, according to the view of government and parliament, was to remain unified.

The social insurance system had its own administrative tribunals for disputes between social insurance agencies and private parties. Labor courts handled some types of disputes between employer and employee connected with problems of social insurance, concerning, e.g., failure of the employer to affix stamps for invalidity and old age insurance, or work certificates required for unemployment insurance.

Arbitration was separated from adjudication. As stated above, the labor courts claimed power to decide an award's legality by judicial review. They interpreted and enforced collective agreements but did not assist in writing them.

PROCEDURE

The controversy concerning admittance or exclusion of lawyers was solved as follows. Lawyers were barred from the labor courts, while members and officials of employers' associations and bona fide trade unions legally empowered to represent their associations were admitted as representatives of their associations and members thereof, provided they did not practice professionally as lawyers. Only members and employees of such associations as were capable of being parties to a collective agreement, or of federations of such associations, were admitted. In summary procedure, or in cases in which dismissal was contested by the works council, the latter could appear.

In the district labor courts, the parties could employ lawyers or be represented by members or officials of an employers' organization or a union under the same conditions as in the labor courts. The works council, when party to a contest, could be represented by a lawyer or the representative of an association. No Federal Labor Court decision clarified the question of whether, in cases of unjustified dismissal (Sec. 84 ff., *BRG*), the right of representation could be claimed by the affected employee's trade union, the union to which belonged any member of the works council or any worker in the plant. According to a Federal Labor Court decision of April 13, 1929,[15] on the ground that Section 36, *BRG*, made the latter responsible for expenses of the works representation, the works council could decide the kind of representation (lawyer or trade union representative), with costs borne by the employer. This led to the awkward situation that when a works council was defeated, expenses were paid by the winner. Interestingly enough, the decision of the Federal Labor Court stressed the value of lawyers as compared with representatives of organizations who had no legal training.

Representation through lawyers was compulsory before the Federal Labor Court.

Any lawyer admitted to the German bar could represent parties before a district or the Federal Labor Court, while in civil procedure in ordinary courts (except municipal courts) only lawyers admitted to the particular court could appear. Counsel could be assigned to poor persons,[16] i.e., those who, without impairment of subsistence for themselves and their families, could not pay for litigation. In such cases, the state paid the fees of the lawyer. These fees were regulated by statute but were lower than regular fees. By Emergency Decree of October 6, 1931,[17] such assignment of counsel was restricted to cases which did not appear hopeless and wanton. It could be denied whenever the party would, without such assignment, have refrained from suing for the whole sum. Lawyers' fees in poor law cases were cut.

As in the former industrial and commercial courts, procedure was, in general, based on ordinary civil procedure but was more informal and had to be expedited in all phases.[18] Court vacations had no effect on proceedings. Complaints could be filed in writing or orally with the clerk. No written reply was required. Parties might appear at regular sessions without summons and make a complaint. In conflicts about dismissals (BRG, Sec. 86-87; cf. n. 59, p. 210), either the worker or the works council (workmen or salaried employees' council) could bring an action. The chairman could direct the parties to appear in person at any stage of a suit, and he could examine the parties in an informal way. Judgment could be granted by default, objections to be filed within three days. The chairman could refuse to admit a representative if the parties defied an order to appear in person.

The statement of the parties as well as the hearing of witnesses and pronouncement of judgment were public unless public order, the safety of the state, or public morals would thereby be endangered, or unless the parties objected to publicity because business secrets were involved. If there was ground to fear prejudice, a member of the court might be barred from a case by decision of the chamber.

The emphasis on conciliation was reflected in the fact that the chairman, acting as sole judge, first tried to effect an amicable settlement. This could either be a compromise, a withdrawal, or abandonment or admission of the claim. The chairman could, furthermore, decide alone if judgment was given without a hearing in the above-mentioned cases, or if the decision could be given, on the request of all parties, in the course of the trial immediately following the conciliation procedure.

When an agreement was reached, the conciliation procedure had to be entered into the record. When the attempt failed, the case proceeded as a law suit before the full court with two assessors. Assessors, called according to the roster, sat until the case was concluded. Fines could be imposed by the chairman if an assessor failed to appear without sufficient excuse or otherwise evaded his duties. The law obligated the chairman so to conduct hearings as to conclude each case in a single session if possible. The chairman endeavored to extract from the parties complete statements of fact and evidence. He could summon witnesses and experts, obtain official statements and secure documentary evidence. Throughout proceedings before the full court, efforts had to be made to bring about an amicable settlement. Decisions were by majority vote. It was the task of the presiding judge to voice the court's opinion, which contained a statement of facts and the reasons of the decision. Dissenting opinions are unknown to German law.[19] On the contrary, the presiding and associate judges may not talk about "the secrets" of the court's deliberations. It was even questioned whether a presiding judge might state that a decision was unanimous.

Costs and the sum or value involved in the action were assessed in the judgment. Court fees were fixed by law with a view to making the administration of justice cheap and to discouraging frivolous complaints. They were fixed for courts of first instance on a low sliding scale, beginning with one mark for a claim up to 20 marks, two between 20 and 60, three between 60 and 100, up to a maximum fee of 500 marks. Full or partial exemption was granted in actions terminated by conciliation (even if preceded by hearings), by admission or withdrawal of a claim or in summary proceedings. No fee was charged in unsuccessful cases of works councils against dismissals because the dismissed worker was not party to the suit. Fees were in all instances payable at the conclusion of the case.

Besides court fees, the defeated party had to compensate the winner for his expenses. But no claims for compensation for loss of time or counsel's fees could be allowed. The item, therefore, amounted to nothing, in most cases, or might cover the traveling expenses of the party or his witnesses and the expert's fees.

Execution of labor courts judgments was like that of the judgments of other courts. If an appeal was admissible, they were enforceable provisionally, unless the defendant could show that execution would cause irreparable damage. Then the court was obliged to stay provisional execution.

One peculiarity should be mentioned. The Works Council Law provided that in case of dismissal a worker could ask the court to examine as to whether unfair labor practice was involved or whether the dismissal was unjustified from a social point of view. If the worker won, the court had to order re-employment with back pay or require the employer to pay damages fixed by statute. Orders of re-employment were unenforceable. No contempt of court or similar procedure was open to the worker.

Appeal to the district labor court was possible when the object of litigation, as finally fixed by the labor court, exceeded 300 marks, or when the labor court granted an appeal because of the matter's general importance. The granting of an appeal was usual in suits concerning matters likely to recur. It was mandatory whenever, interpreting a legal provision, the labor court deviated from a judgment given for or against one of the parties to the dispute and cited in the proceedings. It was also mandatory when a decision involved interpretation of a collective agreement concluded by one of the parties and extending beyond the jurisdiction of the labor court. The object was to protect large enterprises from having legal relations with its workers regulated according to different principles in different areas. It should be noted, however, that the question of whether an appeal was permissible was decided by the same court which gave judgment.

The sum required for appeal (300 marks) was higher than in the ordinary courts, where until 1931, it·was 50 marks.[20] The sum had been fixed as high as the average monthly income of a medium-salaried employee in order to prevent protraction of a suit brought by a little man concerning his salary. The right to appeal was not always exercised, however. In 1928, appeal was granted in 4,910 cases because of the importance of the principles involved, but in only 3,970 cases were appeals lodged.

Only about 3.5 per cent of all cases were appealed in 1928, one per cent because of their fundamental importance. An appeal could not be based on defects in the procedure for the appointment of assessors or on circumstances which precluded the appointment of an assessor to exercise his functions.

If the terms of a collective agreement were not clear and led to disputes, both parties—as a rule before judgment was announced—asked for leave to appeal even if the sum involved was small.[21] In cases of dismissals, the works representation could appeal only if it had originally lodged the complaint with the labor court. If the works representation did not use it, the dismissed worker had the right of appeal. In case of denial of the right, the plaintiff might apply to the Federal Labor Court for leave. Proceedings in the district labor courts followed to a large extent the code of civil procedure which governed the procedure before the ordinary district courts with some provisions for acceleration and simplification. Time periods for the appeal, for presenting the arguments, for summoning parties, for fixing the hearing, etc., were made as short as possible. Defects in labor court procedure could not be ground for returning a case to the lower court. Appeals could be based on points of fact or law. But as the main aim of an appeal was to check the legal basis of lower court judgments, and since it was desired to prevent protraction of suits, the production of new evidence was rendered difficult. New facts could be produced in the first oral hearings. Later they could be introduced only if they had developed after the appeal arguments were made or if the delay was not the party's fault.

In the district labor courts and the Federal Labor Court, litigation was without cost when amicable agreement was reached.[22] For actions terminated by default, admission or withdrawal of the claim antecedent to hearing before the whole court, only half the usual fee was collected. Contrary to the proceedings in the civil courts, no advance payment of fees was required. Compensation for expenses included lawyers' fees. Appeal for review was allowed (except in BRG cases), when the amount assessed by the district labor court was above the limit required for a civil law case to reach the Federal

LEGAL REGULATIONS

Supreme Court (4,000 marks in 1927; since February 15, 1929, 6,000 marks).[23] If the amount involved in the dispute changed after delivery of judgment by the labor court, the district labor court could reassess it in its judgment. The district labor court could authorize review on grounds of fundamental importance. No review was allowed for BRG cases (dismissal pleas and cases of summary procedure) or temporary injunctions.

Appeal for review could be based only on statutory questions or a clause of a collective agreement affecting the terms of individual contracts of employment. The most difficult question was the extent to which the discretionary power of the district labor courts concerning questions of evidence could be subjected to review by the Federal Labor Court. The latter was very reluctant in this respect. Appeal for review could not be based on improper assumption of local jurisdiction, defects in the procedure of the appointment of assessors, or circumstances which precluded the appointment of an assessor. Appeal had to be lodged within a fortnight.

Cases could come directly to the Federal Labor Court for higher appeal without passing through appeal procedure of the district labor courts if the amount at issue was sufficient and the contesting parties agreed to the motion for higher appeal or the Federal Minister of Labor declared an immediate decision of the Federal Labor Court necessary in the public interest (Sprungrevision). This could happen, for instance, in a dispute concerning the interpretation of an important collective agreement which endangered industrial peace. No direct review was possible after the appeal had been filed. The number of direct appeals was very small.

Of all cases handled in district labor courts in 1928, only 5.6 per cent were appealed to the Federal Labor Court, 4.3 per cent of which because of the importance of principles involved.

With some modifications procedure in the Federal Labor Court was similar to that of the ordinary Supreme Court. Appeal for review could be dimissed without hearing if not filed in legal form and within the time limit. If appeal was admitted, date for hearing had to be fixed forthwith.

Summary Procedure

Cases relating to workers' representative bodies under the Works Council Act and involving differences between employers and workers or the latters' representative bodies, were settled by summary procedure (Beschlussverfahren). The Works Council Law was originally planned as a statute regulating the lowest level of an economic hierarchy which should supplement the political constitution of the Reich (Art. 165, Constitution). This idea was given up early in the twenties. The Works Council Act was, however, treated as a part of public law. Controversies arising out of the application of this statute had to be decided by administrative courts rather than by ordinary courts. As a matter of convenience, the labor courts served as administrative courts in conflicts relating to the public law provisions of the works council statute. When the labor courts fulfilled tasks of administrative courts, procedure was modeled on the rules of such courts. Proceedings were instituted on application (not complaint), either in writing or orally, and could be abandoned at any time in the same manner. The law did not speak of parties in such cases but of "persons concerned" (Beteiligte). The employer, the workers, and the workers' representative bodies which, under the BRG, were concerned could be heard or make written statements. Local competence depended on the seat of the enterprise. The chairman could order documents examined, information procured, witnesses and experts heard, and personal inspections conducted by the chamber.

Only complaints on questions of law (Rechtsbeschwerde) could be made to the district labor court. Its decisions were final. In exceptional cases, complaint could be brought before the Federal Labor Court. If the decision affected enterprises extending beyond the area of a single state, or if the Reich had supervisory power over the workers' official status, the Federal Labor Court was competent to hear complaints. This brought all conflicts of works representatives in post offices, railroads, and the institute for salaried employees' insurance, to the Federal Labor Court as court of complaint. A complaint on a point of law could be based only on the ground that the decision of the labor court was based on the nonapplication or incorrect application of a legal provision. It could not be based on defects in procedure. A document embodying the complaint was served on the parties for answer. They answered in writing or could have an oral declaration recorded in the office of the labor court. Reference back to the labor court was not permissible. Only in exceptional cases did the Federal Labor Court decide that an oral hearing be granted the parties. The court decided by resolution on the complaint. No fees and expenses were charged.

EXCLUSION OF LABOR COURT JURISDICTION

The German Code of Civil Procedure encourages parties to a litigation to replace the courts by arbitral tribunals. Whole fields of law are dealt with exclusively by such tribunals. Members of the stock exchange, for instance, settle their disputes exclusively by means of arbitral bodies.

Far from excluding arbitral tribunals the AGG regulated them in order to avoid abuses. It provided that the parties to a collective agreement could exclude labor courts wholly or partially from the settlement of civil law disputes, displacing them by institutions set up by collective agreement. Total displacement was effected by arbitral tribunals (Schiedsgerichte) set up either in general or for particular cases by collective agreement. Their jurisdiction could cover civil actions arising out of the individual labor contracts (including those of apprentices) of members of the contracting organizations (see p. 66). They might also cover disputes between the contracting parties. In order to protect employees who, because of their dependency and lack of business acumen, might be induced to accept arbitral tribunals in which their rights were not fully protected, the law prohibited arbitration clauses in individual contracts. The one exception was salaried employees earning more than the limit provided for salaried employees' insurance (6,000 marks a year; after August 10, 1928, 8,400); such highly paid white-collar employees were not helpless and their conflicts frequently concerned complicated issues to which special bodies could bring more expert knowledge than the general labor courts. There was, moreover, a feeling that assessors from lower paid groups would not do justice to higher-paid workers.

Matters of summary procedure did not come within the jurisdiction of arbitral bodies. Whether dismissal suits based on the BRG or litigation between employees arising out of common employment, could be excluded by collective agreement was a matter of dispute.

Arbitral bodies based on the agreement of parties to a collective agreement, must be distinguished from arbitration bodies similarly established. The former, insofar as collective agreements are concerned, decided on interpretation of a collective agreement, the latter supplemented the agreement. In practice, collective agreements did not always distinguish between the two types of bodies. Theoretically it was also possible for arbitration clauses to be contained in an award rendered by an arbitration body, since collective agreements could be set up by awards of arbitration bodies if the awards were accepted by both parties or imposed by authority.

In the guiding principles for the establishment of arbitral tribunals by collective agreement,[24] the Federal Minister of Labor declared that the displacement of the labor courts or official arbitration bodies by tribunals of the contracting parties was possible only by collective agreement. While the establishment of arbitration bodies was recommended, that of arbitral tribunals was declared less desirable lest it endanger the unity of justice. Compulsory awards should not stipulate arbitral bodies of the three types;[25] arbitral tribunals, conciliation authorities, and expert opinion bodies as described below. Only full agreement of the parties could displace official courts. Hence agreed arbitral (and arbitration) bodies were not extended to outsiders even when the Minister of Labor might declare an agreement binding for a whole industry or area.

In order to prevent abuse, the law fixed the composition of arbitral tribunals. In the absence of special agreement to the contrary, they were to consist of an equal number of employees and employers, to which impartial members could be added. Or, instead of setting up their own tribunal, the parties could designate any existing authority whose composition met these requirements.

The existence of an arbitral tribunal prevented disputes from being brought before the labor court unless one of the parties to a dispute or collective agreement failed to nominate arbitrators, or unless the tribunal failed to act within a certain time, or unless the tribunal notified the parties that a decision was impossible because of a tie vote.

The procedure was even simpler than in labor courts. The arbitral tribunal could fix procedure at its discretion but, if not regulated otherwise, had to hear parties orally. The parties could appear in person or send a representative with power of attorney. The tribunals were entitled to examine witnesses and experts. Oaths could be taken only in courts.[26] Award was by majority vote, except when otherwise provided. A copy of the decision had to be filed with the labor court. The award had the same force as decisions of the labor courts insofar as the problem of *res judicata* was concerned. Awards could not be appealed. Execution, however, had to be ordered by the chairman of the labor court after hearing the opposing party.[27]

A plea for setting aside an award, which automatically stayed execution, could be made in a few exceptional cases, e.g., if the arbitral procedure was impermissible, if documents were falsified, conduct of judge or counsel was found culpable, witnesses were perjured, and finally if an award was obviously contrary to a *jus cogens* provision of a statute.[28] The labor court had the final power to set aside an award.

In part, the jurisdiction of labor courts could be excluded by providing a conciliation authority (Gütestelle) by collective agreement. Jurisdiction was the same as for the arbitral tribunals, but only the conciliation proceedings of the labor courts were displaced. Composition could be agreed upon. Parties had to appear in person. If they failed to come to an agreement, the full labor court took over.

Another form of partial exclusion of the jurisdiction of

labor courts was possible by agreement for expert opinions in arbitration (Schiedsgutachtenvertrag.) In this case the parties referred certain matters of fact (for instance, classification within the wage schedule) to an extra-judicial agency whose findings were binding upon the labor courts. The latter then gave judgment only on questions of law. This agency corresponded in composition and procedure to the arbitral tribunals, but never became popular. The idea that questions of fact should be decided by another board than decided questions of law, and that the activities of the judge should be restricted to application of law, is contrary to the German idea of ordinary court procedure.

Chapter IV

THE SYSTEM IN ACTION

TERRITORY OF COURTS AND CHAMBERS

AFTER THE ENACTMENT of the law, organization plans were worked out by the state ministries of justice in agreement with the state social ministries and with consent of employers' organizations and trade unions. The defining of territory to be covered was left to the states. They could give the labor court the same territory as the ordinary courts with a part-time chairman, or increase the territory and provide a full-time chairman. The first method, which the law regarded as typical, was in the interest of the parties involved, because they need not travel long distances to the court and because local conditions could be better understood. Combination with local courts was supposed to simplify organization and administration, because the premises and furniture, as well as the judges of ordinary courts, could be used. Disadvantages were a less specialized chairman and, therefore, perhaps less qualified adjudication. The second method had the advantage that the judge could be a specialist and the assessors become better acquainted with the law they had to apply.

The trade unions favored the second solution because they feared that, with a single person acting as judge of the ordinary and the labor courts, the latter's independence would be less protected. In rural districts, workers were less well organized and the selection of assessors might have presented difficulties. With a more centralized labor court, unions could provide specialized assessors and counsel at the seat of the court and protect members' legal claims. That the unorganized worker who could not afford to pay for traveling expenses would be less protected, seemed justifiable to organized labor.

No uniform method was adopted. In Prussia, Saxony, Hesse, Thuringia, Brunswick, Oldenburg, the Mecklenburgs, Anhalt, Lippe, and Waldeck, as many courts were set up as it was thought would fully occupy the chairman's time. Here the territory of the labor court was equal to that of anywhere from three to eight ordinary courts.[1] In order to obviate long journeys, some courts went on circuit. The southern states aimed at getting the number of courts as near as possible to that of the ordinary courts, with special consideration for scattered agricultural labor. For not more than one or two of the ordinary courts' territory, one labor court was established in Bavaria, Wurtemberg, and Baden respectively.[2] The same method was applied in setting up the courts of appeal.

On July 1, 1927, there were set up 527 labor courts (in 1932 reduced to 452) for 1,745 ordinary courts (1,737 in 1932) of first instance[3] as against 582 industrial courts, 339 commercial courts and 260 labor court chambers in 1926. Eighty district labor courts were established for 156 ordinary district courts[4] —later reduced to 60 (for 159)—and the one Federal Labor Court in Leipzig.[5] In large cities, the premises of the ordinary and labor courts were usually separated; in medium-sized and smaller cities the courts were connected, offices were in the same buildings and the chairmen of the labor court also functioned in the ordinary court.

The business of the various courts was very unequal.[6] Development showed the southern method to be uneconomical. At the beginning of the depression (1930) the number of courts was reduced since some had very few cases.[7]

The creation of special chambers presented problems similar to those involved in fixing districts of the courts, and they were solved in a similar way. The law provided for special chambers for salaried employees and journeymen in order to compensate these groups for the abolition of commercial and guild courts. It permitted special chambers for other occupations and industries because the complexity of industries demanded

THE SYSTEM IN ACTION 85

specialized assessors. A barber could not be expected to judge conditions in the metal industry, nor a manufacturer to judge mining. The technical complexity of mining had been the reason for setting up special courts before the enactment of the AGG. In general chambers, that side would have an advantage whose assessor happened to be familiar with the trade. In special chambers, the chairman could always be familiar with the conditions and needs of the industry. A compromise had been considered during the discussion of the bill which would have made it possible to depart from the usual sequence of assessors in order to make available a person familiar with the trade, a device provided in the statutes of many industrial and commercial courts. This arrangement, however, was rejected in order to prevent arbitrariness and the chairman was not permitted to deviate from the roster.

Against the plan of a large number of special chambers were raised the arguments of high costs and possible delay. To call in assessors for one or very few cases would have increased expenses; to wait until many cases in one industry were ready to be discussed, would have meant protraction. The law, therefore, provided that special chambers need not cover the same territory as the labor courts. Moreover, technical knowledge was needed only in a few cases. A general knowledge of labor, especially of wage conditions, and close contact with the social strata of the parties were, in most cases, sufficient. With a great number of special chambers, organization would have become cumbersome and confusing. With the development of craft into industrial unions, union officials were no longer specialists. Socialist unions favored not differentiation but unification of conditions of work. Unlike other unions of salaried employees, that of the socialists saw it as an achievement of labor adjudication, that differences between the social status of wage earners and that of salaried employees, were reduced, as when the Federal Labor Court recognized short-time work for salaried employees despite fixed salaries.[8] Most cases concerned wages and dismissals which needed no trade knowledge for a decision.

The provision of the law permitting establishment of a

single chamber was applied in eleven cases, ten in East Prussia.[9] Thirty salaried employees' chambers, seven handicraft and thirty-two industrial covered several labor courts in 1932.[10] Thuringia, Anhalt, Oldenburg, Lübeck, Mecklenburg-Schwerin set up special chambers for workmen, salaried employees, and journeymen, and Saxony and Brunswick for workmen and handicraftsmen. In practice, little use was made of the specialization possibility. Chambers for special trades were established only for workers in national railroad systems by railroad administration districts. About eight chambers for commercial employees were set up (replacing 339 commercial courts), which the largest union of salaried employees, the Deutschnationaler Handlungsgehilfenverband (DHV),[11] had urgently demanded, pointing to the fact that 60 per cent of all salaried employees' disputes were those of commercial employees.[12] Saxony, Thuringia, and a few other states had no industrial chambers. With the exception of Berlin, which included twenty-four local court districts and set up thirty-seven[13] special chambers, later increased to forty-eight, Prussia had in only three courts one special chamber each for commercial employees and apprentices. Bavaria, Wurtemberg, Brunswick, Mecklenburg-Strelitz, and Hamburg had a relatively high number of special chambers (mercantile, domestic service, agriculture). Bavaria alone had chambers for mining. Prussia refrained from establishing miners' chambers after the diet resolved against them on May 10, 1927.

Thus, most labor courts worked with assessors who heard cases of various industries. When technical difficulties arose, experts could be consulted. In fact, the assessors adapted themselves to the role of associate judge and did not show bias against special industries or occupations. The leading employees, however, and the commercial employees organized in the DHV, and some groups with special customs (e.g., the theatrical), were not quite satisfied with the solution.

CHAIRMEN AND ASSESSORS

Employees' assessors, insofar as not nominated on combined lists, were provided by unions as shown in Table 15.

TABLE 13

NUMBER OF CHAIRMEN AND JUDGES

YEAR	LABOR COURTS			DISTRICT LABOR COURTS		FEDERAL LABOR COURT
	Number of chairmen	Laymen included	Number of vice-chairmen	Number of chairmen	Number of vice-chairmen	Number of judges
1927	641	36	622	15	89	104	8 (one president and 7 associate judges)
1932	590	19	687	10	76	124	12 (2 presidents and 10 associate judges)

TABLE 14
Number of Assessors in 1928[14]

	Total	Employers	Employees
Labor Courts................	19,933	9,966	9,967
District Labor Courts..........	1,703	851	852
Federal Labor Court...........	38	19	19
In all courts............	21,674	10,836	10,838

Labor Courts			
Wage earners chambers........	8,709	4,354	4,355
Salaried employees chambers....	5,094	2,547	2,547
Combined chambers...........	934	467	467
Craftsmen's chambers..........	5,196	2,598	2,598
Total..................	19,933	9,966	9,967

Labor Courts			
Nominated on combined lists...	7,596	5,052	2,544
Nominated on separate lists....	12,337	4,914	7,423
Total..................	19,933	9,966	9,967

District Labor Courts			
Nominated on combined lists...	541	339	202
Nominated on separate lists....	1,162	512	650
Total..................	1,703	851	852

Federal Labor Court			
Nominated on combined lists...	37	18	19
Nominated on separate lists....	1	1	....
Total..................	38	19	19

THE SYSTEM IN ACTION

TABLE 15
Union Affiliation of Employee Assessors, 1928
Labor Courts

	Total	ADGB	Afa	DGB	Ring*	Other lists
Wage earners' chambers	3,090	2,345	...	490	149	106
Salaried employees' chambers	2,109	8	726	730	570	75
Combined chambers	421	200	43	125	32	21
Craftsmen's chambers	1,803	1,416	7	262	56	62
Totals	7,423	3,969	776	1,607	807	264

District Labor Courts

	650	334	66	145	87	18

*Gewerkschaftsring Deutscher Arbeiter-, Angestellten- und Beamtenverbände, Confederation of Workers, Salaried Employees and Civil Servants.

TABLE 16
Union Affiliation of Employee Assessors, 1927

Organization	Labor Courts	District Labor Courts	Federal Labor Court	Total
DHV	708	79	1	788
Other Gedag* organizations	243	29	1	273
Christian trade unions	1,258	100	2	1,360
Total DGB	2,209	208	4	2,421
GDA†	714	78	1	793
Hirsch Dunckers unions	211	22	1	234
Total RING	925	100	2	1,027
Afa	937	108	2	1,047
ADGB	5,422	414	11	5,847
Total Free Trade Unions	6,359	522	13	6,894
Others	106	4	...	110
Total	9,599	834	19	10,452

*Gesamtverband Deutscher Angestelltengewerkschaften (Christian Salaried Employees' Federation).
†Gewerkschaftsbund Der Angestellten (Trade Union League of Salaried Employees).

90 THE DEVELOPED SYSTEM

The DHV[15] in its 1927 report surveyed trade union affiliations of 10,452 employees' assessors, as shown in Table 16.

How great was the variety of professions represented may be seen by an inquiry which revealed that 470 Afa assessors were distributed as follows: ZdA,[16] 190; of foremen, 168; of technical employees, 75; of foremen in the building industry, 12; of chorus singers and ballet dancers, 5; of bank employees, 7; of stage employees, 2; of artists, 7; of mine machinists, 4.[17]

When dealing with these problems the expert for labor court questions in the Prussian government, Georg Flatow,[18] found 179 women among the 9,480 assessors in labor courts, 42 employers' assessors (38 for wage earners' and 4 for handicraft chambers) and 137 employees' (wage earners', 41 or 2 per cent; salaried employees', 94 or 7.1 per cent; 2 in joint chambers). Eight women were in the district labor courts on the employees' side, one in the Federal Labor Court, representing the Verband weiblicher Handels- und Büroangestellten (Association of Women Commercial and Office Employees, Christian Movement).

Flatow estimated that, of 414 employee assessors in the district labor courts, about 292 were officials of trade unions, at least 140 of employers' organizations. In some cases the same persons had been nominated to the labor courts and district labor courts. In mining and agricultural districts, assessors frequently were from the trade. The DHV had a principle of sending as many assessors as possible from the offices. Of its 788 assessors, only 28 were union officials.

Of the 1,162 Berlin[19] assessors (1,018 labor courts, 144 district labor courts), 320 of the 509 employees were still in their trade and 189 were union officials. In the workmen chambers, 162 were working at the bench, 165 were union officials. In the chambers for salaried employees 158 were in the trade, 24 were union officials, commercial employees, 90 to 8. (DHV, 31 to 1.) Of the 72 district labor court employee assessors, 13 were in their profession, 59 were union officials, among them one workman and 44 officials of workmen's unions; 12 were working salaried employees and 15 were officials of their unions. "Assessors" who were not trade union officials were to a considerable degree members of works councils in great enterprises and could spend full time on such duties (Freigestellte Betriebsräte).

According to an inquiry made in 1931, salaried employees had more assessors working in the profession than did wage earners. Only women salaried employees had a higher percentage of trade union officials. Some trade union officials claimed that they had accepted the position merely because nobody working in the profession could be found.[20]

The number of assessors in the labor courts was too large. Of 1,486 wage earners' assessors who answered a 1931 questionnaire, about 100 had only two or three meetings in a few years, about 100 more had only from two to six meetings;[21] of 2,154 salaried employees, 736 had less than six meetings a year.[22] In the handicraft chambers figures were still lower.[23] Twelve was considered a normal number of meetings to give the assessor experience and training.

In the Federal Labor Court, because of the difficulty of doing justice to all trade unions, the body of lay assessors had been made so large that they were summoned during the first year only once every eight months,[24] which was not often enough to give them experience.

Assessors were generally trained in special courses of the local trade unions before appointment or in the Academy of Labor (cf. n. 4, p. 213). Other means were meetings of assessors, especially in cities with discussion of cases or, among assessors of one court, with the chairmen, who lectured before discussion. Most wage-earner assessors had been union functionaries in social insurance bodies or lay assessors in criminal courts or in industrial, mining, or guild courts. The best means of further training was the work itself. Here too few meetings could be a handicap.

Many salaried employees had some knowledge of law, on account of work. Further training was prevailingly in the hands of unions. Non-trade-union training (e.g., in universities) was frequently financed by the unions. Many assessors had been active in social insurance and the courts. For both groups, periodicals were a valuable source of instruction. Assessors in handicraft chambers had less training.

Another opportunity of education was provided by the

general meetings of the Association of Labor Courts (Verband deutscher Arbeitsgerichte), the successor of the German Association of Industrial and Commercial Courts, a union of professional and lay judges (3,000 members in 1928). It published a periodical, *Das Arbeitsgericht*, as successor to the *Gewerbe- und Kaufmannsgericht*. Labor law questions were frequently discussed in the periodicals of the unions. The free trade unions published a periodical, *Arbeitsrechtspraxis*, exclusively devoted to labor law. Authorities in the field, among them several trade union officials who had won high reputation as experts, published articles on current questions therein. Decisons of the courts were reprinted and case notes were added. Besides this leading trade union labor law periodical, several more specialized labor law reviews were published by individual unions. Wilhelm Herschel who was close to the Christian trade unions published regularly notes on labor cases in the periodical, *Schlichtungswesen*.

THE WORK OF THE COURTS IN THE LIGHT OF STATISTICS[25]

The figures[26] of labor court cases show a great increase after 1927. But they are not strictly comparable because of the enlargement in jurisdiction.

Only in 17.5 per cent in 1927 (19.1 per cent in 1932) was a final verdict delivered; in about 60 per cent in 1927 (about 55 per cent in 1932) was a settlement by compromise or formal judgment reached. The percentage of preliminary amicable settlements was declining slightly. In Prussia, labor courts achieved about twice as many agreements as ordinary courts. In the former, the ratio of judgments to agreements was one to 22, in the latter one to 3.69. The percentage of agreements differed considerably in the districts of various labor courts, however. It must be recalled that many cases which ended in the labor courts by agreement might have been discouraged and brought to compromise by lawyers instead of being brought into the ordinary courts. From 57 to 69 per cent of all cases were expedited in less than one month and only a small percentage required more than one month. The majority of cases handled by the labor courts concerned sums of less than 100 marks (from about 51 to 65 per cent).

TABLE 17
NUMBER OF CASES PENDING AND FILED UNDER NORMAL JUDGMENT PROCEDURE

Year	Total	Filed by Workmen		Filed by Salaried Employees		Concerning Journeymen	
		Number	Percentage	Number	Percentage	Number	Percentage
1927*	164,618	107,953	65.6	39,645	24.1	17,020	10.3
1928	379,689	252,833	66.6	89,796	23.6	37,060	9.8
1929	427,614	277,640	64.9	109,880	25.7	40,084	9.4
1930	438,449	277,022	63.2	123,552	28.2	37,875	8.6
1931	441,243	268,262	60.8	138,648	31.4	34,333	7.8
1932	371,952	225,247	60.6	120,177	32.3	26,168	7.1
1933	261,530	150,864	57.7	91,049	34.8	19,617	7.5
1934	200,052	115,616	57.8	64,895	32.4	19,541	9.8
1935†	188,908	105,645	55.9	64,371	34.1	18,892	10.0
1936	174,476	103,330	59.2	53,709	30.8	17,437	10.9
1937	167,895	101,560	60.5	48,738	29.0	17,597	10.5
1938	151,577	92,057	60.7	44,795	29.6	14,725	9.7
1939	122,795	73,316	59.7	39,093	31.8	10,386	8.5

*July 1—Dec. 31.
†The Saar Territory is included in figures for 1935 and subsequent years.

A slight prolongation of suits took place during the period. Speed, however, was remarkable in view of the fact that the only cases recorded were those decided by formal judgment, which required more time than did agreements. A comparison for 1928 shows that the labor courts closed about two-thirds of all cases in less than one month and only 5.9 per cent in more than three months. In the ordinary Prussian local courts, 48.7 per cent required more than three months. In the district court procedure which, depending on the sum involved, corresponded to about 10 per cent of labor court cases, nearly one-fourth of all cases required more than one year.[27]

The figures show that the great majority of cases arose out of contractual relations and unlawful acts connected with employment, and that collective disputes constituted only a small

TABLE 18
TERMINATION OF CASES IN LABOR COURTS (JUDGMENT PROCEDURE)
(In Percentages)

	1927	1928	1929	1930	1931	1932	1933	1934	1935	1936	1937	1938	1939
By compromise { in amicable settlement	28.6	27.4	25.2	23.5	21.8	22.6	24.4	39.4	36.3	38.1	39.4	40.1	40.9
By compromise { in formal procedure	12.4	12.8	12.3	12.5	11.9	11.6	12.3	....	....	....	....	....	....
By withdrawal of complaint	21.5	21.4	21.2	22.5	23.4	24.2	24.4	15.5	15.4	15.8	16.0	15.2	14.4
By formal judgment	17.5	18.2	17.8	18.8	18.9	19.1	16.5	13.3	14.0	14.6	14.9	14.7	14.4
By default	12.4	12.4	11.3	11.1	10.7	10.0	8.8						
By abandonment	0.4	0.4	0.2	0.2	0.2	0.1	0.1						
By admission of claim	2.9	2.4	2.5	3.0	3.9	3.3	2.9						
Other method of settlement*	4.3	5.0	9.5	8.4	9.2	9.1	10.6	31.8	34.3	31.5	39.7	30.0	30.3
Unsettled	17.2	10.0	9.2	8.9	9.7	9.5	7.2	7.7	9.1	9.9	10.5	10.5	11.8

*From 1934 onward, this column includes termination by withdrawal of complaint.

TABLE 19
CASES SETTLED THROUGH FORMAL JUDGMENT
(In Percentages)

DURATION	1927	1928	1929	1930	1931	1932	1933	1934	1935	1936	1937	1938	1939
Less than one week	6.2	5.1	4.5	3.8	3.7	3.9	5.2 ⎫ 17.6 ⎭	23.2	21.9	18.6	16.6	15.4	16.3
One to two weeks	24.7	22.2	18.8	16.9	16.6	17.0							
Two weeks to one month	38.9	39.1	38.0	37.6	37.0	35.7	35.1	35.6	37.5	36.4	35.1	32.9	30.1
One to three months	26.2	27.7	31.5	32.7	33.1	32.6	30.6	30.8	30.3	33.5	35.1	35.7	37.1
Three months and more	4.0	5.9	7.2	9.0	9.6	10.8	11.5	10.4	10.3	11.5	13.2	16.0	16.5
VALUE OF THE SUM INVOLVED													
Less than 20 marks	19.2	18.2	16.5	14.1	13.5	14.4 ⎫	74.5	....	....	....	....	....	....
20–60 marks	28.4	26.9	25.4	22.9	21.6	21.5		....	....	....	....	....	....
60–100 marks	17.6	16.9	16.8	16.7	16.3	14.5		....	....	....	....	....	....
100–300 marks	20.7	21.8	22.7	23.3	22.8	20.9 ⎭		....	....	....	....	....	....
300–4,000 marks	13.4	15.0	17.6	....	....	....	....	....	....	....	....	....	....
300–6,000 marks	....	....	....	22.1	24.9	27.8	24.6	....	....	....	....	....	....
More than 4,000 marks	0.7	0.9	1.0	....	....	....	....	....	....	....	....	....	....
More than 6,000 marks*	....	....	....	0.9	0.9	0.9	0.9	....	....	....	....	....	....

*Since Feb. 15, 1929.

percentage. To be sure, the latter were of far greater significance than the former. When the court interpreted a provision of the metal collective agreement for the northwestern district, about 400,000 individual cases were automatically settled.

TABLE 20
APPEALS GRANTED BY THE LABOR COURTS

Year	Number granted	Out of cases with value below the appealable sum
1928	4,910	318,381
1929	4,792	348,362
1930	4,672	347,371
1931	3,862	327,507
1932	2,705	264,930
1933	1,428	194,799
1934	983	
1935	1,346	
1936	1,551	
1937	1,619	

TABLE 21
OBJECT OF COMPLAINT IN LABOR COURTS
(In Percentages)

	1927	1928	1929	1930	1931	1932
Cases arising out of disputes concerning contractual relations and out of unlawful acts	95.2	94.8	94.2	91.3	88.4	85.5
Dismissals of workers (BRG)	3.9	4.3	5.2	8.2	11.3	14.0
Cases between parties to a collective agreement arising out of the agreement	0.7	0.7	0.4	0.3	0.1	0.2
Employees out of common employment	0.2	0.1	0.1	0.1	0.1	0.1
Extended jurisdiction	0.1	0.1	0.1	0.1	0.1	0.2

THE SYSTEM IN ACTION

TABLE 22
CASES FILED FOR SUMMARY PROCEDURE

YEAR	NUMBER	DISTRIBUTION (in percentages)		
		Workmen	Salaried employees	Craftsmen
1927	1,076	89.1	9.7	1,2
1928	2,935	86.4	12.5	1.1
1929	3,247	82.4	16.4	1.2
1930	3,968	74.4	24.4	1.2
1931	6,056	69.5	29.3	1.2
1932	4,075	64.2	34.7	1.1
1933	1,601	54.7	44.2	1.1

TABLE 23
DISTRIBUTION OF CASES IN SUMMARY PROCEDURE

	Number	1928 Percentage	1932 Percentage
End of membership in works representation	377	12.9	6.3
Dissolution of works representation	101	3.4	1.8
Convening of provisional bodies	80	2.7	0.7
Setting up and dissolution of works representations	49	1.7	0.3
Imposition of fines	376	12.8	6.0
Infringement of hiring principles	55	1.9	0.6
Setting up, composition, activities and elections	1,348	45.9	17.5
Supplementing the consent of works representations to dismissal of their members	549	18.7	66.8

Before the depression, most cases concerned the setting up, composition, and activities of works representation and elections. During the depression, the question of substituting a court decision for works representation consent to the dismissal of members became most important. The figure doubled from 1930 to 1931.

TABLE 24
CASES IN SUMMARY PROCEDURE

TERMINATED	1928 Percentage	1932 Percentage
By withdrawal of application	46.3	35.9
By resolution	50.1	49.4
In some other way	3.6	14.7
UNSETTLED	7.9	7.9
DURATION OF FORMAL SETTLEMENT		
Less than one week	6.0	4.1
One to two weeks	20.0	15.1
Two weeks to one month	38.1	40.5
One month to three months	30.7	33.6
More than three months	5.2	6.7

TABLE 25
REPRESENTATION IN LABOR COURTS

	INDIVIDUAL EMPLOYMENT CONFLICTS		DISMISSAL CONFLICTS	
	1931	1932	1931	1932
EMPLOYERS				
Representation by members and officials of employers' organizations	148,155	40,892	10,219	7,627
Court officials assigned as counsel to poor	2,489	1,673	355	1,063
Other representatives	25,411	24,912	3,429	8,253
EMPLOYEES				
Representation by members and officials of trade unions	93,455	72,293	14,441	13,685
Court officials assigned as counsel to poor	16,505	13,925	214	219
Other representatives*	18,008	16,091	2,070	2,290
WORKS COUNCILS				
By members and officials of trade unions			14,634†	15,395
Other representatives			1,860†	2,412

*This figure covers such cases as that of a father representing a minor child, a husband his wife.
†Out of 24,500 complaints filed by works councils.

TABLE 26
DISTRICT LABOR COURTS—CASES 1928–1932

	1928		1929		1930		1931		1932	
	Number	Percentage	Number	Percentage	Number	Percentage	Number	Percentage	Number	Percentage
Appeals lodged in judgment procedure............	13,497	....	16,738	....	20,042	....	20,633	....	17,220	....
Settled by trial and judgment..	6,097	....	7,289	....	8,775	....	8,874	....	7,223	....
Sum less than 300 marks.....	.....	29.4	.....	26.6	.....	21.5	.....	19.6	.....	17.2
Cases in summary procedure...	324	....	360	....	441	....	561	....	461	....
Judgment complaints........	810	....	1,308	....	1,062	....	1,221	....	1,236	....
Complaints in summary procedure.............	460	....	569	....	742	....	808	....	759	....
Appeal for review*.........	804	....	693	....	690	....	610	....	497	....
Duration:										
Less than one month.........	.....	28.3	.....	22.5	.....	19.0	.....	20.1	.....	19.1
One to two months...........	.....	53.9	.....	48.2	.....	50.7	.....	48.9	.....	49.3
Two to three months.........	.....	13.4	.....	17.1	.....	15.0	.....	14.3	.....	15.6
Three months and longer.....	.....	8.9	.....	12.2	.....	15.3	.....	16.7	.....	16.0

*Appeal for review granted by district labor courts for cases below the appealable sum.

TABLE 27

DISTRICT LABOR COURTS—CASES 1934-1939

	1934		1935		1936		1937		1938		1939	
	Number	Percentage	Number	Percentage	Number	Percentage	Number	Percentage	Number	Percentage	Number	Percentage
Appeal lodged in judgment procedure	7,373	....	7,105	....	7,015	....	6,079	....	5,549	....	4,315	....
Settled												
by compromise	1,344	21.1*	1,171	19.9	1,123	18.9	1,029	20.5	921	19.9	711	19.9
by informal judgment	471	7.4*	447	7.6	447	7.5	328	6.6	355	7.7	237	6.6
by formal judgment	3,120	48.9*	3,211	54.6	3,274	55.1	2,693	53.7	2,493	54.0	1,953	54.8
otherwise	1,443	22.6*	1,050	17.9	1,098	18.5	962	19.2	848	18.4	665	18.7
Unsettled†	995	13.5	1,226	17.3	1,073	15.3	1,067	17.6	932	16.8	749	17.4
Cases in summary procedure	....	....	....	....	....	....	....	....	....	....	....	....
Judgment complaints	1,002	....	1,142	....	1,171	....	966	....	855	....	603	....
Appeal for review‡	235	....	241	....	273	....	284	....	321	....	306	....
Duration:												
Less than one month	....	24.2	....	33.9	....	29.4	....	30.9	....	....	....	....
One to three months	....	59.4	....	53.0	....	54.2	....	54.2	....	....	....	....
Three months and longer	....	16.4	....	13.1	....	16.4	....	14.9	....	....	....	....

*In percentage of settled cases. †In percentage of cases appealed.
‡Appeal for review granted by district labor courts for cases below the appealable sum.

THE SYSTEM IN ACTION

TABLE 28
Cases in 1932

Objects of Complaint	Number
Conflicts arising out of employment and tortious acts	14,788
Litigation between the parties to a collective agreement	72
Disputes between fellow-workers	56
Disputes concerning dismissal (BRG)	2,293
Extended jurisdiction	11

Settlement	Number 1932	Percentage of Cases Settled 1932	Percentage of Cases Settled 1935
Settled by formal judgment: Total	7,233	48.1	54.6
Sustained	1,670	11.1	....
Rejected	4,690	31.2	....
Mixed	873	5.8	....
Agreement	3,406	22.6	19.9
Default	817	5.4	....
Otherwise (e.g., dismissal for incompetence)	3,603	23.9	25.5

		Percentage of Total Cases 1932	Percentage of Total Cases 1935
Unsettled	2,161	12.5	17.3

Many chairmen were not fully occupied with labor cases. In complaints concerning cases of summary procedure (Rechtsbeschwerden), the works council frequently did not know that it could not produce new facts. Speed, however, as compared with ordinary courts, was remarkable. In 1931, only 16.7 per cent of appeals needed more than three months in the district labor courts, while in the ordinary district courts, 31.9 per cent needed more than six months.[28]

THE DEVELOPED SYSTEM

TABLE 29
Federal Labor Courts

Year	1928 Number	1928 Per cent	1929 Number	1929 Per cent	1930 Number	1930 Per cent	1931 Number	1931 Per cent	1932 Number	1932 Per cent	1933 Number	1933 Per cent
Number of appeals for review	762	....	959	....	953	....	982	....	831	....	479	....
Direct appeal	6	....	6	....	4	....	2	....	3	....	3	....
Revision complaint	38	....	72	....	118	....	119	....	151	....	64	....
Complaint in summary procedure	61	....	64	....	92	....	120	....	110	....	....	....
Appeals admitted	....	78.0	....	76.5	....	78.5	....	76.1	....	70.0	....	....
Object of Appeal — more than 4,000 marks	....	22.0	....	....	....	....	....	....	....	....	....	....
more than 6,000 marks	....	....	....	23.5	....	21.5	....	23.9	....	30.0	....	....
less than 300 marks	....	43.2	....	39.1	....	38.5	....	34.1	....	29.0	....	....
Object of complaint — Contractual relations and tortious acts	....	91.7	....	92.4	....	95.9	....	96.6	....	95.9	....	....
Collective agreements	....	7.5	....	7.2	....	3.7	....	3.2	....	3.9	....	....
Between employees	....	0.4	....	0.2	....	0.2	....	0.1	....	0.2	....	....
Extended jurisdiction	....	0.4	....	0.2	....	0.2	....	0.1	....	....	....	....
Method of Settlement — Formal judgment	293	....	524	....	470	....	525	....	478	....	260	....
Other method	100	....	196	....	143	....	162	....	202	....	136	....
Unsettled	369	....	239	....	340	....	295	....	151	....	83	....
Duration — less than three months	....	18.8	....	2.7	....	3.4	....	2.7	....	18.2	....	35.4
three to six months	....	81.2	....	97.3	....	64.7	....	42.8	....	61.5	....	51.9
Six to twelve months	....	....	....	....	....	31.9	....	54.3	....	19.9	....	12.7
More than one year	....	....	....	....	....	....	....	0.2	....	0.4	....	....

TABLE 30
FEDERAL LABOR COURTS

YEAR	1934 Number	1934 Per cent	1935 Number	1935 Per cent	1936 Number	1936 Per cent	1937 Number	1937 Per cent	1938 Number	1938 Per cent	1939 Number	1939 Per cent
Number of appeals for review	350	....	407	....	397	....	410	....	424	....	459	....
Direct Appeal	....	....	....	....	....	....	....	....	....	....	....	....
Revision complaint	....	....	....	....	....	....	....	....	....	....	....	....
Complaint in summary procedure	....	....	....	....	....	....	....	....	....	....	....	....
Appeals admitted	....	....	....	....	....	....	....	....	....	....	....	....
Object of Appeal — more than 4,000 marks	....	....	....	....	....	....	....	....	....	....	....	....
Object of Appeal — more than 6,000 marks	....	....	....	....	....	....	....	....	....	....	....	....
Object of Appeal — less than 300 marks	....	....	....	....	....	....	....	....	....	....	....	....
Object of complaint — Contractual relations and tortious acts	....	....	....	....	....	....	....	....	....	....	....	....
Object of complaint — Collective agreements	....	....	....	....	....	....	....	....	....	....	....	....
Object of complaint — Between employees	....	....	....	....	....	....	....	....	....	....	....	....
Object of complaint — Extended jurisdiction	....	....	....	....	....	....	....	....	....	....	....	....
Method of Settlement — Formal judgment	175	....	207	....	208	....	215	....	184	....	232	....
Method of Settlement — Other method	84	....	108	....	70	....	77	....	70	....	56	....
Method of Settlement — Unsettled	91	....	92	....	119	....	118	....	170	....	171	....
Duration — less than three months	....	36.6	....	30.4	....	23.6	....	4.6	....	....	....	....
Duration — three to six months	....	54.3	....	63.3	....	66.3	....	82.8	....	....	....	....
Duration — Six to twelve months	....	9.1	....	6.3	....	10.1	....	12.6	....	....	....	....
Duration — More than one year	....	....	....	....	....	....	....	....	....	....	....	....

TABLE 31
Guild Committees

	1931	1932
Number of cases*	7,135	6,406
Method of settlement		
By agreement	4,662	4,134
Decision	2,473	2,272
Complaint against decision in the Labor Courts	770	822

*Not reported before 1931.

TABLE 32
Cases of Berlin Committee for Apprentice Conflicts
(It included most Berlin Guilds[29])

Year	Total	Settled by compromise	Decision	Appeal to Labor Courts
1927	103	29	74	5
1928	105	70	35	11
1929	79	56	23	18
1930	137	88	49	22
1931	237	70	167	34
1932	223	73	150	58
1933	120	52	68	17
1934	80	25	55	9
1935	165	56	109	19
1936	215	48	167	19

TABLE 33
Statistics of the Berlin Labor Courts in 1928[30]

Chamber for	Cases in Judgment Procedure	Cases in Summary Procedure
Salaried employees in insurance and banks....	965	11
" " " railways...............	62	11
" technical employees in metal industry.	856	3
Other technical employees, including foremen.	1,083	1
Artists (stage and film)......................	1,161	..
Other salaried employees (excluding industry, trade, handicraft)........................	3,433	38
Commercial employees......................	11,577	20
Journeymen in clothing industry.............	1,752	1
" " leather, cellulose, graphic industry........................	436	1
" " building industry...............	1,496	1
" " metal industry.................	1,323	4
" " food, cleaning..................	1,518	..
Workers in clothing industry.................	1,787	14
" " leather and millinery.............	774	8
" " graphic industry.................	1,581	20
" " building industry................	4,283	10
" " woodwork industry..............	2,115	8
" " metal industry..................	4,629	58
" " food, cleaning...................	1,159	13
" " lodging, refreshment.............	4,712	25
" " transportation...................	1,802	17
" " cars, bus, subways..............	119	..
" " trade and those not belonging to other chambers...............	3,513	34
" " ceramic and chemical industry....	559	11
" and salaried employees in agriculture and forestry.....................	1,132	3
Domestic servants..........................	5,252	..
Janitors...................................	1,504	..
Total.............................	60,582	312

Chapter V

APPRAISAL

BETWEEN THE FOUNDING of industrial courts in 1890 and the end of the war, Germany's economic and social conditions underwent tremendous changes. In 1890, small-scale industries needed help to regulate labor conditions. In 1918, the workers of large-scale industries were in power and trade unions had acquired unexpected political and economic importance. It was the trade union movement under the leadership of the mass-industry unions which largely influenced the shaping of labor law. Socialistic ideas of centralization, concentration, and unification seemed appropriate to an industrialized country. A court, such as described by Lautenschlager, into which employers and workers came informally to talk over troubles with a judge and learn from him whether or not to file a complaint, had no place in the new picture. The new system, unified and centralized, extended its jurisdiction to collective labor law.

Appraisal of the new system must distinguish between technical organization and the interpretation of law by the judiciary. Within the latter, we must distinguish between the large amount of every-day litigation arising out of the employment contract—matters in general not subject to review by higher courts—and cases which necessitated interpretation of the new collective labor law.

APPRAISAL

STRUCTURE AND PERFORMANCE

Technical Structure and Every-day Litigation

According to the general view, the structure of the new system represented a great step forward. From the point of view of unification and concentration, the improvement was obvious. With unimportant exceptions, all employees were covered. Appeal was to courts specializing in labor law, in which representatives of employers and employees served as lay judges. In the Supreme Court the lay element was an innovation. Decisions of the Federal Labor Court unified the interpretation and application of labor law. The social administration co-operated with the administration of justice in supervising the courts. Chairmen had to have special knowledge and experience of social matters. All this meant that the special nature of the labor contract was recognized. The compromise between independence and integration with ordinary courts met with general approval, although a closer contact with factory inspection and placement service might have been desirable. Shortcomings due to the largeness of areas were the result of more defects in representation (cf. p. 121) than of the structure of the court system.

Court personnel, too, met with general approval. As in the industrial and commercial courts, assessors did not regard themselves as class fighters, but as judges. Only in fundamental questions concerning collective labor relations did they often defend opposing interests. Large-scale employers did not, as a rule, identify themselves with small businessmen who failed to treat employees decently, nor did labor assessors protect unjustified workers' claims. The labor assessors took occasion to show unorganized workers that they were not identified with them. In general, co-operation in the courts, and especially the explanations of the chairman, had an educational influence. When they abused their office, assessors were removed.[1]

For ordinary litigation, the court system maintained the popularity which the industrial and commercial courts had acquired. Litigation remained as speedy,[2] inexpensive, and informal as in the former industrial and commercial courts, and conciliatory efforts were as effective. Appeal was greatly accelerated as compared to the ordinary courts because of the shortening of the period during which it might be filed and prepared. With its informality and concentration, the procedure of the lower courts became a model for ordinary civil procedure. The procedure depended to a high degree on the personality of the chairman, who enjoyed unprecedented discretionary power with respect to procedure and evidence. These he molded in accordance with his ability, his eagerness to effect a compromise, his will to grasp technical details or to appoint and be guided by an expert. Lack of promotion opportunities made older judges hesitant to enter this branch, while young persons could, on completion of their training, hope soon to get a permanent position in this field. There were, nevertheless, few complaints about lack of experience of the chairman. Only occasionally did labor complain that he seemed too close to the employer, or lacking in understanding of the generally weaker position of the worker, or without sufficient knowledge of shop conditions. In general, co-operation with the chairman was satisfactory. Labor assessors had some misgivings about a tendency among chairmen to lean on decisions of higher courts. But, although they insisted that each case be decided on its merits, unions were not, on the whole, opposed to the application of precedents.

Although the percentage of amicable settlements was slightly less than in the industrial courts, organized labor sometimes complained that there were too many and accused the chairman of using pressure, an argument which also had been raised against the industrial and commercial courts. Labor contended that, as compromised in conciliatory proceedings, settlements were unfavorable to their interests. They demanded that such settlements be made only where, without guilt of the parties, no evidence could be provided. In other cases, the plaintiffs should not be induced to give way except after consideration of the justice of the cause. Settlements before the full court were more favorable to the worker. There was always the danger that with a "rage for settlements" (Vergleichswut), as workers called it, splitting the difference might become customary and thus parties be induced to make unjustified or not fully justified demands, in order to have a chance of gaining something.[3] "It is sometimes like a horse trade," said one assessor; "either there is a law or there is none,"[4] a remark typical of the belief of the German worker that each special problem should be decided by statute. Employers were afraid that judges might try to "improve" the law by compromises.[5] At the outset of the industrial court system, Lautenschlager said: "I don't see why a plaintiff whose claim is contested without reason should yield something of his good right and why the defendant against whom are lodged unjustified demands, should pay. People are angrier about a compromise than if they lose a suit. Frequently laziness on the part of a judge who dislikes to write opinions on which decisions must be based, compels parties to settle."[6] Amicable settlement, however, took from the losing party the sense of a defeat. Personal contact of parties in court contributed much to conciliation.[7]

In general, decisions in every-day litigation evoked little criticism. Performances in settlement of the commoner type of litigation—which amounted to about nine-tenths of all litigation—were generally satisfactory. Such scepticism as still existed in 1927 could have been overcome.

Interest in the labor court system was great in small scale business, but big business also recognized its importance. To groups of higher employees or professionals—actors, teachers— it may have meant less than to wage earners and low-paid salaried employees, the more so since these groups largely made use of arbitral tribunals. But all manual workers approved it. Workers thought labor courts indispensable because they saved large sums in wages and preserved many jobs.

When parties could appear in person in the labor courts they felt at ease and were helped by the chairman in working out their idea of justice. The district labor courts and Federal Labor Court had nothing of the intimacy of the labor courts, of course. Labor enjoyed, in all instances, equality with the employer in the courts.

The power of the courts to grant the right of appeal guaranteed that all disputes of importance were brought to the higher courts. In fact, a large part of the cases which came before the appeal courts were admitted by special authorization. The general opinion of legal literature was that too many appeals were allowed. It was pointed out that the interest in local collective agreements, especially if they were to expire after a short time, was not general enough to justify review by a superior court. The parties could correct ambiguous clauses by negotiating a new agreement. Only for *typical* regulations, or those affecting a large number of workers, was appeal justified. The legislator had not intended to have judges pass dubious decisions along to higher courts, as was frequently done. Moreover, too many similar cases were carried to the Federal Labor Court. This can easily be explained by the desire to get final decisions in important issues diversely decided by local courts before the establishment of the Federal Labor Court. Since, however, it could not be expected that the Federal Labor Court would give up its carefully balanced principles after so short an existence, such reiteration of judgments was unnecessary. Future development would have led to some stabilization. Frequently the court admitted appeal as a sort of compromise in order to get a unanimous court decision.

An important criticism of organization was raised by the legal profession, which was deeply dissatisfied with its exclusion from the labor courts. The great power granted to trade unions in the organization of the courts did not meet much criticism. Both questions are discussed in a special chapter (cf. p. 120).

Interpretation of the New Labor Law

Decisions cannot be judged merely by a study of the Federal Labor Court. Unlike Anglo-Saxon countries, in Germany court decisions even of supreme courts did not create law and were not binding except in the particular case at issue. Nevertheless, lower courts were largely influenced by precedent. Unity of decisions was preserved by the fact that the Federal Labor Court was bound by decisions of any Senate of the Federal Supreme Court (not, however, by its own decisions). Should the Federal Labor Court wish to depart from a Federal Supreme Court precedent, a plenum of all civil senates of the Federal Supreme Court and Federal Labor Court or a plenum of all civil and criminal senates of both courts was required to act.

Theoretically, supreme court decisions could be rejected by inferior courts or even executive authorities. This freedom obliged courts to base opinions on solid reasons and prevented petrifaction of the law. The independence of lower courts made difficult uniform application of labor law and the creation of legal security, resulting in a multiplicity of actions. This was outweighed by the fact that every lower court helped in the creation of labor law. Frequent deviation from a Federal Labor Court decision, if convincingly argued, could bring to the attention of the Federal Labor Court the fact that its decision was considered erroneous by the lower courts.

In general, however, Federal Labor Court judgments were not disregarded by administrative agencies or lower courts. The arbitration decree, for instance, was amended when a Federal Labor Court decision declared customary procedure illegal and thus rendered the system unworkable.[8]

Decisions indicated that the judges desired to follow legal scholarship closely. When deviations from views of prominent scholars indicated elaborate distinction, decisions usually quoted legal literature and Federal Labor Court decisions.

Labor courts in all instances took into consideration the decisions of the Federal Supreme Court for Social Insurance (Reichsversicherungsamt) and did not depart from them without well-founded arguments. Thus, for instance, the definition of "salaried employee" given by social insurance courts was accepted in litigation concerning the protection of such employees from dismissal.

The unification of the labor law system was particularly important because much more was needed than the interpretation of law. Labor law in the pre-war period was poorly developed, especially with respect to collective relations of employers and employees. The Civil Code made no distinction between contracts with independent professional men and a labor contract with a factory worker, treating both as *locatio conductio operarum*. Collective agreements were not mentioned in the Civil Code of 1896, since their importance was not understood. Collective labor law before 1918 was 100 per cent judge-made law.

The labor law created after the revolution of 1918 was partly an emergency measure, incomplete, undeveloped, frequently vague, and in need of completion by judicial action. The statutes, some of which amounted to bare statements of principle (e.g., the collective agreement decree of 1918) did not constitute sufficient basis for case decisions. The labor court system had the task of working out a body of substantive law and translating the actualities of collective bargaining into legal terms, since interpretation and enforcement of collective agreements, where not achieved by the parties, had been transferred from the ordinary to the labor courts. This shift had been made because the ordinary judicial system, operating with the individualist legal principles of the Civil Code, could not do justice to the collective character of employer-employee relations.

Organization and procedure of the labor courts prevented a too rigid and unrealistic application of legal rules to the system of collective agreements. The old contract law could be applied in part. In part, only bold departure from it could do justice to the collective idea. The necessary freedom[9] was provided by section 157 of the Civil Code (Sec. 133, 242) which ruled that interpretation of contracts must be according to the requirements of good faith and ordinary usage, thereby giving the judge freedom to consider the community's prevailing sense of justice.

The labor courts followed a general trend which became apparent immediately after the revolution of 1918. Courts no longer adhered to the theory that each case must be decided by the application of the strict provisions of the civil code. The rather vague provisions of the code, such as Sections 157, 242, 826, overshadowed the whole system of law. The method applied after 1918 may be characterized as a sort of "new equity." Labor courts were even more radical in this respect than ordinary courts, although similar tendencies existed in the law concerning unfair competition, corporations and particularly revaluation questions. It was the inflation which shattered pre-war legal methods.

The inclusion of conflicts between economic associations of employers and employees and between such associations and third parties arising out of collective agreements, made the labor courts competent for practically the whole of collective labor law. Interpretative judgments of the courts acquired value in the negotiations of employers' associations and trade unions. Legal decisions brought collective agreements to the consciousness of the community. Courts judged as if in the market place, "like the praetors in ancient Rome."[10]

The incomplete character of collective labor law obliged the courts to produce new formulations and creative decisions. Hence they had to attempt to grasp the prevailing ethical convictions of the community and to balance conflicting interests. This somewhat experimental task was difficult and ungrateful in a time of social tension, when every group identified its interests and convictions with those of the community. The courts were drawn into controversies between capital and labor. Many decisions were highly controversial. They covered, for example, definition of an "economic organization," of "capacity to conclude a collective agreement," "justification of waivers of the collective wage rates," "gross abuse" as a justification for ousting a works councillor, "undue hardship" as protection against dismissal, etc. All these questions of principle were brought before the Federal Labor Court. In deciding issues touching the nerve center of the conflict between capital and labor, the courts had to compromise irreconcilable views. Employers demanded consideration of economic conditions. In fact, the disastrous economic depression which began two years after the courts started to work did not fail to influence decisions.

On the other hand, according to the ideas shared by all German workers, political democracy had to be supplemented by the idea of social-economic democracy, by an equality in which not the individual but the collective co-operated. According to the free trade unions, only the formation and prevalence of collective entities could guarantee progress and equality. Not the individual labor contract was to be the basis of labor law. Labor law had to take into consideration that the individual worker, although free, is dependent. He had to win his independence by collective representation and action. A purely logical and constructional jurisprudence was considered a means of defending the power of the bourgeois class.

Trying to steer its way through such irreconcilable views expressed in contests charged with emotions, attempting to prevent the breakdown of business as well as to do justice to labor, the Federal Labor Court inevitably met sharp criticism from two quarters.

Employers protested when their deliberate attempts to disqualify their associations from concluding collective agreements were frustrated by Federal Labor Court decisions. Some employers' organizations tried to escape by expressly stating in their constitutions that they could not conclude collective agreements. The Federal Supreme Court and the Federal Labor Court overruled the practice. On April 10, 1929,[11] the Federal Labor Court decided that the law had assigned to certain parties public law duties which could not be abolished by changes of constitution as long as they maintained their character as employers' organizations. Even evasion by dissolution was stopped, when the courts decided that trade unions could demand the citation of individual employers before the arbitration boards and subsequent individual citations could be grouped into a single arbitration procedure. In one case, eighty-five firms were included in an arbitration procedure after their association had dissolved.[12] Arbitration could mean imposition of a collective agreement. Employers protested against the interpretation of leave which, according to uniform decisions consisted of two cumulative claims, the grant of vacation and the claim to wages for a period of leave. Workers, according to the Federal Labor Court, did not lose a claim for compensation as a result of dismissal by way of penalty.[13] Employers felt that an undue burden had been laid on them by the decision that permanently disabled workers had a claim to wages during periods of illness.[14] Employers objected that the courts were too social-minded to apply justice. In their opinion, the judiciary was fundamentally inclined not to seek compromise but "to favor the idea of social protection as against economic consideration of the enterprise." [15]

The criticism of organized labor was more general than that of employers. Labor argued that decisions were still based too much on civil rather than on labor law and that the Federal Labor Court had more sympathy for the works council than for the trade union. Judgments and summary decisions in the field of the BRG were not contested.

One decision heavily attacked was the interpretation of the so-called community of risks of employers and employees. The leading case[16] dealt with the following facts. In the early twenties the workers in the Kiel electrical plant struck for better wages. When the street car conductors, organized in another union having nothing to do with the electrical workers' strike, tried to work they could not run the cars. They asked for their wages, stating that they were prepared to work. They pointed out that the "impossibility" was not due to their fault. The action was based on a special provision of the Civil Code (Section 615). The court did not apply this special rule, but rather the vague provision that all contractual duties are primarily controlled by equitable considerations and the idea of justice. The Supreme Court found the solution of the case in the theory that a community of risks between employers and employees (works community) exists which—although unknown to the code—has found its expression in the trends of modern labor law. By means of interpretation, this theory was derived from the broad principle as laid down in Section 242, BGB.

In a similar decision of June 20, 1928,[17] which concerned a temporary stoppage due to lack of coal (resulting from a strike in the lignite industry), the Federal Labor Court in its decision shared the view expressed in the above-mentioned decision of the Federal Supreme Court. The Federal Labor

Court explained that "the individualistic point of view prevailing at the time of the creation of the Civil Code with respect to master and servant has not its old importance, now that the idea of social community of labor and industry has been recognized not only in legal literature but also by legislation. . . . The individual worker does not confront the employer as a single contracting party. He becomes organically a member of the undertaking. . . . He is no longer a mere tool of the employer but a living member of the works community comprised of the employer and the workers as a whole."

With this declaration, the Federal Labor Court recognized the claim of organized labor to be treated as a collective group, a claim which was not contested in principle by the employer. But the Federal Labor Court did not meet the social views of either party by applying the term "community" to their relations. In using it, the Federal Labor Court merely applied a fundamental conception of the Works Council Law which, however, had been neglected by labor in the law's enforcement. "The worker," said the court, "is no longer in the undertaking as an individual who merely offers labor while otherwise remaining alien to the undertaking. There is a measure of unity between him and the undertaking. He not only puts his labor at its disposal, but he also undertakes to contribute to the fulfillment of its objects and to the maintenance of its economic stability." Labor protested vehemently against the conclusions drawn from the fact of such a community in the last decision: "One who is jointly responsible for the undertaking must also bear the resulting disadvantages," i.e., bear the consequences of interruption of work and, in some cases, risks.

On the question of who bears the risk of lost time, the Federal Labor Court ruled that contractual stipulations had to be decisive in the first instance. Where nothing was agreed, a decision must be based on the community of risk. The employer would have to bear the risk alone when responsible for a stoppage (e.g., in case of failure to provide coal or electric current). On the other hand, employees had to bear the primary risk where the interruption was due to the conduct of a group of working personnel, as in partial strikes. According to the solidarity of labor, it was argued, unemployment caused by fellow-workers would not entitle those willing to work to compensation. This decision, though attacked by labor, met with public approval because of the danger that the employer might be forced to finance partial strikes based on a general labor plan, since it was labor's tactic to call out only key groups and thereby cripple the work of all.

Community of work, however, demanded more sacrifices, according to Federal Labor Court decisions. Workers had to bear their share when the existence of an undertaking was threatened by a long stoppage due to natural or extraneous forces.[18] Thus, employees were made to bear the risk of interruption of electric current in a shipyard due to an unusual and unforeseeable ebb of water.[19]

Decisions based on the community of work within the undertaking, for which the Federal Labor Court had not laid down general rules, were attacked by both parties, as well as in legal literature. The employers resented having to take a larger part of the risk, to prevent wage losses. Organized labor called the community of interests and the organic conception of the undertaking an invention similar to feudal law. They refused to share the risk without sharing the profit. It would become a "community of loss."[20] Legal literature deplored the fact that decisions concerning works community made it impossible to calculate risk.

Similarly attacked was the theory of the Federal Labor Court concerning "waivers" of wages after work had been done and wages were due.[21] Waiver contracts by means of which one party to a contract partly or wholly gives up legal claims without compensation, are legal in German contract law. The question arose whether this general doctrine was applicable to labor contracts regulated by collective agreement. The German collective agreement statute was based on the principle of non-deviability. The individual employer and the individual employee could not agree on employment conditions contrary to the collective agreement unless these conditions were more favorable to the employee than was the collective agreement. But did this statutory provision exclude only agreements with respect to labor to be done in the future, or also contracts regulating payments for labor rendered in the past? The Federal Labor Court recognized in principle the validity of contracts by means of which the employee waived a part of his wages contrary to the collective agreement provided that the waiver dealt with compensation for work done in the past. There was, however, one significant exception. A waiver under duress was declared invalid. The Federal Labor Court interpreted the concept of "duress" very broadly. "Duress" was recognized not only where threat or pressure was exercised on the individual employee, but in all cases in which an employee was motivated by fear of losing a job or similar economic considerations.[22]

The trade unions and many labor law experts criticized this decision of the Federal Labor Court, arguing that an ex post facto waiver was contrary to the principle that collective should have priority over individual contracts. Employers and many contract law experts defended the decision since it saved the principle of "freedom of contract" and because weak entrepreneurs got a chance to keep workers by paying lower wages than set forth in collective agreements.

In practice, however, the "economic pressure" exception to the waiver-contract proved more important than the principle that waiver-contracts were valid. It was hard to imagine a case in which an employee waived wages unless under "economic pressure."

The doctrine of the Federal Labor Court created insecurity and made decisions unpredictable. Here was a true "compromise" decision resented, for different reasons, both by employers and employees.

Another decision, attacked as contrary to the spirit of the collective idea, concerned the capacity of company unions to conclude collective agreements. While the trade unions considered all workers' associations restricted to one undertaking as dependent on the employer by mere threat of dismissal, the Federal Labor Court recognized, in principle, the capacity of such unions to conclude collective agreements.[23] Each case had to be treated on its merits. Size of enterprise, financial resources, and similar criteria should be taken into consideration in judging independence. Similarly, the independence of non-militant unions had to be examined in each case. When a farm workers' union, which rejected the strike as a weapon, won the recognition of the Federal Labor Court[24] (cf. pp. 127-28), there was widespread protest.

Franz Neumann expressed the deep disappointment of left wing socialists with the Federal Labor Court in describing labor law, after five years of interpretation by the labor courts, as a heap of ruins. "The plan for equal participation (gleichberechtigte Mitwirkung) of workers in adjudication has not fulfilled the ideal of reconciliation of workers with the State,"[25] because the men of the Federal Labor Court were not heroic enough to withstand the influence of the depression and the ideological destruction of the idea of democracy and equality (Parität).

The ruins are not those of positive labor law, was the answer of another labor jurist (close to the employers), but of castles in the air, of programmatic utopias which, in view of inevitable economic development, could but slightly influence law.[26] Another labor jurist saw in the judgments of the Federal Labor Court a tendency towards fascism,[27] as expressed in the Italian *Carta del Lavoro*, the attempt of the state to suppress irrepressible class fights.

This view, however, remained isolated. Decisions of the Federal Labor Court were not homogeneous enough to justify any such interpretation. The Federal Labor Court had no conscious social ideal but attempted to do justice to two groups and to protect the interests of the community. In facing fights between interested parties, the court attempted not only to protect the weaker group within the frame of existing laws, but to prevent economic and social disintegration. The Act was in force for such a short time (only five and one-half years in 1933) that its application could not be tested at all points, especially since the depression influenced decisions and opinions formed about them.

Legislation would have been able to correct Federal Labor

Court decisions considered inadequate by public opinion. The law of collective agreement, for instance, which was supposed to be enacted in due course of time, would have had to solve such contested questions as bargaining capacity, waivers, etc. The Reichstag hesitated before this type of legislation, however, and relied on the courts to find solutions. It was considered their function to prepare the way for future legislation. Since standardization of labor law in a period of such rapid development and fundamental change could easily become a drag on business and even on labor, it was considered preferable that the workers continue under a diversified and complex body of rights with a uniform system of interpretation. Clarification of some moot points was sought in bills pending in 1933 when the National Socialists came into power.

TRADE UNIONS AND THE LABOR COURTS

The spirit of the AGG was to favor trade unionism or, more correctly, recognized trade unions. Economic associations of employers and employees, i.e., bona fide trade unions and employers' organizations, had the right to co-operate in the establishment, organization and supervision of labor courts. Economic organizations had the right to sue and to be a party to a suit in the labor courts whether or not incorporated (AGG, Sec. 10). In ordinary courts this right could be exercised only by incorporated associations. While employers' associations were in general incorporated, the trade unions did not register in order to avoid full liability in case of tortious acts in strikes. Trade unions before the World War, therefore, had not been able to sue or assert claims arising out of collective agreements. Thus a great handicap was removed.

Local competence could be regulated by collective agreement. It thus became possible to concentrate law suits for special industries and territories in one labor court, even for outsiders to whom the collective agreement was extended by the Minister of Labor.[28] Since the labor courts interpreted collective agreements, the trade unions considered their activity in the courts as part of their policy.

Trade unions and employers' associations had almost a monopoly of arbitral labor tribunals. Their role symbolized the progress of the collective idea. "At the threshold of the GGG stood the individual contract, in its place in the AGG stands the collective agreement, protected and promoted by the State as the basis of the large majority of all individual contracts."[29] Leading factors of trade union power in the courts were representation of organized labor in courts of first and second instance and the presentation of lists of assessors for nomination.

Representation in Courts[30]

Trade unions were entitled to represent their members in labor courts and district labor courts, and in the former enjoyed a monopoly of representation.[31] The right was restricted to trade unions (and employers' organizations) capable of being parties to collective agreements,[32] and to federations of such associations. The trade unions had trained a large number of officials in the conduct of cases. Where the local union was large enough, one official usually acted as full-time representative. Smaller unions could get the help of their federations.

The barring of lawyers from courts of first instance was always contested. The campaign for a change was backed by the whole legal profession, including chairmen of labor courts, and by the employers' organizations, although many of the latter could employ a legally trained man to represent them in the courts. The mistake of banning lawyers from the labor courts had been made, it was argued, because the Reichstag had entrusted preparation of the law not to the Committee on Law (Rechtsausschuss) but to the Social-Political Committee, of which only three jurists were permanent members, while the other twenty-five members were prevailingly secretaries of trade unions, political parties, and other organizations. This argument was not convincing since the political parties could easily have changed the composition of the committee by substituting members, as was frequently done when a subject required expert discussion.

All trade unions, including those of higher salaried employees, opposed any change in the law. They were wholly satisfied since the system of representation worked to their benefit. They had favored large districts and heavy concentration of litigation, since otherwise they could not have provided a trained representative for each member. They could point to the fact that representation by officials of trade unions and employers organizations had not prevented parties from appearing in the courts. Representatives aided but did not displace parties; thus close contact of judge and parties was preserved.

To be sure, the system worked satisfactorily in most everyday conflicts of organized employers and employees. The officials of the organizations restricted themselves to a presentation of facts. They did not dispute facts which were common knowledge to everybody in the plants. Occasionally representatives were unable to distinguish essential from other facts. In general, the representatives were close to the parties and to labor matters, and their co-operation was helpful. Trade union officials could speak more freely than workers. That the dissatisfaction with the exclusion of lawyers was growing, nevertheless, may be ascribed to two fundamental shortcomings. One was that the development of labor law was deprived of the help of lawyers in these courts. Secondly, some large groups could not receive the aid of counsel in courts of first instance. Also involved was the slight to the lawyers, who had particularly high standing in Germany.

The system of representation by members and officials of organizations was unsatisfactory wherever fundamental decisions about principles of law had to be made. Even the trade unions felt this, as, for example, in the famous conflict in the northwestern iron industry involving the one-man arbitration award and the interference of arbitration awards with existing collective agreements. Here the official of the powerful employers' organization was a former prosecutor while the trade unions could be represented only by officials, not learned advocates. The unions lost this suit in the first instance. Aided by three lawyers, they won in the second although they lost again in the third.

APPRAISAL

The trained lawyer could have helped the chairman in many cases simply because of the novelty of labor law. Decisions of the labor court in a particular case frequently became *de facto* precedents for a whole branch of industry. A chairman could get no help from lay assessors in creating law, but was left alone with the great responsibility of immediately executable decisions.

The second drawback—that some large groups remained without representation—was still more serious. These underprivileged groups belonged prevailingly to the working class. In 1930, of about eighteen million workmen included in invalidity insurance, only 5,900,000 were organized; of 3,500,000 salaried employees only 1,700,000 were organized.[33] Organized labor considered the hardships of the unorganized just punishment for lack of solidarity. "In the present order of society, social organizations play such an important role that everybody who remains outside eliminates himself. . . . The state, carried today by social organizations, has not been established to create special institutions for those who place themselves outside social organizations."[34] The unorganized party, they said, is unrepresented through its own fault.

Nörpel explained that German justice hitherto had been individualistic, while the trade unions succeeded in carrying their collectivistic ideas into the AGG. The law does away with individualism. "The trade unions have created labor law and cannot admit their principles to be violated by egoists. The unorganized worker who stands aloof cannot complain. . . . In order to make use of his right, he must join a trade union." This would be less expensive than railroad fare.[35] It is not immoral to insist on organization, Nörpel said on another occasion. "Those who remain individualists in a period of collectivism must bear the consequences."[36]

Such views meant an indirect compulsion to coalition and a Berlin Labor Court therefore declared the exclusion of lawyers unconstitutional (July 13, 1928), without, however, citing authority in literature or the courts. Moreover, not all the unorganized could have joined an organization, for instance, a party suing for the wages of a deceased person, divorced wives, pursuing the wage claim of a former husband, or other "third person." Some persons did not fit into existing organizations or might not have been eligible, e.g., the agent, artist, or contractor who, because of economic and personal dependence, was considered by the courts to be an employee. Foreigners who had returned to their home country could not be represented. Trade union employees in conflict with employers or each other could not be represented. An organized employer or worker might not desire to be represented by his organization, because of disagreement with the latter's view or for other reason.[37]

Not all organizations had a continuous network of local offices. Smaller organizations were not always able to provide representatives at all places. For instance, the trade union of conductors of orchestras and choirs had only one office, in Berlin, and could not send representatives all over the Reich.[38]

When persons without organizational aid were at their place of residence, they could appear, and were at a disadvantage only insofar as they had no assistance of counsel. They could get legal advice from lawyers, the few municipal legal aid bureaus or such labor secretariats (of trade unions) as received public funds. The unorganized party whose case came up in a place far from his residence, who could not afford railroad fare and loss of earnings, who knew no one in the court town to act as his representative, was at a clear disadvantage. This happened frequently in cases of transportation workers or workers who had changed their place of work. Memoranda of physicians and artists[39] showed that these groups felt the handicap heavily.[40] An unsatisfied need for representation existed in cases of employers who would have had to close their shop, of employees who had changed jobs and disliked informing the new employer of an old conflict in order to get leave, and of sick or handicapped persons.

The courts tried to meet the need generously. It became their practice to appoint a clerk of the court or a referendar[41] as the paid counsel of an absent party, a device whose legality was disputed.[42] Statistics on such representation show that of 441,243 cases in 1931, court officials represented the parties in 19,543 cases (16,719 of whom were employees). Such representation, then, was granted in 1931 in 4.43 per cent of the cases; in 1932 in 4.54 per cent. Although representation by organizations was much larger,[43] the figures reveal a great gap. They show only part of the need, since representation was granted by some courts only if the worker did not live in the district and was poor, i.e., unable, by the testimony of a municipal authority, to pay traveling expenses without serious impairment of his or his family's subsistence. Parties could be in straitened circumstances without being "poor." Moreover, the districts were so large that traveling expenses could be out of proportion to the disputed sum.

The solution remained a makeshift. Officials were withdrawn from their functions (in Berlin five court officials were permanently employed representatives). Referendars were trained only one month in the labor courts and could not acquire broad experience. They were less qualified than representatives of organizations. A change of representation could delay procedure. This lack of protection was the more inappropriate in that the sum for appeals had been fixed much higher than in ordinary courts. To deprive a person of both representation and the right to appeal was unjustified.

Monopoly of representation in the labor courts strengthened trade unionism not merely by facilitating the drive for members. Trade unions refused to represent their own members when the latter held deviating views. In undertaking representation, they demanded that wherever the interest of the individual deviated from that of the organization the client follow directions and put his interest below that of the organization. In such cases, then, the individual was not protected.

Although some amendments were introduced in the Reichstag, none were passed before the Hitler revolution. Fear of increasing expenses was great during the depression,[44] and trade union members of parliamentary factions in the Reichstag used their influence to prevent amendment. Amendment was bound to come, however, even if not in the form of unlimited admittance of lawyers. Various proposals had been made for admittance of lawyers for persons not residing at the seat of a court, or cases of fundamental importance,[45] etc. A democratic legislator would have found some compromise solution.

Appointment of Assessors

The change from the election to the appointment of assessors worked in favor of the trade unions. Government, employers' organizations, and free trade unions agreed on this change, only the last realizing its revolutionary character. In its 1923 bill, the government proposed indirect election (by district economic councils and National Economic Council) and, as a preliminary, appointment by the social administration. In a few new labor laws, appointment displaced election, as in the Placement Service Law of 1922[46] and an ordinance relating to the Arbitration Decree of 1923.[47] The ordinance provided for appointment of additional assessors to the industrial and commercial courts until new elections.

The 1923 bill gave as its motives the high cost of elections and the poor participation in elections to the industrial courts, without mentioning the fact that this had been due partly to the misery of the inflation period. In 1923, the climax of inflation, the darkest year for public finances, even the Association of German Municipalities (Deutscher Städtetag) came forward with similar suggestions.

After stabilization of the mark, the argument of high costs and small election participation would have lost validity. Costs could have been reduced by holding all social elections on one day (including those for social insurance), and interest in elections would have revived. Nor could the precedence of the arbitration law justify appointment. The arbitration system had to deal—except for a few unimportant works representation cases—with disputes of interests between economic associations. The AGG, on the contrary, dealt with disputes of law, 99 per cent of which concerned individuals in the lower and district courts (in the Federal Labor Court about 90-91 per cent). Moreover, the arbitration decree and its ordinances had been issued during the inflation period, with all the handicaps weighing on a regulation in a time of financial collapse.

The employers organizations always disliked the elections because of the excitement they aroused. They were glad to be rid of them. Since they had to recognize trade unions, they felt that it was simplest to have the unions, which proved a factor of order in revolutionary days, agree on assessors among themselves. They always preferred to deal with one union or a few big unions instead of with such a variety as might have come out of elections.

The free trade unions certainly realized what power would be in their hands with the possibility of barring not only communist and nonmilitant unions, but any special group that might arise. "The trade unions are the representatives of labor; this position need not be confirmed by elections," wrote the official periodical of the ADGB.[48] To cling to elections would mean only "that we are still adhering to individualism." We must stand for collectivism and its consequences. There were lonely voices of protest. Friedrich Kleeis[49] reminded his colleagues of the old socialist demand that judges be elected by the people. He pointed out that elections are an opportunity to explain the usefulness of the trade unions and to arouse the indifferent masses. He argued that there were not yet organizations for all workers. But the temptation of a legal guarantee, instead of a testing of the will of the rank and file, was too great.

The adoption of appointment confronted the government with the task of deciding which economic associations should be recognized. Since the law was based on the recognition of the collective idea, the answer was, "those associations entitled to conclude collective agreements." But, as will be explained below, (pp. 193-94) the definition itself was subject to question.

The fight centered on the "nonmilitant" unions. The bona fide trade unions considered them dependent on the employer. Protest was made by employers' associations and right wing parties against the exclusion of associations whose independence was doubted. The only associations of importance in this group were the agricultural workers' leagues, which did not recognize the strike.[50] When the Federal Labor Court recognized, in 1930, the capacity of the Pomeranian Agricultural Workers League (cf. p. 118) to conclude collective agreements, the organization was admitted to represent its members in courts. Practically, the three powerful movements succeeded in applying the definition which the Miners' Insurance Act[51]—the only law including a definition—formulated. It defined economic associations as those belonging to one of the federations recognized as nominating organizations of the Provisional National Economic Council.[52] This meant that nominations were restricted to wage earners' and salaried employees' unions of the three movements, the socialist, Christian, and liberal unions. The legal provision that assessors be selected in suitable proportions and with due regard for minorities, from nomination lists sent in by the economic associations of employers and employees, protected only unions belonging to these federations.[53]

No difficulties arose on the employers' side, where even chambers of commerce and of craft organizations not entitled to conclude collective agreements presented candidates for nomination.

Another problem was the "suitable" proportion. On the employers' side this meant consideration of the number of workers in the enterprises of members, on the workers' side extent of membership of the trade unions. Examinations of the lists by public authorities preceded nomination. They checked the associations and the relative size of organizations on the lists. Inevitably, trade unions accused each other of manipulation of membership figures. The Prussian Ministers of Commerce and of Justice, in common declarations of August 26 and September 9, 1927,[54] therefore, allowed associations to investigate each others' membership figures in cases of complaint but refused to check the figures after assessors were nominated. The authorities were supposed to protect minorities.

The authorities were not entitled to add names to the lists which the associations presented but could negotiate changes

APPRAISAL 129

and settle the order of sequence. After the authorities of Social Administration and of Justice Administration had agreed, the persons on the lists were nominated.

The nomination system deprived unorganized workers and employers of a voice in choosing assessors, which meant exclusion of small entrepreneurs who had not joined an employers' association and of the majority of the working class. The individual was nothing, the organization all. It meant, moreover, the exclusion of many organizations which were too small to appear on the list. The newly organized unions of private teachers, social workers, nurses, etc. were not affiliated with a federation and could not influence selection. Elections would have given them this influence because the big trade unions, in their selection of candidates, would have had to consider the not insignificant vote and moral support of these associations. The trade unions did not realize what an excellent test of the confidence of the rank and file elections represented. Nominations were so convenient and seemed to increase their power, which in fact was weakened by unavoidable petrifaction. It was trade union bureaucracy, not membership that decided. It is no accident that the lively and constantly growing DHV, although not unanimous, was one of the few trade union voices against nomination. It claimed that in labor court elections it always received many more votes than those of its members.[55]

This fundamental change from a democratic to a corporative method aroused remarkably little interest. Few voices of protest were heard[56] against a method which—as Gertrud Israel said—might finally lead to the appointment of parliamentary deputies according to the alleged strength of their parties. The new method was defended by the representatives of the free trade unions not only by practical arguments but also theoretically, which proved again their suspicion against the judiciary. The unions argued that the assessors must not only collaborate with individual judges but must also cope with a strong bureaucratic machine represented not so much by the individual judge, as by the judiciary as an organized body. The unions pointed out that a bureaucratic machine can be controlled efficiently only by an organization wielding a certain power over its representatives. A further justification for the method adopted by the statute was found by the unions in the close connection between the creation of collective rules and the interpretation and application of these rules in the courts. The unions looked on the activities of the assessors in the courts as a part of the work which had to be performed by the unions. Principles of an "individualistic democracy," it was argued, were to be supplemented by those of a "collective democracy," the former characterizing the legislative process, the latter the process of a truly democratic administration and judiciary. Basic for this attitude was belief in the tremendous power exercised by the hierarchical centralized machine of the administration of justice.[57]

The right to nominate assessors gave the trade unions a strong influence on court decisions. Their confidential men were elected and they could control their activities. They educated assessors in trade union courses and discussed important cases in their own labor law periodicals.

Criticism was levelled against the frequent trade union practice of choosing one man to be both assessor and representative of a member to the same court. Employers mentioned instances of a trade union official appealing to the district labor court a case in which he had been judge.[58] In one case, an assessor appealed his own decision. Before the enactment of the AGG it even happened that a trade union secretary, appointed chairman of an industrial court, appeared as an advocate in a very similar case in another court.[59] Such duality of function was not illegal, but could easily undermine confidence in an assessor's impartiality. To act as assessor and representative of a party in one court was generally held permissible by the free trade unions, while others like the DHV,[60] opposed the practice. In the above mentioned inquiry (p. 90) most of the 1,468 workmen assessors who answered the questionnaire were also representatives of parties. Many thought this arrangement helped maintain the assessors' contact with the working class, others felt a difficulty in being both impartial and representative.[61] Among salaried employees, 112 of the 462 Afa League assessors, 77 of the 655 GDA assessors, and

102 of the 1,020 DGB assessors, united the two functions [62] in one chamber.

The assessors' committees (Beisitzerausschüsse), which were supposed to establish close contact between assessors and courts, did not develop much activity or fulfill the hopes placed in them. Moreover, since the law did not prescribe proportionate consideration of minorities, employees were frequently merely represented by one of the several trade union movements interested.

Agreed Arbitral Bodies

In providing for the exclusion of jurisdiction of labor courts by arbitral tribunals, conciliation and expert opinion bodies the AGG had molded itself to the exigencies of a collectivistic period. The former law (KGG, Sec. 6) had prohibited arbitral arrangements for commercial employees—cancelled by November 27, 1922 [63]—and allowed them for industrial workers as in the ordinary civil law procedure (GGG, Sec. 6). The ZPO, however, had been planned for commercial cases, and while it admitted arbitral agreements only between contestant parties in an individual case, it did not provide for permanent tribunals set up by parties to a collective agreement.

Many collective agreements (including about 89 to 91 per cent of all workers covered) had provided for some arbitral tribunal. Many of these institutions remained on paper, however, while others were concerned only with conflicts between the contracting parties and did not care to establish costly machinery for individual conflicts. In general, the collective agreement did not distinguish between individual and collective disputes or disputes on right and on interest. Arbitral tribunals were very much diversified. In some unions with old traditions they were organized on three levels. Their competence was not always well defined. Because of the lack of clear definitions, no figures can be given about their activities. They frequently were concerned with declaratory decisions concerning the norms of collective agreements for which the concluding parties certainly were well equipped.

For workers employed by public authorities, it was usual

to establish special arbitral tribunals, some for all types of conflicts, others only for expert opinions. The collective agreement for salaried employees of the state of Saxony, for instance, set up an arbitral tribunal, composed of an impartial chairman and ten assessors divided among employers and employees. It had three groups of functions: arbitration, interpretation of the collective agreement, and arbitral expert opinion for salary grouping. Litigation went to the labor courts.

Conciliation agencies did not succeed and in practice merely delayed procedure. In general, the trade unions were not inclined to displace the labor courts by agreed bodies. M. Schleicher,[64] a leader of the free trade unions, in contrast to the free trade union press, advocated the development of arbitral tribunals in order to have trade unions influence collective labor law as much as possible. He pointed to the fact that the decision of a tribunal, specialized for the industry, helped build up the collective agreement. Schleicher was an official of the Holzarbeiterverband (Woodworkers Union), a typical craftsman's organization. The industrial organizations, for instance the metal workers union, fought such tribunals. In the metal industry, nearly all arbitral tribunals for labor questions were abolished after enactment of the statute. Clemens Nörpel, the legal expert of the ADGB, refused to have the labor courts become a Cinderella of courts whose decision could not be enforced without help. Arbitral tribunals are only a makeshift where labor courts fail to work. The enforcement of law created by collective agreement and legislation is the task of the state. We will not return to the Middle Ages, he wrote, where guilds were powerful and Kaiser and Reich became a puppet (Possenfigur). Weak trade unions cannot have tribunals of their own. They would face enforcement difficulties if the employers were malicious. Arbitral tribunals, in his opinion, faced a danger of inbreeding and petrification.[65] Adjudication might become disunified.[66] Moreover, the weaker party could easily be exposed to pressure of the stronger. The DHV recommended leaving to employees the choice between arbitral tribunals and labor courts before initiation of procedure. Arbitral tribunals should be agreed upon only if a personal and material guarantee of unobjectionable functioning could be provided. As mentioned above, the authorities, too, considered the displacement of state courts by agreed courts as opposed to the unification of justice.

Since labor courts were popular, and because of the trend toward displacing pure self-governing bodies and activities by those of a public character, arbitral tribunals would probably not have had a good chance of developing had democracy survived.

SUMMARY

The German people in general had confidence in labor jurisdiction and considered it an essential part of German democracy. Because of the privileged position of the democratically-ruled, free economic associations of employers and employees, there existed a democracy half-way between that of the Western countries and a corporate state.

THE PERIOD OF NATIONAL SOCIALISM

Chapter VI

THE CHANGE IN LABOR RELATIONS*

IMMEDIATELY AFTER COMING to power, the National Socialists revolutionized labor relations and the labor court system soon reflected the changes. In constructing the new labor law, the regime proclaimed its opposition to the "liberalistic" *(sic)* philosophy which based employer-employee relations on individual and collective contracts. Against such "dualistic" recognition of separate spheres of employers and employees, was set the "old Germanic community" of leader and follower, its relation of care and loyalty, command and obedience. The free contract, it was argued, had led to class conflict and the uprooting of labor. Equality of capital and labor, the aim of the fallen system, would not be compatible with the leader principle of the authoritarian regime.

In order to break the great political power of the economic organizations of business and labor, the National Socialists conceived the idea of a "community" of employers and employees working in the interest of the nation, i.e., of the National Socialist state. For the realization of their utopia, they had to get rid of all institutions and groups based on the conception of the antagonism of classes. A change of leadership in trade unions and employers' organizations would not have been sufficient, since the very idea of separate organiza-

*The manuscript of this study had been sent in for composition before V-E Day. The present tense in which the chapters on National Socialism were first written have been left unrevised.

tions meant recognition of centers of potential resistance. Under National Socialism none of the groups would be allowed to organize or act without the other's participation or without party control. Trade unions, therefore, were doomed to disappear. Since, however, their sudden destruction would have "atomized the working classes and exposed them to influences hard to control,"[1] some preliminary solution had to be found which, in the minds of the workers, would seem to guarantee the maintenance of trade unionism.[2] On May 2, 1933, the ADGB's headquarters was raided and the huge property of the free trade unions confiscated. A large organization, the German Labor Front (Deutsche Arbeitsfront, DAF) was set up.[3]

Employer-employee relations are regulated by the Gesetz zur Ordnung der nationalen Arbeit (National Socialist Labor Act) of January 20, 1934 (henceforth referred to as AOG).[4] The AOG displaced the decrees regulating collective agreements, arbitration, the Works Council Law and Section 152 of the Industrial Code which guaranteed freedom of organization. Parts of the Weimar Constitution were also invalidated by it. The cardinal principles underlying the new legal system of employer-employee relations are in particular the abolition of all democratic means of employee representation in shop and industry and the shifting of the center of gravity to the individual enterprise. Instead of workers' representation, there is prescribed a sort of "shop community," the employer being called the leader and the employees followers (Gefolgschaft). Relations between employer and employees are no longer to be based on a contest, but on a works community (Betriebsgemeinschaft) and a common effort to further the purposes of the enterprise and, thereby, of the nation. Class antagonism is to be completely eliminated. The employer, as chief or leader of the undertaking, is responsible to his followers for all decisions affecting his business, and must seek to promote the welfare of his employees who, in turn, are required to serve him loyally. The DAF shop stewards are responsible to The German Labor Front and thereby to the National Socialist Party for the National Socialist conduct of the shop communities which are supervised by the Trustees of Labor (Reichstreuhänder der Arbeit, RTA).

The RTA,[5] loyal National Socialists, appointed for large economic areas (at present fifteen in the old Reich territory), have taken over most of the functions of associations of employers and employees. They are federal officials under the supervision of the Federal Minister of Labor bound by instructions and directions of the federal government. The Minister of Labor may appoint special trustees to perform, temporarily or permanently, particular tasks. Special trustees have been appointed among others for home workers, for public enterprises, for coal mining, the cigarette industry, and other industries.

The DAF was first organized as a federation of fifteen wage earners' and nine salaried employees' organizations, under the leadership of the Party Chief of Staff, Dr. Robert Ley, a veteran of the National Socialist movement. The inclusion of an organization of the employers and a fourth group, the organization of commerce, trade, and handicraft comprising the urban middle class, was projected and first steps taken toward realization in the fall of 1933. In November, however, the whole structure was abandoned and transformed in a process which consumed the entire year 1934. It started with a proclamation issued November 27, 1933, by Ley, together with the Federal Ministers of Labor and Economics and the Chancellor's representative for economic questions. They explained that "the high aim of the DAF is the education of all working Germans to the National Socialist State and to National Socialist principles."[6] This proclamation was followed by the self-dissolution of all employers' organizations, some of which had already joined the DAF. A like atomization was accomplished for the masses of labor by dissolving their organizations above mentioned. This reorganization[7] deprived the DAF of the last remaining vestiges of "class" character and transformed it into a body in which entrepreneur, labor, and urban middle class people were indistinguishably organized as individuals.

The dropping of the "Bureau for Estate Organization" (Amt

für ständischen Aufbau) of the DAF indicated the abandonment of the corporate idea, which had been in the party program. On October 24, 1934, the DAF received its final constitution[8] by decree of Hitler which set its aim as the formation of a real national and working community (Volks- und Leistungsgemeinschaft) of all Germans. The totalitarian pretensions of the DAF were confirmed by the statement that membership in it cannot be replaced by membership in a professional, socio-political, economic, or philosophical organization. Even denominational workers' organizations without trade union character were compelled to dissolve.

The DAF was now divided into eighteen Reich "enterprise communities" (Reichsbetriebsgemeinschaften), i.e., groups of establishments organized on broad industrial lines.[9] Since 1938 the enterprise communities have been called trade offices (Fachämter). They were, in fact, mere departments without regional or local subdivisions. Workers and employers were members of the DAF only, not of the trade offices. Thus old trade union loyalties were disrupted and workers were isolated from each other. Another cause of alienation was the influx of millions of new members, who joined under pressure, fearing loss of jobs. Membership, although legally voluntary, is practically compulsory for both workers and employers, even the small ones.[10]

The individual membership of the DAF allegedly surpassed 19,000,000 in 1938.[11] Four million shops were included. There were also such corporate members as the National Culture Chamber, the Federation of National Socialist German Jurists, and others.

By the so-called Bückeberg agreement of October 6, 1935, the Reich Food Estate (Reichsnährstand) became a corporate member of the DAF and superseded the Reich Agriculture Enterprise Community. The Leipzig agreement of March 26, 1935, between the Ministries of Economics and Labor and Dr. Ley made the handicrafts, trade, and industry organizations corporate members of the DAF. The Ministry of Transportation adhered to this agreement on July 22, 1935. A hierarchy of committees for discussion of economic and socio-political questions (called chambers) was established, with equal participation of employers and employees. It has remained on paper, however.

The DAF is an affiliated organization [12] of the party, divided territorially like the party and under the latter's leadership, with officials appointed from above on a basis of political reliability. Workers and employers pay dues according to income;[13] workers' dues are deducted from pay checks. They aggregate a vast fund, expended as the leadership sees fit and without accounting.[14]

The DAF is supposed to secure industrial peace, educate labor to National Socialism, and increase its efficiency. The first function, prevention of labor unrest, is exercised mainly by shop stewards and legal advisory offices. The second is carried out by a variety of activities, largely those of the Strength Through Joy organization (Kraft durch Freude). The third is advanced by participation in vocational training, plant contests, and annual vocational competitions first staged for the youth, since 1938 for all workers.

The DAF drafts lists of assessors for labor and social honor courts. It has set up separate legal advisory offices (Rechtsberatungsstellen) for its employer and employee members. They [15] give advice on all questions concerning labor relations and social insurance and may represent members in the labor courts and social insurance courts. Advice is given to workers without charge. Employers pay for being represented in the courts. Workers must refund expenses should the office withdraw assistance because of the making of false statements.

By law of December 23, 1936,[16] the offices were authorized to receive applications for old age and accident insurance benefits. In 1937 [17] they received the additional function of advising independent artisans in tax questions.

There were 478 local legal advisory offices in January, 1940,[18] with about 1300 full-time officials of whom more than half had full legal training. Some advisory offices went on circuit. The DAF Auslandsorganisation gives legal protection to members in foreign countries,[19] and supervises them.

In nearly all districts, legal advisors meet every few months for one or two days to discuss their problems. The advisory offices maintain contact with the factory inspection, receiving information about labor laws and, since 1939, with employment offices in order to receive information about allocation of labor. The war increased their work considerably because of the large amount of new legislation, while simultaneously many of their experienced officials were drafted. Compulsion to consult the advisory offices before making a complaint has brought the pursuit of all legal claims under complete party control (cf. pp. 157, 184).

The DAF was not supposed to deal with labor conditions. It did, however, influence them in the early years, especially in the shop. In enterprises of more than five employees, it is represented by the shop steward (Betriebsobmann, formerly Betriebswalter). In smaller shops the Ortsobmann (local Labor Front chief) takes care of these functions. In large enterprises, the powerful DAF steward heads a complicated organization of cell and block stewards. The shop steward is responsible to the NSDAP for the enforcement of National Socialist will in the enterprise.[20] He must see to it that all employees and managers are members of the DAF. He is not employed by the entrepreneur but by the DAF and, therefore, is independent of the employer.

In the course of time, DAF activities have become more and more government or party functions. Acting under strict party control, it is the authoritarian instrument for keeping the party's thumb on employers as well as on labor. At times it had a definite labor bias, but finally it always followed the instructions given by the government or party. The institution which at first seemed to develop a power of its own has been increasingly subjected to government orders.

In 1944 all activities of the DAF (including those of Strength Through Joy), except those necessary for the war effort, were discontinued.

The system of labor relations centers around the shop controlled by the DAF (a party organization) on the one hand, and the RTA (a government representative) on the other. The powers of the trustees are extraordinarily wide.

They are responsible for the maintenance of industrial peace.[21] In order to achieve this task, they may issue and supervise the enforcement of collective rules (Tarifordnungen) for a group of enterprises; these replace collective agreements.[22] They lay down guiding principles for and supervise the observance of shop rules (Betriebsordnungen) drafted by the employer (obligatorily in shops with more than twenty employees). They may authorize lay-offs. They co-operate in the Social Honor Courts (cf. pp. 173-74). They supervise the constitution and procedure of confidential councils and give a decision in any dispute concerning them. If any one repeatedly and wilfully contravenes the RTA's written instructions, he is prosecuted at the request of the RTA and may be punished. Moreover, gross breaches of the written instructions of the RTA are considered grave offenses against social honor and penalized by the social honor courts.

Confidential councils consisting of from two to ten persons who must be members of the DAF are set up in establishments with twenty or more employees. While at first the workers in the shops had to vote yearly for a list drawn up by the employer (in agreement with the Labor Front steward) or to reject it, voting was suspended when it revealed opposition to the regime in 1935. Since then the RTA has filled all vacancies. Together with the employer who is the leader, the confidential men constitute the confidential council.

The confidential council's official functions are to assist the leader with advice, to consider all measures directed toward increase of efficiency, to help carry out shop rules, and to settle grievances. They have none of the functions of the old works councils, which were elected by secret ballot of workers to represent their interests in the shop and to supervise the enforcement of collective agreements. The confidential council cannot, as did the former Works Council, file complaints against dismissals, although protection against unjustified dismissal has been upheld.[23] Under certain circumstances where consultation of the Works Council would have been mandatory, the confidential council need not be consulted by the employer. The employer is not obliged to take the council's advice.

A majority of the council may appeal to the RTA against any decision of the employer concerning conditions of employment which do appear unwarranted by the social and economic conditions of the establishment. The trustee rules on the appeal.

During the first year the confidential men—where they functioned at all—seem to have considered their task not so different from that of the former works councillors. They felt themselves to be representatives of labor in cases of grievance. Meetings of the councils—to which the "leader" of the shop (employer) frequently delegated minor management officials as his representative—dealt predominantly with such questions. In order to eliminate these topics and to create a more general interest, the DAF suggested later common topics of discussion such as "preparation for efficiency contests," "rationalization," and "vocational education."[24]

Since it is the aim of the AOG to center labor relations in the enterprise, shop rules[25] issued by the employer (in place of former works rules which had to be agreed upon with the works council) are supposed primarily to regulate working conditions. Guiding principles set up by the RTA have no direct influence on working conditions. They indicate to employers the main lines to be followed. The RTA can set aside an employer's shop rules if the confidential council appeals to him on the grounds that the rules are not compatible with shop economic and social conditions. Shop rules are rules of law,[26] not unlike the collective rules of the RTA.

While at first the idea prevailed that wages would be regulated by shop rules, only in exceptional cases by collective rules for groups of industries, it soon became clear that employers and workers favored uniform regulations. Employers resented underselling by competing enterprises due to unfavorable conditions of work. Labor resented the power of the entrepreneur who frequently was not socially-minded. In practice, therefore, the collective agreements of the Weimar period were continued as collective rules, and the latter prevailed, with frequent adjustments. Compared to them shop rules were of secondary importance.

Collective rules, thus, became the predominant form of

regulating conditions of work. This meant outright state command. They were, in their legal effect, similar to the old collective agreements, although the Federal Labor Court tried to establish some distinction in claiming that norms of collective rules did not—as collectively agreed upon rules had done—enter into individual labor contracts, but "governed" them, a somewhat artificial distinction. Since the National Socialists claimed that collective agreements had equalized to too great an extent the conditions of work in different enterprises and had not given consideration to weak enterprises, the RTA, since 1935, was entitled to exempt individual firms, departments of such, and even individual workers from collective rules.[27].

By order of June 25, 1938,[28] the trustee was authorized to regulate wages independently of collective rules,[29] to fix maximum wages in specified industries. Shop rules became dependent on his consent. After the outbreak of war,[30] his powers were extended to the issuing of collective rules for individual establishments, and to the establishment of wage ceilings. By order of October 12, 1939,[31] wages were frozen. The development of wage policy shows that the National Socialist government reserves for itself the highest power of regulation and does not shrink from increasing drastic intervention.

From 1938 on, it became obvious that the power of the RTA had to be enlarged. This was due to the importance of a new field of labor law which developed with the increase of labor allocation, which finally resulted in the complete control of the mobility of labor. During the very early phase of the regime, measures aimed at re-employment. Beginning in 1934 with the restriction of mobility of farm labor and young workers, planning was extended to various defense industries after the proclamation of the Four Year Plan. Rational distribution of labor was carried through with the help of the work-book, compulsory since 1935.[32] It contains the complete record of training, work experience, and health of the worker. On April 22, 1939,[33] the last exemptions were removed so that all employees, even contractors and helpers who were members of the family were included. Many law suits arose when employers in some economic branches were authorized to retain work books in cases of breach of contract [34] and thus prevent workers from getting new employment. The worker could sue for restitution in the labor court.

With the growing shortage of labor, a year of compulsory service (so-called duty year, Pflichtjahr) was introduced for girls before they took up gainful employment.[35] Voluntary labor service for young people was transformed into compulsory service for boys from 18 to 25 years of age on June 26, 1935,[36] and for girls on September 4, 1939.[37]

When the building of the West Wall necessitated a large labor force unobtainable in the market, compulsory labor for adult workers was introduced in 1938[38] and extended in February, 1939.[39] Partially since March, 1938, and totally since the outbreak of war, change of jobs came under the control of the employment offices, which since 1935 have had a monopoly on placement. These various measures brought recruitment and allocation of labor under such complete control that the shift to full war economy could be achieved with but slight changes. The huge amount of work of the trustees necessitated the establishment of outside agencies for the RTA. These had been largely factory inspectors, with whom the RTA had, in any case, to co-operate in many fields.[40] In August, 1939,[41] they were displaced as commissioned agencies of the RTA by the 340 employment offices and their approximately 40,000 officials. The employment offices were supposed to suggest appointment and removal of confidential men, draft rules regulating conditions of work, and make investigations for social honor courts. This new arrangement revealed how much the interest of the RTA had to shift during the war period to the planning of labor supply. The power of the DAF and its relationship to the RTA decreased in conformity with the inflation of the trustees' own agencies.

When in 1942 the former party district leader of Thuringia, Fritz Sauckel, was appointed Commissioner-General of Manpower (Generalbevollmächtigter für Arbeitseinsatz) the employment and wages departments were transferred from the

Ministry of Labor to the Commissioner-General.[42] The offices of the trustees and heads of regional employment offices were merged and the entire administration of labor, with the exception of factory inspection, thus brought under the direction of one government agency. In 1944, Sauckel was subordinated to Goebbels as the Plenipotentiary for the Total War Effort (Reichsbevollmächtigter für den totalen Kriegseinsatz).

Many statements[43] reveal that the AOG anticipated a new social order which could not be accomplished. By shifting responsibility for regulating wages and other conditions of work to the establishment, the AOG assumed a degree of employer responsibility and social-mindedness which certainly did not exist and could not be created by Hermann Goering's and other National Socialist leaders' threats.

In 1935 Dr. Ley wrote: "There are still many who have not been drilled in the new spirit." If the confidential man goes to the employer and the latter consults his lawyer, the confidential man loses his position of confidence. "We ourselves know that the AOG came into existence too early. . . . Woe to the leader who looks upon the confidential man merely as a dummy or who pays less wages than the laws prescribe. We National Socialists punish hard and severely." [44]

In January, 1935, the RTA of Brandenburg, Dr. Daeschner, stated that it was easier to fight Marxism than the liberalism of the employer, whose egoism he blamed for many of the difficulties of the RTA.[45]

In the 1937 yearbook for National-Socialist Economy Helmut Egloff states that three years are too short a time in which to judge the success of a law. However, he complains about shop rules which are unsatisfactory and which even violate laws.[46] Still more severe is the criticism of the RTA for Westphalia, who speaks about lack of initiative, refusal to accept responsibility, schematism devoid of National Socialist spirit,[47] and a consequent backsliding to "mass" regulations and narrowing of the margin of social policy left to the undertaking. As a conclusion drawn from all these facts, it was frequently stated that it would take generations to educate the employers.

The AOG set up only the most important principles and institutions of the new system. It was supposed to be followed by other laws concerning the labor contract, labor protection, training, etc. None of these materialized before the outbreak of war, however. A youth protection law enacted on April 30, 1938,[48] had to be partially suspended on the outbreak of war. The law concerning the labor contract, for which the Academy of German Law[49] had prepared a draft, was not worked out because there was no clear opinion of its nature. A Homework Law enacted on March 23, 1934[50] was essentially based on a draft of the previous democratic government. Other changes dealt mainly with the prolongation of hours of work in the military interest.

The development of labor relations in the National Socialist period may be summarized in the following trends:

(1) A huge propaganda has been carried on during the whole period of Hitlerism in order to win over the workers for the regime. It was at first almost exclusively political in character. After the creation of work for the unemployed, the raising of a generation of young workers who knew nothing except National Socialism, and the growth of a belief among the leaders that the older generation had been now at least neutralized, the propaganda showed mainly a mixture of political indoctrination and incentive for highest occupational efficiency.

(2) The aim of the regime has been to militarize industry and to create a "soldier of labor" equivalent to the army's soldier. The National Socialists hope that this has been achieved to a certain extent by military sports in and outside the shops,[51] exercises of uniformed shop troops, and roll calls (Betriebsappelle) for all workers, including the employer.

(3) Self-government of employers and workers by representatives of their own choice has been abolished. In so-called "self-government" (the chambers of the Leipzig agreement, the advisory bodies of the RTA, the confidential councils), office-holders are appointed, do not act on their own initiative,

and have merely an advisory function. The DAF became, for a short period, a powerful instrument supposedly neutral as far as labor relations are concerned, although politically, of course, ardently National Socialist: a "community," in the National Socialist language. In many cases it showed, nevertheless, tendencies similar to those of the former trade unions. Frequently the shop steward, the alleged representative of the "community," felt that he had more in common with the worker than with the employer. The enterprise communities boasted of achievements formerly rejected by employers. The government, however, has remained the supreme power able to defend its policy against such orientations whenever that policy has seemed to be threatened.

(4) Class war has certainly not been overcome. The threat of merciless prosecution of offenders, the spy work of party members and other careerists, the intimidating power of the Gestapo, have, however, had effect. The suppression of the opposition has, in time, had an appeasing influence. Appeals to national honor and patriotism may have worked in the same direction. In some cases, the gap between employers and workers was bridged by mutual dissatisfaction with the regime.

(5) The regime concentrated efforts on increasing efficiency by vocational training. The worker, "physically hardened" by military sports and mentally drilled in the National Socialist way of thinking, was vocationally trained to become the world's "aristocracy of labor."

(6) An improvement in working and living conditions was achieved by removing unemployment through rearmament, making the employer beautify the shop, establish canteens and common rooms, provide warm meals, help establish homesteads, contribute to recreation trips, etc. These "collective" income increases have been considerable and are appreciated by the workers.

(7) The levelling down of other classes, particularly the lower bourgeoisie, and giving social privileges to labor, definitely raised the prestige of the German worker. The same effect was achieved by the creation of a class of pariahs, Jews and enemies of the state, whose miserable living conditions

proved to labor that it was not at the bottom of the ladder. Moreover, newspapers, films, and radio exalted the social status of the German worker. Physical labor has been glorified in art. Uniforms and decorations helped overcome old feelings of inferiority. In line with this development, a few shop rules abolished the former distinction between wage-earner and salaried employee,[52] thus raising the former into a group which it always had regarded as of higher status.

Chapter VII

LABOR COURTS IN THE JUDICIAL SYSTEM

THE NEW ROLE of the labor courts is not indicated by the amendment of the AGG. It must be understood within the framework of the new Reich's conception of justice which destroyed the rule of law and due process.

National Socialism claims to be a new world outlook which revolutionizes all spheres of life and culture. It recognizes no "isolated ego," allows the individual to exist only as a "collective being,"[1] deriving his value and obligations from the ethnic, racially-pure community called the people. The will of the people is expressed by the Führer, acting through the party or the state machinery. Moreover, because of their racial superiority, the Germans are a master-race, entitled to claim world leadership. Hence the right of the Führer and the group supporting him to subject to his will, not only all Germans, but other nations as well. The German system of justice is an expression of this world outlook.

The new justice is based on the abolition of the division of powers. Executive, legislative, and judicial functions are united in the Führer, and their assignment to separate agencies is merely a technical device. The Führer is the supreme source of law. He is bound by no law. No constitution restricts his will. No bill of rights protects the individual against executive encroachments. The leader personifies the people. "Law is what is useful to the German people."[2] "The vital root of law reaches down into the secret depths of the national conscience and thence furnishes its inner validity and affirmation." [3] Thus law is transmitted by blood, given application by statute. Since National Socialist philosophy is the purest expression of the Germanic spirit, all that is not in conformity with it is illegal. Right is whatever promotes the interests of the regime. From the basis of this unified power of a leader representing the will and expressing the spirit of a nation, emanate some of the characteristics of the new justice.

The Führer himself may act by sovereign jurisdiction or by way of legislation or through the party expressing his will. In the purge of 1934, he assumed judicial functions and acted as the German nation's supreme judge (oberster Gerichtsherr des Volkes) [4] and executioner in order to suppress an alleged revolt. The same right was exercised by Hitler during the present war after the German defeats in Russia in the winter of 1941-42. In his Reichstag speech of April 26, 1942, Hitler explicitly claimed the right to act at will, regardless of whether written law is in accordance therewith. The Reichstag took notice of this declaration and confirmed his unlimited power.[5]

The Führer's will may be expressed in government laws and decrees or in his official statements or in those of other prominent party chiefs. His orders are binding, even when not issued in prescribed form. He may transfer his powers to important party bodies or chiefs.[6] In appointing Otto Georg Thierack, Minister of Justice in August, 1942, Hitler gave him power to set aside all written law. Thus the minister may simultaneously make law and pronounce judgment, may interfere in any department. He may make special regulations in individual cases.

The normal type of legislation is a government decree passed by the Cabinet (based on the Enabling Act of March 24, 1933,[7] and the National Reconstruction Act of January 30,[8] 1934) and unfettered by any legislative machinery. The decree frequently proclaims only a general principle and delegates detailed regulation to subordinate authorities. Thus many decrees restricting mobility of labor were issued by Dr. Friedrich Syrup, then President of the Federal Institute for Placement and Unemployment Insurance.

The judge is bound to the written laws enacted under National Socialism. Pre-1933 statutes which continue to exist, including some provisions of the constitution, must be applied only insofar as they have not become obsolete through National Socialist development.[9] They shall be interpreted according to National Socialist philosophy and thereby changed in application. It therefore became necessary to free the Federal Supreme Court from the elaborate safeguarding rules which had to be observed in departures from its own previous decisions. The Act of June 28, 1935,[10] provides as follows: "It is the task of the Federal Supreme Court to see to it that, in interpreting enactments, regard be given to the change of philosophy of life and law brought about by the reform of the state. In order to place the court in a position to carry out this task, unfettered by the application of past decisions sprung from another philosophy of life and law, be it enacted that, in deciding a question of law, the Federal Supreme Court may depart from a decision given prior to the coming into operation of this act." Safeguards must be observed, however, in any departure from decisions issued in the new spirit.

JUSTICE AND LABOR LAW JURISDICTION

On coming into power the National Socialists did not abolish the labor court system but merely purged it of persons and functions undesirable from the viewpoint of their collective labor law. Labor court *procedure*, with its speed and directness, fitted Nazi principles. In fact, the reform of ordinary civil procedure of October 27, 1933,[11] took labor court procedure as its model. The courts, however, have been deprived of so many *functions* as now to appear rather insignificant.

In April, 1933,[12] the National Socialists started to break the monopoly of bona fide trade unions by authorizing the Federal Minister of Labor, acting in agreement with the ministers of Economics and of Justice, to place other organizations on an equality with the three federations of trade unions as labor representatives in the courts. A series of orders issued in pursuance of the act conferred upon nonmilitant [13] and quasi-political organizations, such as the Steel Helmet Self-Help [14] and the National Socialist Shop Cell Organization,[15] the right to present workers before the courts.[16]

On May 18, 1933,[17] the Administration of Justice was authorized in agreement with the Social Administration to promulgate provisions governing the appointment and the dismissal of assessors in all three instances. They could depart from the former rule that assessors in the district labor courts must have held the post of labor court assessor for at least three years. The Federal Minister of Labor was authorized to replace the assessors in the Federal Labor Court. All rules requiring consultation of economic associations (of which at that time only the employers' existed, trade unions having been transformed early in May) were repealed.

On April 10, 1934, the AGG was adapted to the requirement of the new order by amendment.[18] The new regulation came into force on May 1, 1934.

The number of local and district courts has remained the same for the old Reich territory. After the return of the Saar territory the former were increased in 1935 by three, the latter by one.

The organization of the courts was but inconsiderably altered. The most important change consists in the transfer of the administration of Justice from the states to the Reich. All courts, including the labor courts, thus became federal courts.[19] Powers formerly exercised by the state ministries were taken over by federal authorities. The powers of appointment and supervision were largely delegated to officials in the Reich Department of Justice,[20] which at the same time was authorized to delegate those powers to inferior authorities. In consequence, the power of supervision was given to the presiding committee (Präsidium) of the district court. All functions of employer organizations and unions, such as giving advice before establishing courts and chambers, issuing rules, etc., have been repealed.

By law of November 24, 1937,[21] such self-government as previously existed was taken from the German courts. This included in particular the power of assigning duties, which had frequently belonged to the oldest chairman of the labor court. Now it was given to the president of the district court (in exceptional cases to the president of the local court). In the district court this power was taken from the presiding committee and given to the president. The activity of the committees had been understood as a judiciary activity, but now the chairman and president were to act in the interest of the administration and under the instructions of the Federal Ministry of Justice. Thus, the leadership principle was established. The independence of the courts was endangered by a provision that assignments might be changed not only for such reasons as illness but also in the interest of the administration of justice.

According to the AGG of 1934, assessors were to be appointed from nomination lists of the DAF by the superior administrative authority in agreement with the president of the district court. The DAF was to choose entrepreneurs and employed persons in equal number, and wherever a corporative organization of the economic system would be created (Reich Food Estate, Reich Chamber of Culture), would have to consult the proper corporation.

Under the National Socialist regime nobody deprived of the right to head an enterprise [22] and no member of a confidential council may perform the function of lay judge. The formation of assessors' committees in the labor courts and district labor courts became optional; election gave way to appointment. Assessors in the Federal Labor Court do not participate in assigning duties.

The fundamental step of abolishing assessors in the local courts "in order to speed up procedure during war time," was taken on September 1, 1939.[23] This meant a revolutionary change in the system. No changes were made for district labor courts or the Federal Labor Court. In 1940 the tenure of assessors in higher courts was prolonged until termination by the Reich Ministers of Justice and of Labor.[24]

The same decree raised the minimum suit value appealable from 300 to 500 marks and the minimum reviewable by the Federal Labor Court from 6,000 to 10,000 marks. Pending suits were to be discontinued when an interested party was drafted. Distraint was restricted.[25] The mandatory grant of appeals (AGG, Sec. 6) was abolished. These measures may have an emergency war-time character, but they were considered as permanent.[26]

No change has occurred with respect to the question of who is subject to the jurisdiction of the labor courts. Those whose economic status is similar to that of employed persons are defined as economically dependent. This corresponds to the former interpretation and has failed to clarify a much contested question.

The labor trustee may, in issuing collective rules, give jurisdiction to a labor court in a locality in which it would otherwise have none. He may order the displacement of jurisdiction by arbitral tribunals or conciliation or expert boards. This means that a federal official can negate the jurisdiction of federal courts. This, for instance, was done for seamen, whose disputes had always been decided by special tribunal.[27] By decree of August 23, 1937,[28] the RTA became entitled to refer the execution of awards of marine offices to labor instead of to ordinary courts. Actors were another group for whom special tribunals continued.[29] For the cigar industry, a classification agency (Einstufungsstelle) was set up by decree of December 14, 1935,[30] to grade all cigar-makers into wage classes under the supervision of the special trustee for this industry.

The question of what cases should be decided by the labor courts underwent fundamental changes because of the fact that freedom of coalition, collective agreements, works councils, economic organizations, and legal strikes or lockouts no longer existed. The courts, therefore, no longer had power to deal with such matters. Their practical importance has been thus diminished. The only conflicts they can deal with are between employers and individual employees or between two workers.

Changes in procedure have been less important. With the disappearance of works councils the summary procedure became obsolete. The reform of civil procedure reduced the difference between the procedure of labor and ordinary courts by speeding civil trials, simplifying civil procedure and reducing costs.

The right of representation was fundamentally altered. In the district labor courts, representation by lawyers was made mandatory, as in the Federal Labor Court. In the labor courts, members of the legal consultation offices established by the DAF for entrepreneurs and employed respectively, may serve as representatives provided they do not otherwise plead professionally in ordinary courts. In addition, lawyers may be authorized by the DAF to represent a party in any particular case.

Permission for representation by lawyers was to be given only if the case was important from the viewpoint of law or fact. Very little use is made of the possibility. Only such lawyers may be admitted as are members of the National Socialist professional organization (which accepts only those of "pure blood").

In its domination of representation in the labor courts, the DAF is limited by only two reservations: 1) The Federal Minister of Labor, in conjunction with the Ministers of Justice and of Economics, may accord to other organizations the same right of representing their members which the DAF enjoys; this has never been done. 2) By an amendment of March 20, 1935,[31] the chairman of the labor court is authorized to admit a lawyer or other suitable person to represent a party when representation by the DAF is impossible. According to the guiding principles issued by the Federal Minister of Labor on June 13, 1935,[32] this would apply to persons, members neither of the DAF (e.g., aliens) nor of a corporately affiliated organization (such as the Reich Chamber of Culture), or to persons to whom representation has been refused by the DAF. This is necessary in all cases in which the DAF itself is a party to the dispute. The DAF may refuse to represent in a case alleged not to be in accord with labor's principles of honor. A client's lack of confidence in the DAF is not recognized as adequate reason. The chairman has discretionary power to determine whether admittance of a lawyer is appropriate and whether a particular lawyer is admissible.[33]

The advisory offices of the DAF must determine whether

a complaint has a chance of success and is in accordance with National Socialist principles. It is supposed to prevent unnecessary litigation. It discourages disputes and often achieves compromises. It may prevent any suit not in the interest of the NSDAP. Once the legal advisory office has been notified of a complaint, the party may not seek other advice, withdraw, or settle. He is obliged to act in agreement with the advisory office.

The offices of the DAF also provide lawyers for the second and third instances. When necessary, they provide poor law counsel.[34] Such counsel was restricted by a law of October 27, 1933,[35] to cases with "sufficient" chance of success (formerly simply "chance of success") and which do not "appear" wanton (formerly "are not" wanton).

The legal profession remained dissatisfied with the regulation of legal representation in the labor courts. They found the system too complicated and arbitrary[36] and disliked the intermediate role of the DAF.

In addition to the labor courts, the guild committees continued to function for apprentices.

In 1944 labor litigation was considerably curtailed in the course of the combing-out process inaugurated by Goebbels as plenipotentiary for the totalitarian war effort. In line with the simplification of the total system of justice, only litigation which concerned the war effort was permitted. Suits not essential for the conduct of the war, had to be postponed. Since postponement was supposed to be the rule, only few labor conflicts may have been admitted to the courts. Moreover, the district labor courts were abolished. Appeal for review to the Federal Labor Court was admitted only if expressly granted in the labor court decision. This admittance was restricted to cases of principal importance and under consideration of war conditions.[36a]

Proposals to change the labor court structure were made in conformity with the reform of the whole court system. There was a strong movement to apply the leadership principle to court organization. This would not mean the abolition of collegial courts, but of collegial decisions. Assessors would

LABOR COURTS IN THE JUDICIAL SYSTEM 159

be deprived of the vote and a judge would decide alone. Roland Freisler,[37] a leader in this movement, calls "the game of counting ballots" (das Abstimmungszahlenspiel) as a basis of judgment incompatible with National Socialism, and a last bulwark of liberalism. "National Socialism cannot stop at the door of Justice; it cannot tolerate a decisive influence of the anonymous and lack of responsibility in jurisdiction. The leader state does not recognize majorities, but only personalities." Freisler has attacked not only gambling with "majorities," but the fact that discussion is given too prominent a place in intellectual consideration. In criticism of this demand for abolition of the collegiate system, the danger of erroneous or arbitrary decisions is pointed out.[38] For labor courts of the first instance the leader principle has been fully established since the outbreak of the war. The decline in legal procedure has led to the demand to abolish chambers, since, having but few complaints, they meet only infrequently and hence decisions are delayed.[39] This might have been only the first step towards merging labor with ordinary civil courts. The decreasing importance of the labor courts has not stimulated proposals to alter the system.

Looked at from the outside, German labor law has not undergone revolutionary change. Collective agreements have been displaced by collective rules. The confidential council appears as a shadow of the works council. Arbitration continues extralegally and without publicity. The politicalization of the system has, however, had revolutionary effect. Moreover, the requirements of war preparation to which the economic system was dedicated in 1933, as well as the National Socialist world outlook, resulted not only in a change of interpretation, but also in a shift in types of litigation. Questions concerning allocation of labor, breaches of contract,[40] restrictions of employment, gradually came to the foreground. Co-operation with employment offices was made the duty of legal advice bureaus. The extension of vacation claims led to an increase of litigation in this field.

The trend of court decisions revealed a tendency toward

obliterating the demarcation between public[41] and private law such as might be expected in a totalitarian state in which the sphere of private life is gradually disappearing as political domain expands and in which contracts have lost their private character. Unification of public and private law was demanded in the interest of the unity of *voelkisches* law.[42] Private law applying to cases between individuals correspondingly diminished. "Welfare duty" and "loyalty" are public law concepts. Collective rules are fixed by act of the state. National Socialist ideology called for the displacement of the concept of labor's "contractual duty"—"Romanistic"—by the "Germanistic" concept of "public duty." Strikes became a criminal offense and, correspondingly the employer had a social duty to provide for his employee (Fürsorgepflicht). The law is more interested in stressing obligations to community or party than in protecting rights. With the state allocating labor, i.e., determining engagement and dismissal, the labor relation has ceased to be a private one. According to National Socialist ideology the place of work becomes a public office (Dienststelle),[43] and workers and employers are transformed into "trustees of work" necessary to the maintenance and defense of the nation.

The most characteristic representative of National Socialist legal theory in this field, Wolfgang Siebert,[44] anticipates developments today evident only in germ, when he demands the separation of labor law from the law of contract in the Civil Code, because of its greater affinity to family law.[45] The labor contract, says Siebert, should be abolished and labor relations based merely on the functioning of the works community. The labor contract—as part of the law of contracts—is based on the theory that employer and employee confront each other without inner connections and represent conflicting interests. The works community, however, is a "concrete and living order," a sort of autonomous body under its own law. He thinks it not feasible to treat labor protection as public law and the labor contract as private law.

The courts have not accepted this theory and have not supplanted the labor contract by community loyalty, which would have meant abolition of the distinction between civil servant and private employee. But they minimized the "materialistic conception" which had substantiated contractual relations between employer and employee. Thus the Federal Labor Court did not derive a pension right of an employee from the rather vague general "welfare duty of the employer" but rather clung to the principle that every concrete legal claim must be based on a special legal argument.[46] In accordance with earlier decisions, however, they admitted that binding norms could be derived from custom.

The courts have recognized the "works community" as a source of legal obligations, especially in decisions concerning notice, dismissal, and re-employment. The Gelsenkirchen Labor Court decided that an employee of long standing who had been dismissed during the depression was entitled to re-employment because of the loyalty obligation.[47] The Federal Labor Court decided that an old employee, for whom strenuous work has become too much of a burden, has a right to another type of work.[48] The same was decided in the case of a pregnant woman. Dismissal without notice was considered only as an ultimate means. The rules concerning payment of wages during periods of illness, compensation for accidents during the May 1 celebration, and liability for damages to health have been strictly interpreted. Interruption of work due to a sterilization operation was adjudged an innocent misfortune subject to compensation by the employer.

The theory that certain "loyalty" duties between employer and employee form a part of the labor law, had been recognized long before 1933. Thus, former decisions placed the risk of stoppages on the employee as well as on the employer.

The shift in court decisions from the concept of obligation to that of loyalty can best be followed with respect to vacation rights. National Socialism had recognized that every worker is entitled to vacations, but the question has been regulated by law only for young workers (1938). In the first years after 1933 the court followed the old theory according to which a worker has a double claim to the privilege of being freed from work and to compensation. Although the courts hold that the worker has no claim to a vacation[49] without special provisions, these decisions already stress that the labor contract is characterized by highly personal relations between the parties, based on the state of loyalty. On October 20, 1937,[50] the Federal Labor Court stressed that the aim of vacation is recreation. On February 16, 1938,[51] the Federal Labor Court recognized that compensation must be paid even if vacations cannot be taken during the period of employment. The reversal comes with the decisions of March 16, 1938[52] and May 21, 1938,[53] that sickness during vacation should not restrict the worker's right to full recreation. Formerly the worker could receive vacation money and leave his job for another (although collective agreements tried to prevent this).

One labor court even recognized a claim to vacation after one-half year's occupation in the shop,[54] not based on law or collective rules, a decision which the Federal Labor Court would not have confirmed. On the other hand, a widow was denied her claim to compensation for vacation time due to her husband.[55]

The Federal Labor Court decided that the individual worker could not waive the rights granted to him in a collective rule, a decision which was hailed as a great achievement.[56] A loophole was left in the recognition of forfeiture (Verwirkung), however. The Federal Labor Court recognized clauses in collective and shop rules limiting claims to certain periods.[57] On July 25, 1934, and March 16, 1938, the court admitted a waiver after the employment relation had ended on condition that no pressure was used and that full knowledge of the claim existed.

The RTA wrote forfeiture clauses into nearly all collective rules,[58] especially concerning compensation for overtime work, vacation, and the placing of employees in incorrect wage brackets.[59] In a decision of May 17, 1939,[60] an arrangement (Vergleich) made between an individual employer and his employee in which other conditions were agreed upon than those set forth in collective rules if not made under pressure or

LABOR COURTS IN THE JUDICIAL SYSTEM 163

against good morals was admitted as an interpretation of the collective rule rather than as a waiver of the individual rights. This decision was criticized by Nipperdey[61] as turning away from the principle of nondeviation.

While the jurisdiction of labor courts has become restricted, the work of the court has to a certain extent become more difficult because certain interpretation problems have become more complicated. Although collective rules have in general been issued for larger areas and have been simplified, they are in many cases valid only for certain groups. Their scope may be restricted to individual establishments or departments of establishments. Since 1934 wages of homeworkers may be individually regulated.[62] After the order of June 25, 1938,[63] authorized the RTA to regulate wages and conditions of work independent of collective rules, the courts had to deal with innumerable individual regulations, differing widely from the area of one trustee to that of another.[64] All collective rules and shop rules are treated as sources of law, i.e., as legal rules. The great variety of such legal rules makes uniformity of interpretation very difficult, especially since, in September, 1939, the RTA was empowered to issue collective rules for particular firms.[65] Retroactive effects of collective rules were another source of difficulty, e.g., when collective rules were changed retroactively during a suit.

POLITICAL JUSTICE

The confusion, insecurity, and arbitrariness which characterize German justice are due to two main causes: First, those powers supposed to represent the Führer and execute his political will are removed from the field of justice; justice is not entitled to interfere with their activities. Second, the German government is not so much a dictatorship as a series of rival dictatorships.[66] The NSDAP has sovereign functions and can create law beyond the realm of its members for the whole nation.[67] Its law is of equal validity to that promulgated by the Reich government. Hitler has occasionally delegated to the party tasks which the government was un-

164   THE PERIOD OF NATIONAL SOCIALISM

able to perform (e.g., the solution of the "race question" in 1935 and later).

To express the dualism of political arbitrariness and legal order which were characteristic of German law in the early years of the National Socialist regime, Ernst Fraenkel has coined the phrases Prerogative State and Normal State. The former means a "governmental system which exercises unlimited arbitrariness and violence unchecked by any legal guarantees," and the latter "an administrative body endowed with the elaborate powers for safeguarding the legal order as expressed in statutes, decisions of the courts and activities of the administrative agencies." [68] While the sphere of arbitrariness was constantly growing, the remaining narrow sphere of a quasi-legal order was continuously reduced until it disappeared completely during the war.

The main ways in which arbitrariness invaded the previously existing legal order may be reviewed briefly as follows:

(1) *The political sphere is removed from the jurisdiction of law.* It is not governed by legal rules but is arbitrarily regulated. Officials exercise discretionary prerogatives. Acts of the Gestapo (the Secret State Police), supposed to investigate and suppress activities dangerous to the state, are subject to no judicial review.[69]

The lawyers of the regime have called acts of authority unfettered by control "Justizlose Hoheitsakte" (sovereign acts exempt from justice).[70] Those sovereign acts are immune from judicial control, says Huber,[71] which defend the order of life (Lebensordnung) of the German people, including the state and party constitution, against any danger to their very existence (existenzielle Gefährdung), especially treason and attack, but also economic distress. "The security of the national order of life," writes Prof. Otto Koellreutter, must be given precedence "over the security of individuals and individual legal claims." [72] Defense of the order of life, however, has no well-defined boundary. The "interest of the state" and "change of circumstances," have been used to negate apparently unimpeachable claims.

The scope of the political sphere beyond judicial control

can be arbitrarily widened. The courts are subordinated to political authorities.[73] Laws can be applied only insofar as political authorities do not exercise an opposing power. "The so-called private sphere is only relatively private; it is at the same time potentially political." [74]

The superiority of police and party authorities to the courts is especially evident in interferences with pending court procedures[75] and disregard of court decisions. Courts have been prohibited from trying defendants, who are often kept in jail indefinitely. Cases have been withdrawn from the ordinary courts[76] when judges tried to give preference to law in contradiction to government policies.[77] Acquitted defendants have been arrested by the Gestapo for further treatment.

The NSDAP and its affiliates enjoy special legal status. The party is in the domain of public law. Although no general exemption of the NSDAP from court jurisdiction has been recognized by the Federal Labor Court,[78] actions of party officials do not fall within the jurisdiction of ordinary courts.[79] Practically, the power of the party bureaucracy is beyond control. Members of the party or one of its structural parts (SA, SS, etc.) may not, without the sanction of the Führer's deputy, be examined as witnesses or experts before the courts on matters labelled confidential by the party.[80] Members occupying certain posts are forbidden to give evidence without permission, which is given only if the welfare of the state and party are not jeopardized. Party members have benefited most from the government's power of pardon and amnesty.

(2) *The infusion of politics into law and the judge's obligation to follow the dominant political creed, have put an end to the objectivity, impartiality, and independence of the judge.* "Only in the frame of a given world outlook can and must justice be independent." [81] "The objectivity of the judge receives its new value from being rooted in National Socialist principles and there finds, simultaneously, its natural boundaries." [82] In 1933 Hitler solemnly declared that the government would strictly adhere to the principle of independence of the judge.[83] In fact, the judge is not independent in his

decisions. He is "Hitler's soldier in plain clothes."[84] "The judge must be a model National Socialist."[85] "He is the vehicle of the eternal blood laws of the people."[86] "National Socialism protects the judge in his independence on the soil of National Socialist philosophy." "National Socialism does not tolerate a so-called independent jurisdiction fluttering above us in timeless space; it demands that jurisdiction be part of the community of our people."[87] Roland Freisler frequently has demanded displacement of impartial by "fighting" jurisdiction.[88]

As early as April, 1933, the judicial personnel was considerably changed by purges based on the law "for the restoration of the civil service."[89] It provided that "officials who, because of previous political activities do not offer the guarantee of defending the national state without reservation, may be dismissed from service."[90] Based on this provision, the non-aryan clause, and the clause that officials might be pensioned in the interest of the service or simplification of administration, Jewish, socialist, liberal, and pacifist judges were dismissed and their places filled with National Socialist partisans. No appeal to courts or administrative tribunals was allowed. Moreover, the threat of dismissal forced those remaining in office to conform. Not a few judges retired. Party district leaders and officers of the SS have intervened in connection with dismissals and appointments of judges. A special Act of April 7, 1933,[91] provided for the disbarment of many Jewish lawyers. A new clause in the lawyers' code of December 20, 1934,[92] opened the possibility of excluding lawyers whose personality does not guarantee reliable professional work.

Women were practically excluded from the careers of judge, lawyer, or state attorney.[93] To mitigate the consequences of this measure, it was proposed to allow graduate law students to become secretaries in courts. University training had not been required for this service.

Judicial positions are open only to loyal supporters of the regime. On June 30, 1933,[94] it was ruled that "as civil servant only he may be appointed who guarantees that he will at all times fully identify himself with the state of the national revolution."

LABOR COURTS IN THE JUDICIAL SYSTEM 167

According to ministerial orders, preference is to be given to those who have distinguished themselves in the National Socialist struggle and who will educate others in the spirit of National Socialism.[95] The Civil Service Law converted the civil servant into an instrument of the party. In contrast to the constitutionally safeguarded political integrity of the civil service in the Republic, officials must pledge personal allegiance to the Leader.[96] "He is the executor of the will of the state borne by the NSDAP." The district party leader must be consulted in appointments in order to manifest the unity of party, nation, and state.[97]

Although the law forbids removal by reason of the material content of a judicial sentence, such sentence may be considered contrary to the interests of the regime and an indication of unreliability, a basis for removal. In fact, whenever sentences have displeased the party, judges have been removed or demoted to inferior positions and thus driven to resign.

Staatsanwaltschaftsrat Ebert expressed the view of the co-ordinated judiciary in 1934: "We are not less National Socialist than any other 'estate' (Stand) of the German people. As workers of law, we refuse to drag the dust of obsolete liberalistic views with us after the leader flung open the doors of the Third Reich." [98]

Thus the German judiciary has gradually fallen into line with National Socialist dogmas, to which reference is frequently made in judgments, even where no political issues are involved. Slogans about the priority of public welfare to individual interest are used; "the bond of community between shop leaders and followers" is stressed. In some cases these slogans herald a departure from principles upon which former decisions were made; in others they are thrown in only to prove the judge's loyalty to the movement or disguise the meaning of his decisions. The last step was taken on April 26, 1942, when Hitler asserted the right to remove at will such judges as fail to understand the "demand of the hour." (Cf. n. 5, p. 224).

(3) *Equality before the law has been abolished.*[99] When party members or enemies of the state are involved, impartiality must suffer. Especially the "old party fighter" claims legal

privileges. Extenuating circumstances are recognized when one who "deserved well of his country" "makes a false step." The manhandling of workers by foremen and employers has been punished as an offense against social honor, but when a party member was involved, the social honor court has decided that a certain roughness is in line of duty. A former SA Sturmführer, a married man who frequently made advances to female employees, was treated gently by the Federal social honor court because of his services to the party.[100] Tax offenses have not been prosecuted when the offender had served National Socialism during the fight for power. That untruthfulness in an employee must be excused when he is the sole National Socialist in a shop in which employers and employees have not yet found the way to the new state, was the decision of a labor court.[101]

On the other hand, a large category of enemies of the state, "destructive forces" which threaten the nation, have been deprived of all legal protection.[102] Against those who did not fall in line with enthusiasm, "the full strength of the law has been applied." They do not "deserve any generosity."

No contract or right of ownership can protect those ousted for political reasons, which frequently means that a man high in the Nazi ranks is eager to get his hands on a certain position or business or to oust a competitor or personal antagonist. Thus editors of newspapers, owners of businesses, high-salaried employees, have been removed without notice, without recourse. Often the person to be ousted has been arrested and, by threat of concentration camp, induced "voluntarily" to waive legal claims.[103] In other cases courts have upheld arbitrary actions either by recognizing delegation of state functions to party officials or by acknowledging lack of legal restraint on police power.

"Political" judgments have been issued against so-called enemies of the state—Jews, Communists, Freemasons, Jehovah's Witnesses (Ernste Bibelforscher), pacifists "who do not understand the heroic attitude of the nation," and lawyers who had the courage to defend such "enemies". Dissatisfaction with the new order has been sufficient reason to establish the character of a person as dangerous to the state or to label him Communist.

Wherever political interests have been involved, ordinary, labor, and social honor courts have acted without consideration of legal principles. One Bavarian court of appeal declared that "the protection of state and people is more important than adherence to formalistic rules of procedure." [104]

Most enemies of the state were given the opportunity to change their minds and to fall into line. One group, however, has been doomed because of its unalterable "blood." [105] In the first stage of the development the Nazis tried to uphold at least something which looked like "legality." By means of legislation issued as early as 1935 Jews were barred from public office. In their first decisions most courts applied the racial idea only within the limits of these statutes, although, from the beginning, ambitious judges secured their career by anti-Semitic decisions. In the first period, the right to dismiss Jews without notice and without compensation was recognized only in public and not private enterprise, although the Federal Labor Court admitted that "the new attitude of the people toward the Jew differs fundamentally from its former attitude." [106] The Nuremberg laws of 1935 tightened the grip; the Jew was eliminated from family and household relations with non-Jews. Courts yielded to party pressure. Older judges, slow in adjusting to the revolutionary principles, were displaced. Others saw that their office and personal security depended on the application of the Führer's will. Courts began departing from the letter of the statutes to apply the "new morality."

Gradually Jews abandoned appeals to courts because they could expect no protection. On March 20, 1937, the Federal Labor Court justified the subjugation of Jews to the state, declaring that "the racial principles expounded by the National Socialist Party have been accepted by the broad mass of the population, even those who do not belong to the party." [107] The Federal Supreme Court had, in 1936, dissolved the contract of a Jewish stage manager which was supposed to be terminable only by sickness or death, arguing that the deprivation of rights—inflicted on the Jews living in Germany—can be described as civil death. "The racial characteristics of the plaintiff were likened to sickness and death." [108] With the extirpation of Jews from economic life and the loss of all possibility of earning a living—a development which found its climax in the pogrom of November 10, 1938—law suits concerning dismissals or damages disappeared, and the labor courts no longer had the task of dealing with Jews.[109]

Dismissals without notice of former officials of trade unions were upheld,[110] but former membership in the Social Democratic Party or in a trade union was not considered sufficient justification for dismissal without notice.[111] Decisions to the contrary would, in fact, have meant laying off at least one-third of all the manual workers. The National Socialist government gave former political adversaries in the working class a chance to become co-ordinated but dealt mercilessly with those who refused to do so. Employers were held justified in dismissing workers whose political views were suspect, since such suspicion would render them useless.[112] Communist activity was considered a culpable breach of loyalty.[113] The following reasons for dismissal were recognized; defamation of political leaders; refusal to allow children to join the Hitler Youth; refusal to give the Hitler salute;[114] listening to a Russian radio station;[115] refusal to contribute to the winter relief, [116] to join the DAF, [117] and to take part in works community meetings.[118] Workers showing a nonco-operative attitude toward National Socialist functions might be accused of maliciously disturbing the spirit of the works community.

Testimony of party functionaries has been considered of higher significance than that of other persons. Opinions of party district leaders as to political reliability have been accepted by some courts.[119] The Federal Labor Court argued that the opinion of a district leader did not relieve the court of its duty of independent investigation. It admitted, however, that "unfounded charges and even an unjustified suspicion coming from influential quarters may carry enough weight to constitute a major cause for dismissal." [120] Other courts have ruled that the opinion of the district leader, even in violation of a law, cannot be disregarded.[121] Thirty-three district leaders, 760 sub-district leaders and 100,000 local, block, and cell leaders, can give the courts quite a variety of opinions which they are supposed not to disregard.

The shop steward frequently has assumed the right to exercise pressure to dismiss persons for political reasons. In a decision of February 13, 1940, the Leipzig Labor Court confirmed a dismissal by demand of the DAF, although the relation of the employee to the employer was a good one. The charge was that, although she paid membership dues, she had taken no part in DAF activities and discontinued a subscription to a party periodical.[122]

True conformity with National Socialist tenets is shown in some judgments concerning eugenics and employment of women. At the beginning, dismissals of women in order to provide jobs for unemployed men were upheld as in accordance with the government's wishes.[123] Dismissal because of pregnancy, however, was rejected because it showed lack of understanding of woman's moral responsibility to nation and state.[124] In the course of time, especially from 1938, women's occupation was considered a necessity.

A memorandum opinion reflecting the eagerness of the courts to conform was rendered by the Federal Supreme Court for Social Insurance (Reichsversicherungsamt) on June 13, 1936,[125] recognizing sterility as a disease. The opinion was rendered without a case having been brought before this administrative court, but as one of fundamental importance.[126] The court explained that heretofore sickness insurance safeguarded the interest of the insured and his family by removing or reducing sickness and suffering, or by preventing it from becoming worse. "According to National Socialist conceptions, the well-being of the community takes precedence over personal interests." "As sterility can be considered a disease only if it is in the interest of the community that it be removed, it is necessary to consider whether the hereditary disposition of the woman in question makes it undesirable for her to have children. . . ."

Where judgments have displeased influential party groups, pressure has been used. Thus the Schwarze Korps has published frequent violent SS criticisms of the courts. The DAF has issued its own collection of labor court decisions (DAF Entscheidungssammlung) in which judgments were discussed mainly for the instruction of DAF officials and in order to influence courts and legislators.

DISPERSAL OF JURISDICTION

One of the means of destroying the old system of justice has been the creation of courts which intensify control over the individual and substitute decisions by partisans for those of judges who could traditionally be expected to be independent. These courts are designed to protect the strata for whom they are created from destructive persons (Schädlingen) and educate to "honorable behavior."

In the interest of the works community, gross violations of any of the rights or duties of followers or leader, may be prosecuted as violations of honor in a special set of courts, the social honor courts (Soziale Ehrengerichte).[127] These are quasi-criminal courts similar to the disciplinary courts which had existed before for civil servants and members of the professions, rather than labor courts. It is their duty to safeguard the social honor supposed to govern relations between each enterprise's "leader" and his "followers." Social honor means loyalty to the works community. Serious violations of social duties naturally arising from a works community, are punishable by the social honor courts as offenses against social honor. Such offenses are deemed to have been committed when (a) employers or others in a position of authority, by abuse thereof maliciously exploit the labor power of employees, e.g., by compelling illegal overtime or insulting employees' honor; (b) "followers" endanger the peace of an enterprise by maliciously inciting other "followers" or by continuously or maliciously disturbing its spirit of community, and as confidential men, by deliberately and improperly interfering with, the conduct of an enterprise; (c) members of an enterprise repeatedly and frivolously address unfounded complaints or proposals to the labor trustee or obstinately act in defiance of his written instructions; (d) members of the confidential council communicate without authority information, or manufacturing or business secrets which have come to their knowledge in the execution of their duties and which are designated confidential.

Penalties are warning, reprimand, fines up to 10,000 marks, disqualification as leader of an undertaking or member of a confidential council, dismissal, transfer to inferior work. Disqualification as leader means that the employer may be forbidden permanently or temporarily to function as employer, although he may retain his property and his entrepreneurial functions. Someone else must then take over the function of employer; the owner must then obey him as far as employer functions are concerned.

A social honor court is set up in each labor trustee's district. It consists of a judge as chairman and one enterprise leader and one confidential man as assessor. The assessors are appointed by the chairman from lists of the DAF.[128]

The court of appeals, the Federal Social Honor Court (Reichsehrengerichtshof) consists of two judicial officials, one as chairman, the other as associate, and three assessors, one an employer, one a confidential councillor, and one nominated by the federal government.

The administrative work of the social honor court is performed by the labor court office situated where the social honor court has its headquarters, and of the Federal Honor Court by the district labor court office in Berlin.[129]

Procedure is governed mainly by the provisions of the Code of Criminal Procedure (Strafprozessordnung), but is more informal and flexible. Complaints are made in writing to the RTA in whose districts the enterprise is located. The RTA who receives the notification, or in some other way becomes aware of a breach of social duties, must investigate, hearing the accused and deciding whether or not to refer to the social honor court.

Should he decide to do so, he acts as prosecutor, i.e., presents charges in writing. The presiding judge, after having investigated, may dismiss a charge as unfounded, pass judgment at a preliminary hearing where he may even impose light penalties, or refer the case to the full court. Many decisions—102 out of 155 in 1936—are made by the chairman alone (nine such cases were protested in 1936). If the application is dismissed, the RTA may appeal; where sentence is passed the defendant may do so. Arrest, temporary detention, search, and seizure are barred.

The court decides by oral public procedure. It procures evidence and may examine witnesses and experts under oath. The public may be excluded. The RTA may attend the trial and make recommendations. He may withdraw a case before a decision is rendered. The defendant may be represented by counsel holding power of attorney. Should he have none, the chairman may ex officio assign counsel. The court may compel the attendance of the defendant. The court decides at its discretion.

The RTA or the defendant may appeal to the Federal Social Honor Court in Berlin, the defendant when a fine has been levied exceeding 100 marks or expulsion from a confidential council, removal from place of employment or disqualification as leader has been ordered. The Federal Social Honor Court in Berlin has full discretion in appeals. Even if the appeal was made by the defendant the court may change the decision to his disadvantage. Such *"reformatio in peius"* is one of the National Socialist principles introduced after the revolution of 1933 into the German criminal law and extended later on to similar proceedings.

Enforcement is supervised by the RTA. Pardon may be granted by the Minister of Labor in agreement with the Minister of Justice.[180] A person sentenced may be required to pay part or all costs of the proceeding.

After a period of uncertainty, during which it was frequently claimed that the provisions of the act are indicative rather than exclusive, the Federal Social Honor Court ruled that punishable violations are enumerated exhaustively in the act and that, therefore, no violation may be included by analogy.[181] The Federal Social Honor Court did not follow the revised criminal code which provides that punishments can be inflicted in cases of analogy.

The social honor courts are supposed to decide only cases in which attempts of the RTA to persuade employer or employee fail. Practically, however, they have interfered whenever they felt "that the true spirit of the works community was endangered," especially if anti-National Socialists were involved. They inevitably encroached on the field of the labor courts.[132] Many cases coming before the social honor courts concern exploitation, such as substandard wages, illegally long hours, bad housing conditions. Here the labor court competes jurisdictionally. In disputes of this type, the social honor court is supposed to act only with regard to unsocial motives, abuse of authority and malicious intent. Honest differences of opinion, underpayment made in good faith, are not to be decided in the social honor courts. Persistent payments of wages below the rates of collective rules, irregular payment and neglect of payment of insurance fees have been considered malicious exploitation of labor with abuse of authority,[133] except when the employer was unable to pay.[134] An employer who drank and paid low wages was punished. But even in a case of failure to provide decent housing facilities the "unsocial" motive had to be proved.[135] An unsocial attitude is assumed when offenses are frequent and cumulative. Punishment in a social honor court is supposed to be "educational."

The courts have been used chiefly against employers.[136] (Cf. p. 178.) Most cases concern abuse of authority: beating of workers, kicking, boxing ears, abusive language, immoral advances toward [137] and sexual relations with female employees even with consent.[138] Such attitudes have been punished as remnants of an older class attitude. In accordance with National Socialist views on the functions of women, sexual relations are considered an offense only if they constitute an abuse of authority. A woman employee was presumed to have offended the social honor of her employer when she complained to his wife of improper advances.[139] Punishment for these offenses have been inconsistent, however. Boxing of ears is not always a misdemeanor.[140]

A serious offense is a contravention of instructions of the RTA. Of 141 cases punished in the first two years, 74 concerned failures to promulgate shop rules, three violations of hour regulations, the others of other collective rules.[141] In 120 cases in 1935, penalty was imposed; in 34 the complaint was withdrawn; eight ended in acquittal.

Occasionally violation of protective laws may be punished. The courts are especially proud of cases in which remedies in labor courts or punishments by ordinary courts would have been impossible, e.g., when a farmer refused transportation to a hospital for an employee's seriously ill children,[142] or when an employer put workers under tension by driving, nagging,[143] and using insulting language,[144] or when an employer, hiring a worker, pretended to give him a permanent position but discharged him at the end of a season.[145]

Lack of adequate training of an employee was punished only in exceptional cases.

Cases against workers have dealt with disturbance of social peace (e.g., strike agitation)[146] "stirring up bad feelings in industry," "interference with business management, overbearing attitude toward fellow workers, quarrelsome behavior, undermining the authority of foremen," etc. Cases involving members of the confidential council have been based on unco-operative and quarrelsome behavior and interference in management.

By far the most common penalties are fines.[147] In general, penalties were more severe in lower courts than in the Federal Court. Particularly, disqualification as leader has been resorted to only in rare cases, "when other penalties do not correspond to the gravity of the offense or when the possibility of the employer altering his ways and attitude toward his employees appears beyond realization." [148]

The social honor courts, which seemed impressive innovations when introduced, became much less significant than was intended. They do not seem to act in big business at all. About three-fourths in 1935, nine-tenths in 1939, of all cases involved handicrafts, agriculture, and small industrial enterprises,[149] in which personal relations are relatively close. In 1939 only

12 of 120 charges lodged against employers concerned industry.[150] In 1938 the RTA were advised to pay special attention to the housing conditions of agricultural workers. The institution may have had some significance, although not a great one, for improvement in this field.

The figure of 128 decisions by all courts in 1935 (156 in 1936) is astonishingly low as compared with the figure of 20,500,000 workers with sickness insurance in that year.[151] Cases do not indicate fully the courts' influence, because their existence may have worked to discourage abuses. Examination of cases shows their middle-class character, however.

It has been the aim of the social honor courts to prevent social unrest due to unsatisfactory relations between employers and employees. The primary task of maintaining peace is entrusted to the labor trustee. When he meets resistance, he can resort to the social honor courts. The somewhat vague conception of social honor has made it possible to deal with some cases which would have escaped prosecution in the regular courts. But the social honor courts are basically mere show. The party has swifter and more efficient weapons with which to attack offenders. Here it demonstrates social-mindedness at the expense of the little businessmen.

There are other disciplinary courts in addition to the social honor courts. The Weimar Constitution abolished special military courts. One of the first steps of the National Socialists was to re-establish them. Disputes concerning government officials are handled by the National Federation of German Officials, an organization directly affiliated with the Party. The SS, the Labor Service, etc. have their own disciplinary rules and courts which enforce the subservience of the individual and hermetically seal the organizations against outside influences.

The DAF has its own Code of Honor[152] and special courts (district courts and a Supreme Court) for its members and officials. These courts, generally composed of a full-time chairman, two honorary assessors, and a full-time *rapporteur*, may consist exclusively of lay judges. Nonpayment of dues for more than three months, unsocial behavior, lack of comradely

TABLE 34
CASES BROUGHT BEFORE THE SOCIAL HONOR COURTS

	1934[153] (Since May)	1935[154]	1936[155]	1937[156]	1938[157]	1939[157]	1940[158]	1941[158]	1942[159]
CASES									
Brought before the courts............	61	204	251	542	232	142	72	66	29
(Involving persons)............	...	...	...	...	...	...	80	...	34
Cases against employers or their deputies............	56	164	189	...	...	120	59	...	22
Cases against supervisory personnel (managers and foremen)............	3	41	35	...	...	19	16	...	8
Cases against other workers............	2	18	54	15	...	14	5	...	4
CHARGES									
Malicious abuse of authority............	22	95	167	105	...	44	55	...	25
Malicious exploitation of labor............	15	34		74	...	22	3	...	1
Malicious abuse of both............	8	41		...	...	16	9	...	...
Contravention of instructions of the RTA (some involving exploitation).	16	20	75	68	...	48	...	...	...
Endangering industrial peace.........	1	5	...	9	...	...	...	...	...
Charges against confidential men.....	1	1	...		...	...	...	...	...
Malicious disturbance of the spirit of the works community............	...	8	...	...	...	12	4	...	3

TABLE 34—Continued
Cases Brought before the Social Honor Courts

	1934[153] (Since May)	1935[154]	1936[155]	1937[156]	1938[157]	1939[157]	1940[158]	1941[158]	1942[159]
Termination									
Judgments............	13	128	156	...	...	73	54	...	22
Complaints withdrawn...	...	34	35	...	...	49	5	...	5
Death of participants...	...	...	...	...	...	...	2	...	1
Penalties									
Disqualification as leader...	3	9	6	14	...	7	...	3	2
Deprivation of employment...	2	1	3	...	...	...	...	...	...
Fines..................	...	76	117	222	...	60	37	23	14
Warning...............	...	13	11	...	...	1	...	...	1
Reprimand.............	...	21	14	...	...	1	...	...	1
Acquittal..............	...	8	4	13	...	3	...	5	3
Appeals...............	...	28	26	...	...	10	5	...	2

feeling, are grounds for action against employer or employee, and may result in temporary or permanent expulsion. In many respects the decisions of the special courts of the DAF have a far greater significance than those of the social honor courts. Since the "closed shop" principle controls the whole German industry, exclusion from the DAF means permanent unemployment. Officials of the DAF may be given notice only if action against them is simultaneously brought before the DAF or party courts. Cases involving high officials of the DAF are decided in the Supreme Court as first and final instance. At the end of 1944 the courts of the DAF were empowered to deal with breaches of contract and ordered to mete out punishment which really hurt.[160]

Among other honor courts, the most important are those of the NSDAP for members.[161] The party had already a private arbitration system before the seizure of power, the Investigation and Arbitration Committees (*Untersuchungs- und Schlichtungsausschüsse*), briefly called Uschla.[162] In 1934 the system was reorganized. It has three instances, Kreis and Ortsgerichte as local courts of first instance, Gau (district) courts of appeal and the Supreme Court of the NSDAP in Munich (Oberstes Parteigericht). The district courts act as appeal courts for local courts and as first instance for the middle strata of the party bureaucracy. The Supreme Court is a second appellate court for the lower and the sole appellate court for district courts. It acts as a court of original jurisdiction for high party leaders.[163] No party official may refuse to appear. Each chamber has a chairman and two or more assessors, of whom one must belong to the SA if the defendant is a member of the SA and must outrank the latter. The local courts are generally composed of lay judges; in the higher courts learned judges prevail. Women are not appointed judges. Ordinary courts must give legal aid to the party courts. Standards are extra-legal and political. In making decisions the judges are bound only by their National Socialist conscience. "The Party courts derive their jurisdiction and related powers from the NSDAP, which, in turn, is independent of the state and itself an originator of law, subject only to the will of the Chancellor acting in his capacity as party Führer."[164]

LABOR COURTS IN THE JUDICIAL SYSTEM 181

The party courts prosecute persons (1) who commit dishonorable deeds, (2) who give offense by immoral behavior, (3) who act contrary to the aims of the NSDAP, (4) who cause quarrels within the political community, (5) who fail to pay dues for three months in succession, and (6) who show lack of interest.[165] In fact, they have frequently taken jurisdiction in civil matters involving a party member. "The party courts always have to consider themselves the iron clasps of the movement which hold together the proud structure of the NSDAP built up in laborious efforts by the political and SA leaders; to preserve it against damaging cracks and shocks is their primary task." [166]

Penalties are warning or reprimand; loss of the rights of holding party office, carrying weapons or speaking in public; expulsion. These tribunals are among the most powerful institutions of the government. Expulsion may mean economic ruin or worse.[167] Execution lies in the hands of the party organization.

Because of jurisdictional confusion, conflicts sometimes arise between the social honor courts and ordinary civil and criminal courts, labor courts, estate honor courts, and the party courts. All may function simultaneously and consecutively. Sentencing by an ordinary criminal court is no obstacle to prosecution for the same offense in a social honor court. The AOG provides that where there is simultaneous action by a regular prosecutor (e.g., in a case of manhandling of an employee), action before the social honor court is to be temporarily suspended. If the defendant is convicted in the criminal court, the chairman of the social honor court decides whether the case shall be tried therein. If acquitted, he may still be tried in the social honor court. Frequently offenders have been punished by both courts. In cases of simultaneous action by social honor and DAF courts, action before the latter is temporarily suspended but may be resumed subsequent to the decision of the former. Here, too, punishment by both courts is possible.

The possible multiplicity of jurisdictions has been exemplified by a hypothetical case of a lawyer who was, at the same time, a notary public, a member of the NSDAP, and the editor of a law journal,[168] and who maintained an office in which he employed a young lawyer as a clerk. Should the honor of the employee be offended by the employer, who also is a member of the bar and the Party, the case may come under seven jurisdictions: ordinary courts, if the lawyer brings a libel action, which he can do only with the consent of the Party court since both parties are members of the NSDAP. The social honor court could act on application of the trustee of labor. Since the offender may have violated the honor of his profession, the disciplinary court for members of the bar could intervene; the courts of the press, of the economic field, and of notaries could act for the same reason.

The question of precedence is regulated only for ordinary courts. Party courts have a separate precedence. When others are involved, the courts must agree upon which action shall be suspended. Any court may act, however, and would in such a complicated case. No court is bound by the decision on the evidence introduced in another. That multiplicity of jurisdiction has not led to serious confusion and complication, is due mainly to the fact that the social honor courts have remained unimportant and that, in practice, the importance of labor courts has been greatly diminished. Another restriction of labor court activities is due to the great power vested in the Commissioner General of Manpower. Decisions of his agencies concerning hiring and firing of labor cannot be appealed except when based on fraud.[169]

The considerable decrease in cases coming before the labor courts does not confirm the claim of National Socialists that the new order has cut litigation. It rather is an indication of the reduced jurisdiction of the labor courts and of the concurrent jurisdiction of other agencies and the change of character of the courts into executive agencies of the government. In the old order, grievances of individual workers were thrashed out between works councils and employers, and, when no settlement could be achieved, were taken to the labor court. Collective disputes were handled by trade unions and employers' organizations and, if they failed to settle them, by arbitration authorities.

LABOR COURTS IN THE JUDICIAL SYSTEM 183

Today only conflicts on rights are recognized. Conflicts on interest are supposed to have disappeared.

The AOG delegates the task of maintaining industrial peace to varying institutions—the confidential council, the DAF, and the RTA. The works community is obligated to settle disputes within itself. The confidential man, although not meant to be an opponent of the employer, is a representative of labor in fact. In disputes of general importance and complaints against decisions of the leader, appeal may be made to the RTA. Use of this means has been limited by safeguards, however; before the confidential council appeals to the RTA there must be consultation within the council, i.e., under the chairmanship of the employer. The employer himself must lodge the complaint and may add his own point of view. This means powerful pressure on both to come to an agreement. Moreover, members of a works community who make repeated unfounded or frivolous complaints to the RTA are guilty of a violation of social honor. Because of these restrictions, little use has been made of the right of appeal to the RTA. Only in the first period, when everybody appealed everything to the RTA, was he flooded with complaints. In 1934 one could see in the office of the RTA at Berlin a printed statement that the latter had no jurisdiction in landlord and tenant cases, libel suits, alimony proceedings, etc. For a short period the RTA was as popular as the conciliation committees had been in 1919. Warning and the trustees' practice of working only on complaints frankly discussed in meetings of the confidential council led to a considerable decrease of cases. Conflicts submitted to him were originally only of a collective character (concerning, e.g., wages below standards fixed in collective rules). No individual disputes were submitted, and therefore he was hardly in competition with the labor courts in conflicts between employer and employee. He has absorbed part of the labor court's jurisdiction since he decides disputes concerning confidential men and their dismissal or removal from office and now, also, individual cases (cf. p. 145).

To what extent the authorities try to settle disputes within the shop is revealed by a circular of the Minister of Labor of May 19, 1937.[170] He states that many complaints indicate the nuisance of frequently seeking the help of agencies outside the plant and instructs the RTA to first seek settlement within the shop. The confidential council, in particular, must act. In disputes of general importance which cannot be settled in this way, the RTA should be appealed to.

The DAF is authorized to reduce the number of disputes brought to the labor courts. It has done so with the help of various organs. The shop stewards, supposed to be neutral, have frequently dealt with grievances and have been powerful enough to achieve settlements. District stewards and trade offices (Reich Enterprise Communities) intervened in disputes of a more collective character.

Another reason for the reduction of court cases has been the monopoly of representation in the labor courts by the legal advisory offices of the DAF. Since they accept only such cases as have a chance of success and which are in accordance with the principles of National Socialism and the honor of labor, they may refuse any representation.[171] In thousands of cases they can deprive the worker of his right. The employer suffers less from these powers of the DAF since in nearly all cases it is the employee who is the plaintiff. Since the DAF can refuse to provide counsel, it can use pressure to effect compromise or withdrawal or recognition of a claim. Before the war this pressure was especially effective since assessors, too, had to be provided by the DAF. The advisory office was backed by the whole power of the DAF. Thus they "settled" many cases before they reached the courts. The director of the offices claimed that in 1935 over three million employers and workers used the offices (3,657,046)[172] and that 195,000 cases were settled outside the courts,[173] although such compromises were not enforceable.

The large group of complaints was reduced when the employment offices began to control dismissals. As discharges became more dependent on their consent (full control was established September 1, 1939), the labor courts decided fewer of such conflicts. This meant a further restriction of labor's right to protest against injustice in the courts. No formal complaint or appeal to courts is possible against the employment authorities, but only such complaint to supervisory authority as is permissible against any administrative decision.

The decline in labor court cases is, furthermore, due to the competition of special courts which handle some conflicts formerly in the jurisdiction of the labor court. Furthermore, the Gestapo has the duty of maintaining "peace" in the enterprises. Since the Gestapo controls the most efficient means of compulsion, it is the most efficient guardian of industrial peace.

The decrease in litigation testifies to a decline in confidence in justice, and to the terror which controls the life of the greatest part of the population. People try to avoid contact with state authorities regardless of whether they are courts or administrative agencies. Those who belong to the groups discriminated against may be afraid of partiality.[174] Those in power do not need them. Political contacts, intrigue, pressure on Party members, have been more efficient.

SUMMARY

The National Socialist government faced, in the German judiciary, a power which, like those of army and church, might have proved a stumbling block to the revolution. The tradition of court independence and objectivity and impartial civil service efficiency, seemed to guarantee the rule of law. The regime has succeeded in breaking it by restricting the field of justice and reforming the personnel. The first has been achieved in various ways: (1) executive decrees were issued on special cases, e.g., confiscation of Jewish and Communist property, degenerate art, etc.; (2) cases were taken away from courts and dealt with by government departments whose decisions would not be challenged; (3) cases were transferred from ordinary or labor courts to special courts; (4) where law and court decisions lagged behind the regime's desires, extra-legal pressure was brought to bear.

Purges, political threats, and the dismemberment of the field of justice succeeded in forcing the judiciary into submission. This process has been most successful in criminal law. In civil and labor law, tradition and habits constituted obstacles. Even if one admits that many judges have shown considerable courage, they have capitulated when threatened personally. The German judiciary has produced few martyrs ready to suffer for the ideas they had sworn to protect: the rule of law, the independence of the courts, and the idea of justice.

APPENDICES

Appendix I

LABOR LAW BEFORE 1918

Up to the outbreak of the First World War, labor law had not won recognition corresponding to the development of industry. The attitude of the state to the trade unions was not far from hostile. In spite of the freedom of association granted by law to industrial workers,[1] trade unions were tolerated rather than recognized. The Industrial Code[2] of 1869 imposed penalties for coercing workers, not only by violence or threat or other means, to participate in or to refrain from withdrawing from a union. Restriction of organization affected agricultural and domestic help, railway workers, and other public employees, and civil servants. The criminal code and police rules were applied to restrict trade union activities, especially by prosecuting pickets and protecting strike breakers. Collective bargaining was voluntary and private. The worker was in theory a party to an individual, freely concluded contract. Protection was secured for him only as the weaker party.

Protection of manual and nonmanual workers began in Germany with social insurance against illness, accidents, invalidity, and old age. This system, introduced with its own courts during the 1880's, was extended in scope and codified in 1911.

Protective legislation for the industrial worker which had earlier existed only in the form of some regulations concerning children, young persons, and women, began in 1891 as an amendment to the Industrial Code. Protection of women and children,[3] restriction of hours of work for these groups, for young workers, and for all workers in unhealthful occupations; Sunday rest; provisions for the protection of life, health, and morals; the obligation to draw up works rules; and the prohibition of remuneration in kind—these were a few of the achievements. Employees in commercial undertakings were protected by similar regulations included in the Commercial Code,[4] miners by state mining laws, home workers in a Home Work Act.[5] These special laws superseded the provisions of the Civil Code[6] governing labor contracts. The latter was the only statute protecting those workers outside the scope of special laws, e.g., farm and domestic workers, manual workers in small handicraft shops, and office employees in noncommercial undertakings. The Civil Code regulated giving of notice and included a minimum of health protection and safety rules.

The war was a milestone in the relations of state and trade unions. Overnight the latter were publicly recognized. Section 153 of the Industrial Code, which had severely handicapped trade union activities, was abrogated.[7] Trade unions were no longer to be treated as political organizations[8] and thus were freed from restrictions which had especially hampered the organization of young workers. Railway workers were allowed to organize. Restrictions on the use of foreign languages at union meetings (which had inhibited the organization of Polish workers), were removed. The military authorities put pressure on employers to conclude collective agreements with trade unions and frequently made contracts conditional on the acceptance of a minimum wage. General male labor conscription, introduced by the Auxiliary Service Act of December 5, 1916,[9] brought another step. In compensation for organized labor's consent, the trade unions were officially recognized as representatives of labor. Shop committees were made compulsory in establishments of more than fifty employees and conciliation boards, organized on the basis of employer-employee participation, were established to settle disputes.

Appendix II

LABOR LAW UNDER THE WEIMAR REPUBLIC

The revolution following the First World War was a turning-point for labor law. A proclamation of the revolutionary government of November 12, 1918,[1] abolished all restrictions on the right of coalition and assembly. These rights as well as the right of collective bargaining were sanctioned by the Weimar Constitution.[2] Collective replaced individual bargaining in employer-employee relations.

A joint agreement of the Federation of Employers Associations and of the trade unions signed in November, 1918, guaranteed, among other things, recognition of trade unions as the representatives of labor, the setting up of collective agreements, works councils, arbitration and the eight-hour day. As compared to their pre-war attitude, this was a complete surrender of employers to organized labor. Corresponding legislation followed. Existing laws were expanded and entirely new areas added, affecting, for example, collective agreements, works councils, arbitration, farm labor, and disabled veterans.

One set of laws concerned regulation of the labor market and the worker's right to his job. Employers were obliged to re-engage war veterans employed on the outbreak of war. Such veterans were protected against dismissal for three months.[3]

The Closing-Down Order of November 8, 1920,[4] restricted the freedom of employers to order lay-offs; they must furnish proof of necessity and observe certain time limits before being entitled to close completely or partially. Authorities could order a reduction of hours of work during the period of delay.

These laws, intended to facilitate the rehabilitation of soldiers in economic life, were repealed or amended at the end of the demobilization period.

The right to lay men off continued to be restricted. The Act Concerning Disabled Men[5] compelled the employment of a certain percentage of disabled men and protected them against dismissal. During the depression additional protection against dismissal was afforded salaried employees.[6] It provided for three months' notice of termination of employment for salaried employees over twenty-five years of age who had been in one employ five years or longer. After eight years of service, four months' notice was required; after ten years, five months; after twelve years, six months.

Dismissals could be subjected to a judicial review after the works councils had dealt with them in a preliminary procedure (cf. n. 59, p. 210). A network of public employment offices was spread over the country. Another group of statutes protected health, safety, wages, and working hours. The eight-hour day was legalized in 1918-19 (amended 1923).[7] A Provisional Agricultural Labor Decree[8] for the first time provided special protection for farm workers. Protection for home workers was expanded[9] and minimum wages fixed for them. All branches of social insurance were extended in scope and benefit provisions. Unemployment insurance, displacing the unemployment relief system, was added.

By far the most important branch of labor legislation developed in the post-war period around collective labor relations. By decree of December 23, 1918,[10] collective agreements were legally recognized and three principles were established: (1) Only employers and economic associations of employers and employees (i.e., bona fide trade unions) might conclude collective agreements. (2) The principle of nondeviation stipulated that the parties must live up to the terms of the agreement. Departures were admitted only if authorized by the agreement itself or if they favored the worker. (3) By a special decree of the Minister of Labor, the agreement might be extended to outsiders within its geographical and industrial scope.

Eligibility to be party to a collective agreement became one of the most disputed points. What was involved was not simply competence to conclude a collective agreement, but the right to apply for arbitration, to send members of the organization to labor courts of the first two instances, and to delegate representatives to various social and economic bodies, e.g., placement and arbitration bodies, labor courts, and others.

The Collective Agreement Statute [11] gave no definition of eligibility. In the Joint Agreement of November 1918, the employers organizations had withdrawn recognition from the so-called yellow, nonmilitant, or company unions. The Weimar Constitution guaranteed trade union recognition in Article 165. During the revolutionary period, when every spontaneous group called itself a trade union, the federations of the three trade unions had agreed on a definition, which aimed mainly at excluding nonmilitant unions. Legal literature, court and administrative practice developed rules as to the eligibility of economic associations to conclude collective agreements. According to them, "economic organizations" had to be permanently organized, consist exclusively of employers or employees, and be independent of the opposing interest and to aim primarily at safeguarding the economic interests of members in the field of labor relations. The requirement of "independence" gave rise to a bitter contest concerning yellow, nonmilitant, and company unions.[12]

Labor distrusted shop organizations not incorporated into nationwide unions. Organizations of employees which confined their membership to a single enterprise were regarded as dependent on the entrepreneur because the latter had the power to dissolve the union by closing his shop. Company unions were not treated as bona fide.

Nationwide unions and their locals sometimes concluded collective agreements valid for a single enterprise. Although legal, this method was not very popular. In most cases, collective agreements covered all enterprises of a given branch over a large district.

The Labor Administration recognized as bona fide only those unions which were incorporated either in the "Free," the "Christian," or the Hirsch-Duncker (liberal) unions. The courts did not altogether follow this administrative practice. The conflict between the judiciary and the administration was still unsettled in 1933, when the whole problem became obsolete.

As far as labor was concerned, the individual collective agreement was usually written not by one but by several organizations. If, for instance, automobile factory wages in a certain district were regulated by collective agreement, the agreement was concluded by an employers' organization and by several unions, such as the Free Metal Workers union, the Christian Metal Workers union, the Hirsch-Duncker Metal Workers union, the Free Painters Union, the Christian Painters union, the Hirsch-Duncker Painters union, the Free Carpenters union, the Christian Carpenters union, the Hirsch-Duncker Carpenters union, etc.

Before the unions negotiated with the employers' organization, they came to an agreement with each other.

The three "recognized union movements" collaborated rather smoothly. They were, however, well aware of the fact that the whole system was threatened at the moment when outsiders would be admitted to the status of "economic" organizations.

The "recognized" unions, in fact, were supported by the majority of German workers and the charge of monopoly abuses was unjustified. It should be admitted, however, that the system as a whole was rather complicated and artificial. The idea that only one union should control an individual factory was as foreign to the German situation as the "closed shop" device. No legal provisions existed which regulated relations and settled conflicts among unions.

Any collective agreement consisted of two types of regulations, with normative and obligatory effect respectively, depending on the legal validity. The normative provisions regulated whatever could be included in an individual labor contract—wages, hours of work, holidays, etc. According to predominant opinion, it determined the law on which individual labor contracts were based. The norms were automatically embodied in the individual labor contract. The obligatory part determined the legal rights and duties of the parties, such as regulation of apprenticeship, pension fund, use of special employment agencies, etc. The most important provision of the obligatory part was the mutual promise to maintain industrial peace on matters in the agreement. This was implied in the very purpose of the agreement without express stipulation, in accordance with a general principle of German contract law that the parties are bound to fulfill not only those duties which they have expressly agreed upon, but also all duties corresponding to considerations of equity and usages prevailing in the branch of business.

The principle of nondeviation gave rise to litigation concerning admissibility of waivers and questions as to whether deviating conditions were really more favorable than those agreed upon. The clauses concerning rights and obligations of the parties were not subject to the principle of nondeviation.

The third principle, which gave the Federal Minister of Labor the possibility of declaring norms of predominant importance generally binding within the geographical and industrial scope of the agreement, prevented outsiders, employers as well as workers, from undercutting terms laid down in an agreement. Because of such extension—usually demanded by trade unions as well as employers' organizations —the great majority of German workers (more than twelve million in 1928-31) were covered by collective agreements.[13]

A method of achieving collective agreements aside from conclusion and extension, was imposition by compulsory arbitration award. The Arbitration Decree[14] provided that awards of chairmen of arbitration bodies could be declared binding by the authority "if it appeared just and reasonable with due consideration of the interests of both parties and of its wider economic and social effects." The declaration replaced acceptance by the parties and gave the award the force of a freely-concluded collective agreement; it could even be extended to outsiders. Only procedural regulations and the legal competence of the authority were reviewable by a court, not the necessity, reasonableness, or justice of the award.[15] Concerning the regulation of wages, compulsory came to displace voluntarily concluded agreements to a high degree.[16]

Resentment of employers against the regulation of working conditions by imposed arbitration awards led to the famous law suit in the northwestern iron and steel industry. The basic question was whether the arbitration boards were entitled to change an existing collective agreement by means of a compulsory arbitration award. The decision depended upon the authority of the court to review the proceedings of the arbitration board in order to determine whether the latter had unduly extended its "jurisdiction" by changing existing collective agreements instead of restricting itself to creating new collective agreements. The court decided in favor of the employers' organization and invalidated the award.

In principle, the German trade unions did not demand the closed shop. There was, however, resentment against "parasites" who enjoyed gains without making sacrifices. When the German Actors' Union wrote the closed shop into an agreement, the clause was declared illegal by the Federal Supreme Court [17] because the court considered it immoral to bar anyone from earning a living. The decision was sharply criticized by the union.

Collective bargaining gained in importance when the Hours of Work Order of December 21, 1923,[18] in order to loosen the strict rigidity of the eight-hour day, left it to contracting parties to determine elasticity of hours. The statute allowed extension of the working week from 48 to 60 hours by collective agreement.

In the last period of the Weimar Republic, the system of collective agreement was endangered by complaints of employers against inelasticity, rigidity, and equalization tendencies in the agreements. From December 1, 1930, on,[19] emergency decrees, based on the special national emergency power of the Reich President, began to interfere with existing collective agreements, at first only for public employees. Wage and salary cuts were ordered in the Fourth Emergency Decree of December 8, 1931,[20] and collective agreements expiring on January 1, 1932, were prolonged. The Emergency Decree of September 4, 1932,[21] gave the government unlimited power to change all regulations concerning social policy including collective agreements. The Emergency Decree of September 5, 1932,[22] entitled an employer who increased his staff to cut wages under specified conditions. Nondeviation was abolished, insofar as the latter decree established freedom to reduce wages below the decreed rates. With increasing depression and the decline of labor's power, the courts yielded more and more to the relaxation (Auflockerung) claim raised by business.

Litigation about collective agreements was facilitated by the system of declaratory judgments which rested on Section 256 of the Code of Civil Procedure. Under this provision, any one who had a legal interest in the establishment of the disputed facts could bring an action for a declaratory judgment concerning an existing legal relation.

Legal regulation of collective agreements was incomplete and did not cover such an important question as liability for breach of contract. The statute was considered provisional and was to be superseded by a comprehensive statute. Its development was left partly to the labor courts.

Trade union power under the Weimar Republic was strengthened by an instrument which, during the revolutionary period, seemed to threaten the very existence of trade unionism. Spontaneously emerging in the days of the revolution in opposition to conservative union leadership, the works councils, as finally regulated by the law of February 4, 1920,[23] became the "elongated arms" of the trade unions in the shops. Representative bodies had to be established in practically all undertakings employing at least five persons. In small shops there were stewards and in those with more than twenty employees there were councils. Elected for one year and eligible to re-election, by secret ballot of all employees over eighteen years of age, the councils exercised four types of functions.

First, they co-operated in the regulation of working conditions within the framework of collective agreements or in questions not regulated by collective agreements. They had power to approve the employer's work rules regulating the beginning and end of working hours, rest pauses, kind and amount of fines, etc. They negotiated with the employer regarding grievances.

Secondly, they had the power to co-operate in drawing up general principles for hiring. More important was their right to appeal to the courts against dismissals based on political or trade union affiliation, sex, or religion; those without reason being stated; those unduly harsh, unfair, or unjustified. The works council had to be informed in advance of projected lay-offs and was entitled to co-operate with the aim of avoiding hardship.

The third function, that of collaboration in promoting the efficiency in production, was generally neglected.

The fourth, participation in management, entitled the works council to demand information on business proceedings affecting the labor contract, to see the balance sheet and profit and loss statement, and to elect one or two of its members to the supervisory board of joint stock companies with the same rights (except remuneration) as other board members.

Members of the works council were protected against dismissal. Disputes arising out of the act were decided at first by Conciliation Bodies, after 1927 by labor courts in summary procedure.

Although formally independent of the trade unions, the works councils were in fact closely tied to them. The machinery of the councils was set up under trade union control. Lists of candidates were drawn according to trade union directives. The unions could be consulted in works council meetings. They provided training courses in their schools and information through their press. The works council, on the other hand, supervised the administration of collective agreements. They linked the unions with their members in the shop and provided valuable information.

The councils, however, were not under the complete control of the unions. In restricting themselves primarily to grievances of the workers, they failed to fulfill all the functions provided by law.

Appendix III

TRADE UNIONS

The German trade unions were split into three diversely oriented movements, one socialist, one Christian, one liberal. The socialist "Free Trade Unions" were united in the General Federation of Free Trade Unions (Allgemeiner Deutscher Gewerkschaftsbund or ADBG), which had 4,134,902 members at the end of 1931[1] The ADBG had a cartel agreement with the socialist salaried employees, the General League of Free Trade Unions of Salaried Employees (Allgemeiner Freier Angestelltenbund, Afa League) with 465,591 members. The Christian trade unions (Gesamtverband der Christlichen Gewerkschaften) with 577,512 members in 1931 had united in the German Confederation of Trade Unions (Deutscher Gewerkschaftsbund, DGB) with the Christian Salaried Employees Federation (Gesamtverband Deutscher Angestelltengewerkschaften or Gedag), which had 593,800 members. The liberal Hirsch-Duncker Unions, named for their founders, with a membership of only 149,804, were united with a Trade Union League of Salaried Employees (Gewerkschaftsbund Der Angestellten, or GDA) with 327,742 members, in a Confederation of Workers, Salaried Employees, and Civil Servants (Gewerkschaftsring deutscher Arbeiter-, Angestellten- und Beamterverbände, known as the Ring). At the outset, each of the three movements had a civil servants' section.

In addition to the three main groups, there were some unaffiliated bona fide trade unions (e.g., the Federation of

Executive Employees, Vereinigung leitender Angestellter or Vela, and a Polish union) and nonmilitant, so-called "yellow" unions, not recognized as bona fide. From time to time, Communist unions, also denied such recognition, were formed. They claimed 35,774 members in 1931, the nonmilitants 125,083.

The large majority of manual workers were organized into socialist unions. Nonmanual workers were rather equally divided among the three groups. The largest union of the latter was the German National Trade Union of Commercial Employees (Deutschnationaler Handlungsgehilfenverband, DHV) of the Christian movement. It had 379,590 members in 1930.[2]

NOTES
BIBLIOGRAPHY
INDEX

NOTES

NOTES TO INTRODUCTION

1. *Reichsgesetzblatt* (henceforth referred to as *RGBl*, I, p. 1016.
2. Sec. 157: Contracts are to be interpreted as required by faith and credit (Treu und Glauben) with due regard to commercial usage.
Sec. 242: The debtor is obliged to perform as required by faith and credit with regard to custom.
Sec. 826: Whoever designedly injures another in a manner violating good morals is bound to indemnify the other for the injury.
3. Zivilprozessordnung (henceforth referred to as ZPO).

NOTES TO CHAPTER I

1. I. Jastrow, *Sozialpolitik und Verwaltungswissenschaft*, I, 405 ff.
2. From 1864 to 1873, the twelve courts handled more than 50,000 cases.—(*Jahrbuch für die amtliche Statistik des Preussischen Staates*, IV Pt. II, 210 ff.)
3. Preussische Verordnung über den Mandats-, den summarischen und den Bagatellprozess of June 1, 1833, *Preussische Gesetzsammlung* (henceforth referred to as *PrGS*) pp. 37 ff., Sec. 6 and 66 ff.
4. *PrGS*, pp. 41ff.
5. *Ibid.*, pp. 110 ff.
6. *Handbuch der politischen Oekonomie* (ed. by Gustav Schönberg, 3rd ed. Tübingen, 1891), 621.
7. Richard Bahr, *Gewerbegericht, Kaufmannsgericht, Einigungsamt*, p. 9.
8. *Sächsisches Gesetz- und Verordnungsblatt*, p. 221.
9. *Bundesgesetzblatt*, p. 245; republished July 26, 1900 (*RGBl*, p. 871), and frequently amended; henceforth referred to as "GO."
10. Factory inspectors reported that the Stuttgart court worked very successfully. In 1889 it handled 468 complaints, 77.6 per cent of which were settled without judgment.—*Amtliche Mitteilungen aus den Berichten der mit der Beaufsichtigung der Fabriken betrauten Beamten*, XIV (*Reichsamt des Innern*), (Berlin, 1889) 145.
11. Gesetz betreffend die Gewerbegerichte of July 29, 1890 (henceforth referred to as GGG,)—*RGBl*, p. 141.

NOTES TO CHAPTER II

1. *RGBl*, p. 249. The amended text was republished under date of Sept. 29, 1901.—*RGBl*, p. 353. When the law of 1901 went into effect, 313 Industrial Courts had been established.—*Reichsarbeitsblatt* (henceforth referred to as *RABl*), 1903-1904, pp. 130 and 662. The compulsory clause applied to fifty-four cities which had no industrial courts. About forty-one new courts were established.

2. Little use was made of this possibility. Two such courts existed in 1913.

3. The American reader should take into consideration the fact that Germany has never had a dual system of judiciary like that of the United States. There existed only one federal court, the Federal Supreme Court (Reichsgericht). All others were either municipal or state courts. State courts applied both federal and state law. In fact, however, state law became nearly insignificant after 1900, when private law was, with few exceptions, codified by federal statute. Thenceforth it was possible in nearly all cases to appeal from state courts to the federal court (provided that more than a certain amount of money, fixed by law from time to time, was involved). The National Socialists have abolished the distinction between federal and state courts; all German courts are federal courts.

4. The Berlin court consisted of eight chambers for various industries.

5. Berlin, with 1,800,000 inhabitants, had 420 assessors in 1896.

6. Residual costs of the industrial court of Stuttgart, a city of 139,000 inhabitants (1890) with about 25,000 employers and employees (1882), were 7,000 marks in 1892.—Ernst Lautenschlager, "Die Rechtsprechung im Gewerbegericht," *Schmollers Jahrbuch für Gesetzgebung, Verwaltung und Volkswirtschaft im Deutschen Reich*, XVII (1893), 778.

7. Litigation about deduction of sickness insurance dues was transferred to the social insurance bodies after enactment of the Social Insurance Code (Reichversicherungsordnung, henceforth referred to as RVO) in 1911.—*RGBl*, p. 509.

8. In Berlin in 1911, 9,109 cases concerned payment of wages; 5,281, discharge without notice; 987, failure to return working papers; 601 testimonials of the employer; 75, dissolution or continuation of apprenticeship; 28, the worker's return to work. In some cases, several complaints were combined. The most frequent complaint of employers concerned compensation for damages.—*Aus der Praxis des Gewerbegerichts Berlin*, p. 2.

9. In contrast to the American, the German worker was protected from sudden dismissal by the provision of minimum periods of notice in civil law and in the industrial, commercial, and, after 1918, agricultural codes. All these statutes distinguish between regular and extraordinary dismissal. Regular dismissal is permissible only when notice is given in advance. The period of notice varied for the various classes of employees (manual workers, two weeks; clerks, etc., at least six weeks). The distinction between manual and white collar workers, typical of German labor law, found one of its most significant expressions in the disparate periods

of notice. Additional protection for salaried employees was introduced in the Weimar period (cf. page 192). Labor contracts which may be cancelled at will are legal only for manual workers in case the parties waive the period of notice. The periods for giving notice had to be the same for both parties to a contract.

Extraordinary dismissal was permissible only when cause was established. The statutes set forth causes, such as violence, gross insult, immoral proposals, etc., entitling employer or employee to dissolve a labor contract summarily. Should an extraordinary dismissal be proved unjustified, the employee could claim salary for the period of dismissal. According to German law, the dismissed employee was not restricted to damages.

10. In Stuttgart in 1892, only 6 per cent of all complaints were made in writing (Lautenschlager, *loc. cit.*, p. 782); suits brought by employers amounted to 7 per cent (*ibid.*, p. 792); in Essen in 1893, all but four complaints were made by workers (*Sozialpolitisches Zentralblatt*, IV [1894-95], 10); in Frankfurt in 1893-94 workers brought 1,769 complaints, employers 22; four were made by workers against workers (*ibid.*, p. 229); in Berlin until 1908 the number of suits brought by employers never exceeded 5.75 per cent of the total (*Verwaltungsbericht des Magistrats zu Berlin für das Etatsjahr 1908*, No. 31: *Bericht über das Gewerbegericht zu Berlin*). In general, the ratio did not vary much. (cf. p. 32.)

11. Many statutes provided for four assessors since workers felt safer when they could consult a fellow-worker.

12. In 1913 only 10,016 out of 121,193 cases involved an amount over 100 marks, and only 584 or .05 per cent were appealed (*RABl, Sonderbeilage*, July, 1914, p. 12; cf. p. 34); in Berlin in 1911, 1,278 or 9.81 per cent of the cases were appealable (*Aus der Praxis des Gewerbegerichts Berlin*, p. 3).

13. In 1896, when there were 483 strikes, the courts were called on in forty-two. From 1893 to 1900, they were called in 271 cases, of which 119 were settled.—Jastrow, p. 492.

14. The procedure was slightly modified in 1901.

15. In 1902 they were called on in 144 cases, 119 times by one side only. Thirty-five cases were settled by agreement, four by accepted award. The figures for 1903 were 174, 135, 54, and 7.—*RABl*, 1905, p. 213 Statistics of the conciliation department are of little value since they do not indicate the extent or importance of conflicts. (cf. p. 34.)

16. In 1896 the industrial courts advised in 28 cases, in 1900 in 50; they made 24 and 15 proposals respectively (Jastrow, *Sozialpolitik und Verwaltungswissenschaft*, pp. 533, 536); in 1908, 33 opinions were given and 48 proposals were made by the 469 courts (*RABl*, 1909, p. 617); in 1913, all industrial courts gave 17 opinions and made 9 proposals. From 1914 to 1918 they gave 54 opinions and made 7 proposals (*RABl, Sonderbeilage*, July, 1914, p. 13; *Sonderbeilage*, Jan., 1920, p. 19).

17. GO, Sec. 81a, No. 4; 81b, No. 4; 91-91-b.

18. Jastrow, *op. cit.* p. 436.

19. Wilhelm Stieda, "Gewerbegerichte," *Handwörterbuch der Staatswissenschaften*, 3rd ed. (Jena, 1909), IV, 886.

20. GGG, Sec. 82.

21. The number of mining courts fluctuated between seven in 1902 and ten in 1918.

22. Seemannsordnung (Seamen's Code) of June 2, 1902, Sec. 129, *RGBl*, p. 175.

23. Gesetz betreffend Kaufmannsgerichte (henceforth referred to as KGG) July 6, 1904, *RGBl*, p. 216.

24. It should be noted that German law knows no general principle according to which "restraint of trade" is illegal. As a rule, "restraint of trade" is forbidden only when special circumstances make an agreement *contra bonos mores*. Labor law, however, recognized exceptions to the rule. Both commercial and the industrial white collar workers were protected by special statutory provisions from dangers implied in agreements in restraint of trade. Litigation concerning such clauses was within the jurisdiction of the labor courts (so called Wettbewerbsklausel, competition clause).

25. Litigation concerned especially salaries, dismissals, and content of letters of reference. The conciliation activities of the commercial courts were of no importance. From 1905 to 1918, they were called upon only in forty-one cases, never by employers alone. During this period, they settled twenty cases by agreement. Only the Munich commercial court developed some activity in this field.—*RABl, Sonderbeilage*, Jan. 1920. Administratively they were slightly more active than the industrial courts. In 1913 they gave twenty-seven opinions, from 1914 to 1918, thirty-nine. They made four proposals in 1913, seven from 1914 to 1918.— *Vierteljahrshefte zur Statistik des deutschen Reichs* (henceforth referred to as VH), 1921, IV, 39.

26. In 1918 there were 891 industrial courts, 192 (21.5 per cent) of them obligatorily established (*i.e.*, in communities with more than 20,000 inhabitants), and 699 (78.5 per cent) voluntarily established. Of the commercial courts, 73.9 per cent were obligatory and 26.1 per cent voluntary.

27. Gesetz über den Vaterländischen Hilfsdienst, *RGBl*, p. 1333.

28. A worker quitting without a leaving certificate issued by his employer could get no new employment for two weeks. He could complain to the conciliation committee in case of unqualified refusal of a leaving certificate.

29. *RGBl*, 1917, p. 1017.

30. *RABl, Sonderbeilage*, July, 1914, pp. 2-3.

31. *Ibid.*, pp. 14-15.

32. *RABl, Sonderbeilage*, Jan., 1920, pp. 5 ff.

33. *Ibid.*

34. In Berlin, only 34,388 out of 280,000 eligible workers and only 3,047 out of 80,000 employers registered in 1892, and only 70 per cent of registered persons voted.—*Sozialpolitisches Zentralblatt*, II (1892-93), 145 and 265. In Breslau, 65 per cent of eligible employers and 81 per cent of eligible workers voted.—*Ibid.*, III (1893-94), 71.

35. In the first court elections in Berlin in 1893, the Social Democrats won 219 of 420 assessors' seats; i.e., all workers' seats and nine employers' seats.—*Sozialpolitisches Zentralblatt*, II, 265. In 1908, after the introduction of proportional representation, when one-third of all the assessors were elected, the bourgeois list on the employers' side won 54 seats, the

socialists 16. Of 70 seats on the workers' side, the free (socialist) unions won 64, a metal workers' union one, the Hirsch-Dunckers (liberal) unions three and the Christian unions two.—*Aus der Praxis des Gewerbegerichts Berlin*, p. 5.

36. The bourgeois employers' list for 1908 did not include a single industrialist; it was composed of 14 restaurant keepers, 8 newspaper agents, 8 cigar store keepers.—*Soziale Praxis* (henceforth referred to as *SP*), Dec. 2, 1909, p. 220.

37. *SP*, VII (*Beilage: Das Gewerbegericht*, 1897), p. 19.

38. *Blätter für Soziale Praxis*, I, (1893), 152.

39. For instance, a workman sued for four marks and four pfennig wages, and the company lodged a counterplea for 120 marks damages for a box, whose value was 5 marks.—*SP*, Dec. 26, 1912, p. 380.

40. In Berlin in 1897-98, the employers won 77 per cent of all their cases decided by formal judgment (41 out of 53), the workers only 40 per cent (686 out of 1,732) of their suits.—*SP*, Dec. 22, 1898, p. 322. On the average, in the period 1895-1904, employers won 60 per cent and workers 40 per cent of their cases decided by judgment of the full court. —*SP*, Dec. 7, 1905, p. 267.

41. *Sozialpolitisches Zentralblatt*, IV (1894-95), 367-68, 720.

42. It was the successor of the Verband deutscher Gewerbegerichte (Association of Industrial Courts) founded in 1893.

43. At first *Mitteilungen des Verbandes deutscher Gewerbegerichte* (1894-95) as part of the *Sozialpolitisches Zentralblatt* and its successor, *Soziale Praxis*; since 1896, *Das Gewerbegericht*. From 1899 on, it appeared independently.

44. *SP*, June 15, 1911, p. 1166.

45. Cf. p. 133. Speed was especially remarkable in comparison with the work of the ordinary courts. Jastrow reports a workers' suit for wages in which the Industrial Court asked the ordinary court to hear a witness. The case was held up during the two months' vacation of the latter court.—*Sozialpolitik und Verwaltungswissenschaft*, pp. 453-54. In comparing the speed of the industrial courts to ordinary local courts, Jastrow found that the former ended 57 per cent of all cases in less than one week (in 1900) while the ordinary courts held a first hearing in less than one week in 2.9 per cent of all cases (in 1899).—*Ibid.* pp. 446-47. Landsberger reports that, in ten years, 58.9 per cent of cases settled by agreement and 71.57 per cent of those decided by judgment were finished in less than one month in the industrial courts, while in the ordinary local courts one-half of all suits took three months or more and in the district courts 46 per cent took six months or more.—*SP*, July 2, 1914, pp. 1114 ff.

46. With the following figures compare those of the termination of cases given above (p. 133).

47. In Frankfurt a.M. in 1899-1900, about one-fourth of all cases concerned the building industry.—*Sozialpolitisches Zentralblatt*, II (1892-93), 231. In Wurtemberg, nearly one-third of all cases concerned handicrafts. —*Ibid.*, III (1893-94), 334. Only 6 per cent of all cases in Charlottenburg concerned factories.—*Ibid.*, IV (1894-95), 980. Even at Düsseldorf, seat of heavy industries, only 153 out of 1,529 conflicts were in big industry.— *Das Gewerbegericht*, II (1896-97), 118-19. In Leipzig, in relation to

number of workers, factory owners were sued one-half as much as craftsmen.—*Sozialpolitisches Zentralblatt*, IV (1894-95), 608.

48. Hans Prenner, "Die Gewerbe- und Kaufmannsgerichte in der Beurteilung des 31. deutschen Juristentags und der deutschen Handwerks- und Gewerbekammern," *Annalen für Soziale Politik und Gesetzgebung*, III (1914), 355ff.

49. *Sozialpolitik und Verwaltungswissenschaft*, p. 405.

50. Commercial employees and other white collar workers opposed collective bargaining and workers' councils in the pre-war period. After the war they changed their attitude and looked on post-war statutes dealing-ing with these questions as gains. These groups, however, were by no means inclined to give up special privileges. This holds particularly true with respect to their long dismissal periods. In the later 1920's, a certain tendency was evident among workers also to claim these privileges. The tendency to unify labor law and wipe out the distinction between manual and white collar workers was manifested particularly by the socialist white collar workers' organizations. Similar problems existed in the field of social insurance.

51. In 1925, five courts had no cases, 33 had from one to five, 52 had from six to ten, etc.; 87.5 per cent of all courts had less than 150 cases each (*VH*, 1926, II, 97), when full calendars would have meant a thousand cases each. Only eight commercial courts had more than a thousand cases. Nor were most industrial courts fully employed. In 1925, 20 had one-half of all cases; 12 (2 per cent) had none.—*Ibid.*, p. 96.

52. For domestic workers, there were makeshifts in some cities. In Mainz, the industrial court voluntarily included their litigations. In Breslau, some women's associations and servant associations jointly, in Berlin the employment office established arbitral courts. An order of the Bavarian Commissioner of Demobilization of Dec. 13, 1918, provided for the writing of a collective agreement for domestic workers, and the establishment of an arbitral court by the organizations concluding the agreement.—*Arbeitsrecht* 1920, p. 52.

53. Cf. Appendix 2.

54. Decrees of May 12 and Oct. 29, 1920 (*RGBl*, pp. 958 and 1843), laws of Jan. 14 and Nov. 27, 1922 (*RGBl*, I, 155 and 887), and Mar. 15, 1923 (*RGBl*, I, 193); and decrees of June 16, July 12, and Aug. 9 and 23, 1923 (*RGBl*, I, 384, 614, 765, and 845).

55. By decree of Aug. 30, 1923 (*RGBl*, p. 845), amounts were fixed on a sliding scale so that a basic figure had to be multiplied by the Reich cost-of-living index. By decree of June 6, 1924 (*RGBl*, p. 643), they were fixed in gold marks. Income limits determining jurisdiction for technical and commercial employees were uniformly fixed at 5,000 marks, appeals at 300 marks (*RGBl*, I, 777).

56. *RGBl*, p. 155.

57. The committees of the Auxiliary Service Law had been maintained and modified by decree of Dec. 23, 1918.—*RGBl*, p. 1456.

58. *RGBl*, p. 147.

59. Sec. 84 of the act of Feb. 4, 1920 (henceforth referred to as BRG), gave the right of appealing to the Works Council (Betriebsrat) to employees who suspected that their sex or their political, military, religious,

or trade union activities had been reason for dismissal, or who were dismissed without statement of cause or because of refusal to undertake work other than that agreed to, or whose dismissal appeared unjust and involved hardship, etc. If the Works Council failed to arrive at an understanding, such employees or the Works Council could appeal to the conciliation committee, later the labor courts. If the latter decided that the complaint was justified, it could compel the employer to compensate the worker unless he retained him.

These legal provisions sought to prevent "unfair labor practices." According to Art. 159 of the Weimar constitution, freedom of coalition was protected from infringement not only by federal and state authorities but also by employers. The "yellow dog" contract and dismissals due to union activity were illegal.

60. Verordnung über eine vorläufige Landarbeitsordnung, *RGBl*, p. 111.
61. Reichsversorgungsgesetz of June 30, 1923, *RGBl*, I, 523.
62. Verordnung über das Schlichtungswesen, *RGBl*, I, 1043.
63. Where no commercial court existed, the industrial court was to cover litigation of commercial employees involving the new legislation such as BRG, etc., while complaints relating to labor contracts were to go to ordinary courts.
64. Dec. 10, 1923, *RGBl*, I, 1191.
65. Individual disputes are primarily those between employer and individual worker relating to labor contracts.
66. Frieda Wunderlich, *Labor under German Democracy, Arbitration 1918-1933*, p. 9.
67. Sources: *VH*, 1920, IV, 28ff.; 1921, III, 106ff.; 1922, IV, 33ff.; 1924, I, 70ff. and IV, 65ff.; 1925, III, 117ff.; 1926, II, 96ff.; 1927, II, 68ff.; 1928, I, 126ff.
68. *VH*, 1927, II, 68 ff.; 1928, I, 126 ff.
69. *VH*, 1920, IV, 31.
70. *VH*, 1928, I, 126 ff.
71. *VH*, 1927, II, 68.
72. Paul Wölbling, "Die Neuordnung der deutschen Arbeitsgerichte," *Zeitschrift für die gesamte Staatswissenschaft*, LXXXIII (Tübingen, 1927), 66-88.
73. *Verhandlungen des 32. deutschen Juristentages* (Berlin, Leipzig, 1922) pp. 99ff. Only a few jurists, such as Kaskel, Sinzheimer, and Landsberger deviated.
74. *Vereinigung der Arbeitgeberverbände, Geschäftsbericht erstattet über das Jahr 1922*, pp. 32-33; 1925-26, pp. 63-64.
75. *Korrespondenzblatt des Allgemeinen Deutschen Gewerkschaftsbundes* (ADGB), Berlin, Mar. 11, 1922, p. 125.
76. *Gewerkschafts-Zeitung*, July 1, 1927, p. 366. The Congress of the free trade unions demanded in 1922 "that the Reich government and legislative bodies adopt as soon as possible a new labor law in accordance with the following principles: the law shall apply equally to all manual and clerical workers and state employees. . . . The Congress particularly associates itself with the demand of the speaker (Sinzheimer) that labor courts be set up independent of the ordinary judiciary. They should be in direct touch with the labor authorities and under the supervision of

the Minister of Labor."—*Protokoll der Verhandlungen des 11. Kongresses der Gewerkschaften Deutschlands* (Leipzig, 1922), p. 450.

77. *Afa Angestelltenbewegung,* Berlin, 1925-28, p. 166.

78. Allgemeiner Freier Angestelltenbund, General League of Free Trade Unions of Salaried Employees. A survey of the German trade unions is given in Appendix 3, pp. 200-1.

79. The latter view was expressed in Ernst Fraenkel's *Zur Soziologie der Klassenjustiz* (Berlin, 1927).

80. Ernst Fraenkel, "Rechtsprechung und Gewerkschaften," *Internationales Handwörterbuch des Gewerkschaftswesens* (Berlin, 1931-32) p. 1298.

81. The first courses in labor law were delivered in the early twenties in a few universities, such as Berlin, Leipzig, and Frankfurt a. Main. The classes in labor law introduced during the later twenties in all law schools were characterized by the variety of legal problems discussed. The main topics were labor contracts, collective bargaining, labor conflicts, social insurance, labor administration, labor procedure, works council law, and constitutional questions affecting labor. The classes were attended not only by all law students but also by many students of economics and sociology.

82. *SP,* July 7, 1920, pp. 949 ff.

83. *Protokoll* Leipzig, *op. cit.,* p. 439.

84. *Ibid.,* p. 457.

85. *SP,* Aug. 4, 1927, pp. 777 ff. Likewise, Afa *Angestelltenbewegung,* 1921-25, p. 179. *Arbeitsrecht,* Apr., 1922, p. 223; May, 1922, pp. 267 ff. and 303 ff.

86. *Arbeitsrecht,* June, 1922, pp. 331 ff. and Sept., 1922, pp. 523 ff.

87. Against such unification spoke the fact that most labor law was still provisional and that a unification of all labor offices would have led to the creation of huge and unwieldy bodies. Costs, moreover, would have been heavy.

88. *Arbeitsrecht,* Oct., 1925, pp. 6 ff.

89. The Prussian Ministers of Commerce and of Justice, for instance, decreed on July 31, 1924, that law graduates while in training in the courts should attend classes in labor law and meetings of arbitration boards and labor courts.

90. *Vereinigung der deutschen Arbeitgeberverbände, Geschäftsbericht,* 1925-26, p. 64.

91. Georg Flatow, in *SP,* Apr. 15, 1926, pp. 353 ff.

92. Cf. Appendix 2, p. 193.

93. To the court fee of 3 marks for a disputed sum of 100 marks, 36 marks additional would have to be paid if both parties were to retain lawyers.—Otto Kahn Freund, in *SP,* Mar. 16, 1933, p. 325. It should be noted that fees of German lawyers are regulated by statute.

94. *Gewerkschafts-Zeitung,* Oct. 31, 1925, p. 638.

95. *Ibid.,* Sept. 15, 1928, p. 583.

96. *Ibid.,* Oct. 31, 1925, p. 638.

97. Otto Kahn Freund, in *SP, loc. cit.,* pp. 321 ff.

98. Sinzheimer, in *Juristische Wochenschrift* (henceforth referred to as *JW*), Apr. 15, 1922, pp. 538 ff.

99. *JW*, Jan. 22, 1927, pp. 221 ff.
100. *Deutsche Juristen-Zeitung*, Berlin, Feb. 1, 1926, pp. 220-21.
101. Paul Wölbling, *Die Neuordnung der deutschen Arbeitsgerichte*, in *Zeitschrift für die gesamte Staatswissenschaft*, LXXXIII (Tübingen, 1927), 71.
102. *Gewerbe- und Kaufmannsgericht*, 1921, No. 2. Beilage.
103. *28. Sonderheft zum RABl.*, No. 3 (1923).
104. Arbeitsgerichtsgesetz (henceforth cited as AGG) Dec. 23, 1926, *RGBl.* I, 507.
105. Of the fifteen National Socialists, one abstained, five were absent, nine voted for the bill.—*Stenographische Berichte über die Verhandlungen des Reichstags*, CCCXCI, 8509.

NOTES TO CHAPTER III

1. The term of the first group was extended to three and one-half years by law of Mar. 17, 1930 (*RGBl*, I, 39) in order to make their term of office begin with the calendar year. The AGG took effect July 1, 1927.

2. The decree of June 24, 1927 (*RGBl*, I, 129), later amended on minor points, fixed maximum limits for compensation for lost earnings and expenditures and graduated the latter according to length of sessions and the distance between residence and place of meeting. Railroad fares and overnight expenses were paid. Assessors of the Federal Labor Court received relatively higher compensation than those in the labor courts or district labor courts. Employees' assessors occasionally complained that the employer's compensation for lost earnings were higher than their own, although the employee usually had to make up time lost.—Heinz Felten, "Die Stellung der Laienrichter bei den Arbeitsgerichtsbehörden und die sozialrechtliche Bedeutung des Arbeitsgerichtswesens," *Sozialrechtliches Jahrbuch*, IV, 25.

3. Except in a few cases defined by law, employers could give notice of dismissal or transfer to members of a works council only with the latter's or the labor court's consent. Dismissal of employee assessors for activity in labor courts was not considered unfair labor practice *per se*. In most cases, the employee was, however, protected by the Constitution, which extended the freedom of opinion provision to cases of undue pressure exercised by "social forces." Article 118 of the Weimar Constitution prohibited dismissals based on the fact that an employee had availed himself of "freedom of opinion." That protection proved sufficient.

4. For instance, in 1931 the free trade union of metal workers trained eighty-one labor judges in two courses of ten and eleven days respectively in the residential school of the ADGB.—*Jahrbuch des Allgemeinen Deutschen Gewerkschaftsbundes*, 1931, p. 196. From such courses promising students were selected for further training in schools for economics and administration and in the Academy of Labor, which were joint enterprises of the unions and the state. Here, in courses of longer duration, full-time study on a higher level was provided with the aim of training for trade union political functions. The state financed the training, the unions the maintenance of students and their families.

5. Theoretically, it might have been more consistent to connect the

district labor court with the provincial court of appeals (Oberlandesgericht), from which appeal went to the Supreme Court. But the districts of these courts, which covered a state or a Prussian province, were so large that personal appearance of parties would have been too expensive.

6. *Regierungsentwurf*, 1923 *Begründung*, p. 15.

7. Two assessors of employers and employees respectively would have had to be heard by the presiding officers of the Federal Supreme Court before assignment to senates. Since there was only one senate, no use was made of this rule.

8. For instance, the decision of the Federal Labor Court of Feb. 18, 1933 (*Entscheidungen des Reichsarbeitsgerichts und der Landesarbeitsgerichte* ed. by Hermann Dersch and others, henceforth referred to as *RAG.*, XVII, 420); Federal Labor Court, Aug. 10, 1928 (*RAG*, III, 207).

9. Their disputes were settled by the Marine Offices or by consuls abroad, according to the Seamen's Code (cf. p. 30). It was intended to regulate the question of labor law jurisdiction for seamen in connection with the contemplated general revision of seamen's labor law.

10. The third type will be discussed below, pp. 79 ff.

11. Actions of employees against employers based on industrial accidents belonged, however, only in exceptional cases to the jurisdiction of the labor courts. Since all industrial workers enjoyed compulsory workmen's compensation, claims were made directly against the social insurance agencies. Federal administrative courts had exclusive jurisdiction in such cases. The worker did not have a choice between applying to the social insurance agency and suing his employer in a labor court. The social insurance statute excluded all direct claims against the entrepreneur even in the case of the latter's negligence. Only if the worker could prove that the accident was due to a *wilful* action of the employer, could the latter be sued in a labor court.—Sec. 898, RVO.

12. Cf. pp. 194-95.

13. It may be noted that the ordinary court, which had to decide these cases, recognized the power of the unions to regulate their own affairs and interfered only when associations abused their power.

14. *Protokoll der Verhandlungen des 14. Kongresses der Gewerkschaften Deutschlands* (Berlin, 1931), p. 273.

15. *RAG*, VI., 187

16. ZPO, Sec. 114 ff.

17. *RGBl*, I, 537 (564).

18. The reform of civil procedure in 1923-24 simplified proceedings in ordinary courts.—Decree of Feb. 13, 1924, *RGBl*, I, 135, similar to that of the labor courts.

19. Cf. p. 14.

20. It was raised to 100 marks in ordinary courts by Emergency Decree of Oct. 6, 1931.—*RGBl*, I, 564. In the labor courts appeal was based on the value of the disputed sum as assessed in the judgment, in the ordinary courts on the value of the complaint.

21. While in 1928 only 0.7 per cent of decisions of labor courts and 1.8 per cent of appeals to district labor courts concerned collective disputes, their proportion among Federal Labor Court reviews was 7.5 per cent.

22. The special low scale did only apply to the labor courts, whereas

the essentially higher scale of the Court Fees Act (Gerichtskostengesetz) was applied to the district labor courts and the Federal Labor Court. Moreover, in the higher instances, three different fees could be charged, not one as before local labor courts. Cf. p. 74.

23. Decree of Feb. 8, 1929, *RGBl*, I, 19.

24. *Vereinbarung von Schlichtungsstellen, Schiedsgerichten usw. in Tarifverträgen:* Einige Richtlinien für den Abschluss vonTarifverträgen, ausgearbeitet im Reichsarbeitsministerium, *RABl;* 1928, I, 100 ff.

25. If they were included, the Minister of Labor could impose the other norms of the award while excluding this clause.

26. If the arbitral tribunal could not itself undertake investigation of proof (e.g, if a witness had to be examined under oath), it could ask for the assistance of the labor or ordinary court.

27. It was ordered in 224 cases in 1928.

28. Sixty-five such pleas were made in 1928.

NOTES TO CHAPTER IV

1. In Prussia, 226 labor courts corresponded to 1,003 local courts; in Saxony 20 to 112; in Hesse 11 to 53; in Thuringia 12 to 65; in Brunswick 8 to 23; in Oldenburg 10 to 21; in Mecklenburg-Schwerin 5 to 42; in Mecklenburg-Strelitz 3 to 10; in Anhalt 2 to 11; in Hamburg 2 to 3. Bremen, Lübeck, Lippe, Waldeck, and Schaumburg-Lippe had one each.

2. Bavaria established 172 labor courts corresponding to 264 ordinary local courts; the trade unions had asked 60. The figures for Wurtemberg were 26 and 62, for Baden 25 and 59.

3. *RABl*, 1927, I. 295 ff.; *VH*, 1928, III, pp. 58ff.

4. Thirty-three in Prussia, 23 in Bavaria, 6 in Baden, 3 in Wurtemberg.

5. Of all labor courts in the Reich in 1927,

    143 = 27.1 per cent were established for one ordinary court (1932, 70 = 15.5 per cent)

    2 = 0.4 per cent for parts of one (1 = 0.2 per cent)

    370 = 70.2 per cent for the area of a few (370 = 81.9 per cent in 1932)

    12 = 2.3 per cent for the area of a few States (12 = 2.6 per cent)

Of the district labor courts

    25 = 31.3 per cent were established for one ordinary court (1932, 7 = 11.7 per cent)

    2 = 2.5 per cent were established for parts of one ordinary court (1932, 2 = 3.3 per cent)

    41 = 51.2 per cent were established for several courts (1932, 40 = 66.7 per cent)

    12 = 15. per cent were established for several States (1932, 11 = 18.3 per cent)

Number of committees of guilds:

1927	4,728	1930	12,279
1928	10,217	1931	15,416
1929	11,524	1932	15,894

(Of the 15,416 committees in 1931, 9,579 had an impartial chairman).

District Labor Courts were established in 1927: in 1932:
 for one ordinary district court   25 = 31.3 per cent   7 = 11.7 per cent
 for parts of one district court   2 = 2.5 per cent   2 = 3.3 per cent
 for several district courts   41 = 51.2 per cent   40 = 66.7 per cent
 for several states   12 = 15. per cent   11 = 18.3 per cent

6. In 1928, twelve cities had 41.8 per cent of all cases; in 1932, eleven cities had 36.1 per cent (Berlin with 59,422 had 16 per cent). In 1928, 359 cities (68.1 per cent) had from one to 500 cases; twelve cities had more than 5,000 cases each: Berlin had 62,535 (16.5 per cent); Cologne, 13,129 (3.5 per cent); Dresden, 12,636 (3.3 per cent); Hamburg, 11,820 (3.1 per cent); Chemnitz, 10,028 (2.6 per cent); Breslau, 9,173 (2.4 per cent); Leipzig, 8,174 (2.2 per cent); Munich, 7,038 (1.9 per cent); Frankfurt, 6,666 (1.8 per cent); Dortmund, 5,859 (1.5 per cent); Düsseldorf, 5,803 (1.5 per cent); Essen, 5,573 (1.5 per cent).—*VH*, 1929, II, 112 ff; 1933, II, 106 ff.

7. Bavaria reduced it by 65 labor courts and 16 district labor courts in 1929, Baden in 1930 by 6 and one, Wurtemberg by 3 and 3, Saxony by one labor court.

8. The unions of salaried employees (with the exception of the socialists) had claimed that their salaries were independent of hours of work, in contrast to the wage-earner, whose pay was in direct relation to working time. In fact, they felt that one of their main distinctions as against the wage-earner was a guarantee of a fixed monthly salary. Cuts made by employers corresponding to part-time work were contested in the courts. The Federal Labor Court, in a judgment of Dec. 20, 1930 (*RAG* XI, 121), approved salary cuts corresponding to reductions in hours. (Cf. against this decision, Potthoff in *Arbeitsrecht*, 1931, pp. 129 ff.) During the depression, the legal distinction between wage-earners and salaried employees as expressed in variations in the periods of notice became even more important than before. The crucial question was whether salaries of white-collar workers could be reduced at once when hours were cut, or whether such a change was permissible only after notice had been given in accordance with the labor contract and statute.

9. Of the district labor courts, 74, or 92.5 per cent had only one chamber in 1927; six, or 7.5 per cent, all in Berlin, had more.

10. *VH*, 1932, II, 105. There were 527 chambers in 1927 and 452 in 1932.

11. German National Trade Union of Commercial Employees.

12. *Rechenschaftsbericht des Deutschnationalen Handlungsgehilfenverbandes*, 1927, p. 145.

13. Berlin had separate chambers for workmen (17), salaried employees (13), and journeymen (5) in various industries, commerce, stage and film, and domestic service, one for city transportation and railroad employees, one for agricultural workers.—*VH*, 1929, II, 115.

14. *RABl*, 1929, II, 397 ff.

15. *Rechenschaftsbericht des Deutschnationalen Handlungsgehilfenverbandes*, 1927, p. 147.

16. *Zentralverband der Angestellten* (Union of Salaried Employees), affiliated with the Afa League.

17. Heinz Felten, "Die Stellung der Laienrichter," *loc. cit.*, IV., 8.

18. Georg Flatow, "Die Zusammensetzung der preussischen Arbeitsgerichtsbehörden," *Beilage zum RABl*, 1929, No. 4, Pt. II.
19. *Rechenschaftsbericht des Deutschnationalen Handlungsgehilfenverbandes*, 1928, p. 126.
20. Felten, *loc. cit.*, IV, 9.
21. *Ibid.*, III, 16.
22. *Ibid.*, IV, 12.
23. *Ibid.*, p. 30.
24. *Rechenschaftsbericht des Deutschnationalen Handlungsgehilfenverbandes*, 1927, p. 147.
25. Figures for the period of National Socialism are included; they will be discussed later.
26. *Vierteljahrshefte zur Statistik des Deutschen Reichs*, 1928, III, pp. 58 ff.; 1929, II, pp. 112 ff.; 1930, II, pp. 174 ff.; 1931, II, pp. 114 ff.; 1932, II, pp. 105 ff.; 1933, II, pp. 106 ff.; 1934, II, pp. 160 ff.; 1935, II, pp. 98 ff.; 1936, II, pp. 67 ff.; 1937, II, pp. 97 ff.; 1938, II, pp. 91 ff.; 1939, II, pp. 147 ff.; 1940, II, pp. 65 ff. The figures of 1938-39 have been quoted from *Deutsche Justiz* (henceforth referred to as *DJ*), 1939, p. 1595; *ibid.*, 1941, p. 141.
27. Ernst Roesner, in *Deutsche Juristen-Zeitung*, Oct. 15, 1929, pp. 1404-5.
28. *Justizministerialblatt für die preussische Gesetzgebung und Rechtspflege* (Berlin), 1932, pp. 166, 172.
29. Theodor Rohlfing, "Entwicklung und Sinn der Arbeitsgerichtsbarkeit," *Zehn Jahre Arbeitsgericht* (Berlin und Leipzig, 1937), p. 13.
30. *VH*, 1929, II, 115.

NOTES TO CHAPTER V

1. In 1929 the DHV complained of too much rotation of assessors. Without really knowing the reasons, they believed that fear of dismissal might have been one.—*Rechenschaftsbericht*, 1929, p. 172.
2. The Federal Labor Court was crammed for a short time in 1928, but resumed greater speed when the number of judges was increased and the appealable minimum raised.
3. Jastrow reports that an experienced labor judge, proud of his compromises, heard one person advise another, without hearing the argument, "Go to the industrial court; you always get something." On hearing this, the judge realized the mistake of forcing compromises by any means.—*Sozialpolitik und Verwaltungswissenschaft*, p. 456.
4. Felten, "Die Stellung der Laienrichter," *loc. cit.*, IV, 19.
5. Gerhard Simson, in *Der Arbeitgeber*, July 15, 1932, p. 323.
6. "Die Rechtsprechung im Gewerbegericht," *Schmollers Jahrbuch*, 1893, p. 796.
7. Kahn Freund claimed that settlement procedure with its "suit prophylaxis" (Prozessprophylaxe) was due to a change in the concept of justice, according to which courts no longer needed to find a norm but, as an expression of the constellation of social power (gesellschaftliche Machtlage), were to lay down guiding principles. Decisions are no longer the expression of an unequivocal process of thinking, but are a "welfare function." The court must act in order to protect the parties against dam-

age. Kahn Freund proposed to restrict compromises to cases in which the application of the law (for instance, in dismissal cases), would be a hardship, and suggested that no compromises be made where conflicts about fundamental questions were involved.—*JW*, 1930, pp. 388 ff.

8. Wunderlich, *Labor under German Democracy*, pp. 15 ff.

9. This freedom was not generally recognized by the socialists, who felt that they had more influence on the legislature than on the courts. On the other hand, a socialist lawyer, Ludwig Bendix, expounded the dynamic character of adjudication and considered positivism an expression of the bourgeois will to power.—*Arbeitsrecht*, 1929, pp. 128 ff. The working class, in participating in the power of the state, must have confidence in state functionaries, of which the judge is one. The union between economic foundation and legal superstructure depends on the narrow margin in which the irrational forces of judicial decisions may act.—*Ibid.*, 1929, pp. 673 ff. Another left-wing lawyer, Franz Neumann, found that labor's attitude had been reversed. Before the war, labor fought against the dominant class, which defended its position by rigid application of legal rules. Now labor was defending its gains against the employer who, with the help of legislation and court decisions, was trying to change the legal system (Rechtsordnung).—*Ibid.*, pp. 32 ff.)

10. Ludwig Bendix, in *SP*, July 11, 1929, p. 676.

11. *RAG*, V, 537.

12. *Rechenschaftsbericht des Deutschnationalen Handlungsgehilfenverbandes*, 1925, p. 69.

13. Decision of Mar. 13, 1929, *RAG*, V, 523, and VI, 75; of Jan. 11, 1930, *ibid.*, VIII, 280; and others. Similarly the Reichsversicherungsamt admitted payment of unemployment compensation simultaneously with compensation for leave of absence after dismissal.—Decision of the Reichsversicherungsamt, June 12, 1929, ibid., VI, 3.

14. June 8, 1929, *RAG*, VI, 290, and other decisions.

15. Hans Georg Anthes, in *Der Arbeitgeber*, July 1, 1930, p. 367.

16. Decision of the Federal Supreme Court of Feb. 6, 1923.—*Entscheidungen des Reichsgerichts in Zivilsachen* (henceforth referred to as *RGZ*), CVI, 272 ff.

17. *RAG*, III, 116.

18. Nov. 3, 1928, *RAG*, IV, 149.

19. Dec. 15, 1928, *ibid.*, V, 38.

20. *Afa Angestelltenbewegung*, 1928-31, p. 135.

21. German contract law has no rules similar to the common law "consideration" doctrine.

22. Decisions of Nov. 27, 1929, *RAG*, VII, 464; of Feb. 1, 1930, *ibid.*, VIII, 235; of Mar. 1, 1930, *ibid.*, p. 498; of July 23, 1931, *ibid.*, XIII, 96, and many others.

23. Feb. 9, 1929, *RAG*, V, 217.

24. May 21, 1930, *ibid.*, IX, 487.

25. *SP*, Sept. 1, 1932, p. 1111.

26. Hans Georg Anthes, in *Der Arbeitgeber*, Sept. 15, 1932, p. 417.

27. Otto Kahn Freund, *Das soziale Ideal des Reichsarbeitsgerichts*. Assuming that the judge is directed by his own social convictions, Kahn Freund raises the question of norms guiding decisions of the Federal

Labor Court. He finds them, among others, in the ideals of industrial peace, which denies the class war, of organic community within an enterprise and of individualistic welfare (Fürsorgegedanke) which aims at protecting the weaker party as, for instance, in decisions about leave of absence and wages for the severely disabled. Kahn Freund's interpretation did not win support. It could easily be objected that the trade unions considered themselves instruments of peace, that conciliation legislation aimed at preventing industrial warfare, that the Works Council Law was based on a community of interests of employers and employees within an enterprise.—Clemens Nörpel, in *Die Arbeit* (Berlin), 1931, pp. 561 ff.; Ernst Fraenkel, in *Die Justiz*, 1931, pp. 46 ff.; Anthes in *Der Arbeitgeber*, 1931, pp. 524 ff.

28. The regulation of local competence, could, however, be waived for individual litigation.

29. *Gewerkschafts-Zeitung*, July 2, 1927, p. 366.

30. An elaborate essay on the question of representation in Herbert Herzog, *Die Vertretung der Parteien vor den Arbeitsgerichten im deutschen Reich und im übrigen Europa*.

31. *AGG*, Sec. 10.

32. Cf. p. 193.

33. *Statistisches Jahrbuch für das deutsche Reich* (Berlin), 1931, p. 557; 1932, p. 394.

34. Konrad Stehr, in *Afa Bundeszeitung* (Berlin), Apr., 1928, p. 50.

35. Nörpel, in *Die Arbeit*, 1928, pp. 501 ff.

36. Nörpel, in *Gewerkschafts-Zeitung*, Dec. 5, 1931, p. 780.

37. Georg Baum mentions a case in which the employers' association was identical with a cartel and the employer disliked having the cartel know certain conditions in his plant.—*Gerechtigkeit und Berufsinteresse im Arbeitsgerichtprozess*, p. 13.

38. *JW*, 1932, p. 3597.

39. *Ibid*.

40. For a list of hardship cases, cf. *ibid.*, 1928, p. 1638.

41. The referendar is a law graduate who has passed the first state examination and who serves three years in the courts and lawyers' and prosecutors' offices before being admitted to the final examination qualifying for bench and bar.

42. For instance, by Ludwig Bendix, who argued that it was the intention of the law to have the parties carry on their disputes among themselves without the interference of outsiders such as the referendar.—*Arbeitsrecht*, 1928, pp. 259 ff., 319 ff.

43. Cf. p. 98.

44. Herzog calculates the costs for about 25,000 admissions of poor law advocates at about 500,000 marks a year.—*Op. cit.*, p. 204.

45. *Ibid.*, pp. 199 and 272 ff.

46. Arbeitsnachweisgesetz of July 22, 1922, *RGBl*, I, 657, and its successor, the Placement and Unemployment Insurance Act (Gesetz über Arbeitsvermittlung und Arbeitslosenversicherung) of July 16, 1927, *RGBl*, I, 187.

47. Verordnung des Reichsarbeitsministers zur Ausführung der Verordnung über das Schlichtungswesen of Dec. 10, 1923, *RGBl*, I, 1191.

48. *Gewerkschafts-Zeitung*, Sept. 26, 1925, p. 565.
49. *Ibid.*, Nov. 8, 1924, p. 437.
50. Nonmilitant unions were included in assessors' lists in two Bavarian districts.
51. Reichsknappschaftsgesetz, July 1, 1926, *RGBl*, I, 369, Sec. 184.
52. These were the following: ADGB, Afa League, Gesamtverband der christlichen Gewerkschaften, Gedag, Hirsch Dunker unions and GDA.
53. Some difficulties arose with associations whose members were half-way between employer and employee, as, for instance, contractors. In Saxony, a contractors' organization had been allowed to nominate both employers' and employees' assessors.
54. *RABl*, 1927, p. 489.
55. *Rechenschaftsbericht*, 1926, p. 93.
56. Gertrud Israel, in *SP*, Oct. 8, 1925, p. 894; Max Michel, *ibid.*, Dec. 2, 1926, pp. 1209 ff.
57. Ernst Fraenkel, in *Die Gesellschaft* (Berlin), 1929, VI, 103 ff. According to the same author, "Experience has shown that co-operation of trade unions in the courts through their functionaries secures the influence of the lay judges better than the election principle."—"Rechtsprechung," *Internationales Handwörterbuch des Gewerkschaftswesens*, p. 1299.
58. Walter von Karger, in *Die deutsche Arbeitgeberzeitung* (Berlin), 1927, No. 6.
59. *Geschäftsbericht der Vereinigung der deutschen Arbeitgeberverbände*, 1925-26, Berlin, 1927, p. 63.
60. *Rechenschaftsbericht*, 1928, p. 125.
61. Felten, "Die Stellung der Laienrichter," *loc. cit.*, III, 13-14.
62. *Ibid.*, pp. 4 and 24.
63. *RGBl*, I, 887.
64. *Gewerkschafts-Zeitung*, Nov. 7, 1925, p. 655, and Dec. 12, 1925, p. 727.
65. *Ibid.*, Nov. 14, 1925, p. 669, Dec. 19, 1925, pp. 734-35.
66. Nörpel, in *Die Arbeit*, 1925, p. 507.

NOTES TO CHAPTER VI

1. *Der Sinn des Gesetzes zur Ordnung der nationalen Arbeit* (Berlin, 1934), p. 5. This is the official explanation issued by the Ministry of Labor.
2. That trade unions would not be destroyed was promised under oath in a proclamation of Dr. Ley published on May 6 in the *Informationsdienst*. A collapse would be dangerous, according to the government's view, "for it was just the best workers who, in their associations, also found the satisfaction of a healthy feeling of unity and who would have felt the sudden destruction of their associations, for which there was no immediate substitute, like a loss of their birthright."—*Der Sinn des Gesetzes*, etc., p. 5.
3. Although the DAF was established in 1933 as a substitute for the trade unions and the latter's members and funds were taken over, the Federal Labor Court ruled in several decisions that the DAF was not the

legal successor of the trade unions and therefore did not have to take over their obligations. The assets, it was decided, had not been transferred, but seized. February 28, 1934, *Arbeitsrechtssammlung* (continuation of *RAG* collection of court decisions, henceforth referred to as *ARS*), XX, 102; September 29, 1934 XXII, 97; December 4, 1935 XXVI, 222. Rights of former union officials to old age pensions, etc., had been forfeited, whatever special dues the officials might have paid. By act of December 9, 1937 (*RGBl*. I, 1330) liability was accepted for such claims only insofar as the employment relationships were extended by the DAF beyond September 30, 1933. A provision that persons who had promoted actions inimical to the nation were excluded from compensation, made it easy to deny all claims of the former trade union leaders.

4. *RGBl*. I, 45 and many ordinances. Similar regulations were enacted for public enterprises and administrations in the Gesetz zur Ordnung der Arbeit in öffentlichen Verwaltungen und Betrieben of Mar. 23, 1934.— *RGBl*. I, 220.

The AOG is supposed to be applied—in spirit at least, if not in letter— by German undertakings abroad. It is the task of the foreign branch of the DAF, in close contact with the NSDAP, to secure enforcement.

5. At first regulated provisionally by Act of May 19, 1933 (*RGBl*. I, 285) and Order of June 13, 1933 (*ibid.*, 368); finally in the AOG, Sec. 18 ff. An amendment of the Reich Salary Law (Reichsbesoldungsordnung) of March 19, 1937 (*RGBl*. I, 342), changed their name to Federal Trustees of Labor.

6. *SP*, Dec., 1933, p. 1419.

7. *SP*, 1933, pp. 854 ff., 883 ff., 1000 ff., 1415 ff.; 1934, pp. 135 ff., 203 ff., 1274 ff.

8. *Völkischer Beobachter*, No. 298. This decree has not been published in the *RGBl*. Dr. Ley issued directions on principles (Grundsätzliche Anweisungen) on Sept. 12, 1936 (*Amtliches Nachrichtenblatt der DAF*, Folge 23), in which he interpreted the decree from the Labor Front point of view.

9. A reorganization based on "concern industrialism" had been proposed and accepted at the congress of the ADGB in 1922. The resolution was not carried out because some of the most important unions were unwilling to submit to such a loss of identity.

10. In a discussion between the Ministry of Labor and the DAF Social Office, it was stressed that membership was voluntary but that employers were entitled to restrict employment to members of the DAF by a shop rule (Circular of the Ministry of Labor of Oct. 10, 1935, *RABl*. 310).

11. Ley at the party convention in 1938.—*DJ*, 1938, p. 1471. This figure does not include the Austrian membership.

12. The decree of Oct. 24, 1934, described it as a structural part (Gliederung) of the NSDAP together with SA (Schutzabteilung, Storm Troops), SS (Schutzstaffel, Elite Guard), Hitler Youth, etc. Its enumeration among the "affiliated associations" (angeschlossene Verbände) in the Ordinance of the Führer and Chancellor of March 29, 1935 (*RGBl*. I, 502), changed its status. The question of whether the DAF is a corporation of public law (Körperschaft des öffentlichen Rechts) or an association (rechtsfähiger Verein) has been disputed. The Federal Labor Court decided in

favor of the latter on Dec. 16, 1936 (*ARS* XXIX, 223), and Feb. 15, 1939 (*ARS* XXXV, 223). Against this view see Ernst Rudolf Huber, "Die Arbeitsverfassung des völkischen Reiches," *Zeitschrift der Akademie für deutsches Recht*, 1937, pp. 73 ff., and, "Die Rechtsnatur der Deutschen Arbeitsfront," *ibid.*, 1939, pp. 435 ff. The character of the DAF is of importance for the question of whether the AOG or the Code for Public Enterprises was to be applied to its relations to its staff. The latter was ruled out by the Federal Labor Court. That the DAF, as an association, cannot be compared with other associations, has not been contested. Stewards of the DAF exercise sovereign (hoheitliche) functions, according to court decisions. Actions of its political chief are considered sovereign measures, not reviewable in the courts (*JW*, 1937, p. 3182; *ibid.*, 1938, p. 3159; *ibid.*, 1939, p. 264).

13. Dues range from 60 pfennig a month for persons receiving an income of 40 to 60 marks a month to 12 marks for those receiving more than 740 marks. Unemployed pay 40 pfennig, Hitler Youth, 30. Voluntary contributions may amount to 15-50 marks a month (*Arbeitertum*, Nov. 1, 1936, p. 4).

14. According to the *Neue Volkszeitung* of Oct. 5, 1941, Dr. Ley said in the *Angriff* that the DAF, in the middle of 1939, had a monthly income of 46 million marks; in the first three months of the war the income was reduced to 38 millions, but by the end of 1940 it increased to 50 million a month.

15. Rechtsschutz-Ordnung der Deutschen Arbeitsfront. Wolfgang Siebert, *Das deutsche Arbeitsrecht*, D. 121a. In other legal questions advice is given gratuitously to needy party members by the Rechtsbetreuungsstellen (legal advisory offices) of the NSDAP. Persons applying to these offices must prove that they are without means. Lawyers organized in the NS Rechtswahrerbund must contribute voluntarily to these offices, a so-called fidelity service (Treuedienst). There were 1,600 such offices in 1939. In 1936 advice was given to 343,000.—Ludwig Illinger, in *Der Schulungsbrief*, 1939, No. 5, p. 201.

16. *RGBl.* I, 1128.

17. March 5, 1937; in *Aufbau*, No. 14 (Berlin, second issue of July, 1937), p. 30.

18. *Arbeitertum*, Berlin, January 1, 1940, pp. 4 and 5.

19. Cases of legal advice handled in foreign countries in 1938 numbered 6,933.—Ernst Ludwig Illinger, in *Der Schulungsbrief*, Berlin, 1939, p. 204.

20. *Arbeitertum*, July 1, 1937, p. 9.

21. *Aufruf* of Ley, September 14, 1939, Siebert, *Das deutsche Arbeitsrecht*, Anhang I, 175.

22. In order to avoid sudden changes, the Minister of Labor decreed that collective agreements be prolonged without alteration in the form of collective rules. They may be annulled or amended by the RTA.

23. Employees in shops with at least ten employed persons who, after employment of one year, claim that their dismissal is an undue hardship, can bring action for reinstatement before the labor court. Decisions of the court to nullify the dismissal can be set aside by payment of compensation.

24. *SP*, Nov. 1, 1938, p. 1293. By order of May 5, 1937 (*RGBl*, I, 58), the Minister of Labor provided for the setting up of company councils

composed of confidential men of the separate establishments of the concern. The same order secured a greater protection for confidential men by making their transfer to other shops, in case of disagreement, dependent on the consent of the RTA.

25. Shop rules cover the beginning and end of working hours and breaks; time and type of wage payments; principles for calculating piece wages; fines; dismissals without notice; use of wages forfeited by unlawful termination of employment. They may also include provisions about wages and other conditions of work.

26. The shop rules, like the collective rules, "are the statute legally binding on the members of the undertaking under the provisions of which the conditions of employment are settled. The only difference is that those issued by the RTA rest immediately on a state command while those issued by the leader of the undertaking are the emanation of a special rule-making power (autonomy) conferred upon him."—Judgment of the Federal Labor Court of Sept. 21, 1935, *ARS*, XXV, 103-4.

27. Decree of Oct. 15, 1935, *RGBl*, I, 1240.
28. *RGBl*, I, 691.
29. Collective rules had to be registered and filed at the Ministry of Labor and published in the *RABl*.—Order of Mar. 10, 1934, *RGBl*. I, 187.
30. Sept. 1, 1939, *RGBl*, I, 1683.
31. *RGBl*, I, 2028 and ordinances.
32. Law of Feb. 26, 1935 (*RGBl*, I, 311 and ordinances).
33. Decree of Apr. 22, 1939 (*RGBl*, I, 824).
34. Decree of Dec. 22, 1936 (*RABl*, 1937, I, 13).
35. Decrees of Feb. 16, 1938, *RABl*, I, 46, and Dec. 23, 1938, *ibid.*, 1939, I, 48.
36. *RGBl*, I, 769.
37. *RGBl*, I, 1693.
38. Decree of June 22, 1938, *RGBl*, I, 652.
39. Decree of Feb. 13, 1939 (*RGBl*, I, 206 and ordinances).
40. In Saxony, the RTA had consulted the factory inspection in 3,079 cases in 1936.—*SP*, Feb. 1, 1938, p. 178.
41. *SP*, Aug. 1, 1939, pp. 909, 911.
42. Decree of March 21, 1942, and Order of March 26, 1942, *RABl*, p. 257.
43. See complaints in an article of Dr. Franz Goerrig (*SP*, Sept. 1, 1934, p. 1297), and Goering's threats (*SP*, Nov. 7, 1935, p. 1295); Ley, in *Frankfurter Zeitung*, Oct. 19, 1934.
44. Quoted from *Deutsches Recht* in *SP*, Sept. 26, 1935, p. 1129.
45. *SP*, Jan. 24, 1935, p. 113.
46. Helmut Egloff, in *Jahrbuch der nationalsozialistischen Wirtschaft*, ed. Dr. Otto Mönckmeier (München, 1937), pp. 53.
47. Quoted *ibid.*, p. 59.
48. *RGBl*, I, 437.
49. The Academy of German Law had been established by the National Socialists to prepare the purge of German law of "Jewish-Roman" characteristics and the creation of a pure German law.
50. *RGBl*, I, 214. A decree of Oct. 30, 1939 amended the law *RGBl*, I, 2143.
51. In August 1935, there were already sport courses for 2,270,000 par-

ticipants given by 1,300 sport instructors.—*Arbeitertum*, Oct. 15, 1935, p. 7.

52. *Arbeitertum*, March 15, 1936, p. 13. A Labor Relations Bill drafted by the Academy for German Law does not recognize the distinction.

NOTES TO CHAPTER VII

1. Otto Dietrich, *A Revolution in Thought*, p. 7.
2. Dr. Hans Frank (Minister without Portfolio and Chief of the National Socialist Jurists Association), *Nationalsozialistisches Jahrbuch* (München, 1936), p. 221.
3. Reich Minister of Justice, Dr. Franz Gürtner, in *DJ* 1933, p. 622. "One may call previous juridical thinking mechanistic, logical, factory-like and soulless." Now it follows the national ethos (völkischer Sittlichkeit).—Secretary of State in the Reich Ministry of Justice, Roland Freisler, in *DJ* (1936), p. 1569. "German legal science had lost the knowledge of interdependency of race, habit and justice . . . had debased law to a system of abstract conceptions."—Ludwig Fischer, in *Der Schulungsbrief* (1939), p. 187.
4. *Deutsche Juristen-Zeitung*, 1934, p. 746. The law of July 3, 1934 (*RGBl*, I, 529), which declared these measures legal did not aim to legalize initially illegal acts but was merely declaratory.
5. *RGBl*. 1942 I, 247: "There can be no doubt that in the present period of the war, in which the German people are engaged in a struggle for their very existence, the Führer must possess the right claimed by him, namely, to do everything which serves or contributes to the attainment of victory. In his capacity as leader of the nation, as commander in chief of the army, as head of the government and supreme bearer of the executive authority, as chief judge and as leader of the party, the Führer must therefore—without being bound by existing legal principles—be able at any time, if necessary, to urge any German to fulfill his obligations with all means which appear to him appropriate. It does not matter whether the German is a soldier or an officer, a high or low manual laborer or an employee. In the case of a dereliction of these duties, after a conscientious investigation he must be able, without regard to so-called 'well acquired' rights, to impose the fitting punishment, in particular, without introducing the prescribed procedure, to remove any man from his office, his rank, and his position."
6. A decision of the Hamburg Oberlandesgericht of March 31, 1936, recognized the right of the Federal Press Director, a party official, to dismiss without compensation, although, as the court explained, "it would have been contrary to the earlier conception of law to grant an administrative body power to intervene in existing contractual relations."— *Hanseatische Rechts- und Gerichts-Zeitschrift*, 1936, p. 252. The Federal Supreme Court, slower in accepting "co-ordination," reversed the decision of the lower court because of lack of a legislative form of Führer's instructions.—Decision of February 23, 1937, *ibid.*, 1937, p. 235.
7. *RGBl*, I, 141.
8. *RGBl*, I, 75.

9. Freisler, *DJ*, 1935, pp. 1160 ff.; *ibid.*, 1933, pp. 694 ff.; *ibid.*, 1934, pp. 1333 ff. Carl Schmitt writes: "If, contrary to the governing National Socialist notions of the German nation, other notions, alien or even hostile to them, were to be brought forward, this would be a subjectively arbitrary procedure and a political act directed against the state."—*JW* 1933, p. 2794.

10. *RGBl*, I, 844, Art. II.
11. *RGBl*, I, 1933, 780.
12. Apr. 4, 1933. *RGBl*, I, 161. The orders based on this law ceased to have effect on Apr. 30, 1934, after the enactment of the new Labor Court Act.
13. The recognition of nonmilitant unions, of which the only important group were agricultural associations sponsored by the Reich Agrarian League (Reichslandbund) was a sop to Alfred Hugenberg, the German National Party leader who then was still Minister of Economics, i.e., a member of the coalition government. When these unions tried to win new members, they were attacked by the National Socialists.
14. The Stahlhelm-Selbsthilfe, Steel Helmet Self-Help, was composed of workers belonging to the war veterans' Steel Helmet. It aimed to find employment for and otherwise aid economically its members, and to protect them against prosecution by reason of their political activities. It was dissolved in July, 1933.
15. *NSBO* (Nationalsozialistische Betriebszellenorganisation, National Socialist Shop Cell Organization) was the party organization for wage-earners and salaried employees. Party members and sympathizers in each establishment were united in a cell for propaganda purposes. All cells together formed the NSBO, which was made a division of the National Socialist Party in 1931 and a department in 1932. In reality it was a mere recruiting body of the party rather than a trade union group.
16. *RGBl*, 1933, I, 193.
17. *RGBl*, 1933, I, 276. Similar regulations were to have been promulgated by the higher state administrative authority for the appointment and dismissal of assessors and representatives in home-work committees.
18. *RGBl*, I, 319.
19. Law of Feb. 16, 1934, *RGBl*, I, 91; Dec. 5, 1936, *RGBl*, I, 1214; Jan. 24, 1935, *RGBl*, I, 68; Mar. 18, 1935, *RGBl*, I, 381.
20. Order of Dec. 5, 1935, *RGBl*, I, 1428, and of Dec. 10, 1935, *DJ*, p. 1798. The power to decide about the number of chambers in labor and district labor courts and institution of chambers and allocation of business was delegated to the presidents of the ordinary district courts. Presidents of labor courts and district labor courts had to be appointed like officials by the Department of Justice.
21. *RGBl*, I, 1286; and Decree of Dec. 3, 1937.—*DJ*, p. 1944.
22. Disqualification as leader of an enterprise is one of the penalties which may be imposed by a social honor court.
23. *RGBl*, I, 1658.
24. Decree of Feb. 10, 1940, *RGBl*, I, 348.
25. Decree of Sept. 1, 1939, *RGBl*, I, 1651.
26. Concerning the change in judicial personnel, cf. p. 166.
27. Collective rules of Nov. 15, 1934, *RABl*, VI, 506.

28. *RGBl*, I, 914.
29. Collective rules of April 4, 1938, *RABl*, VI, 422.
30. *RGBl*, I, 1509.
31. *RGBl*, I, 386.
32. *RABl*, 1935, I. 203.
33. Of 15,000 cases brought into the courts in Berlin by the DAF (out of a total of 35,000) in 1935, lawyers were admitted in 1,900 (in 1936, in 900 of 14,000 complaints brought into the labor courts by the DAF out of a total of 25,000).—Erich Burkhardt, "Die Prozessvertretung vor den Arbeitsgerichten," *Zehn Jahre Arbeitsgericht*, p. 28.
34. It has been contested whether poor-law lawyers are admitted in the labor courts.—*JW*, 1935, p. 679.
35. *RGBl*, I, 780.
36. Ministerialrat Martin Jonas, in *DJ*, 1935, p. 1822.
36a. Verordnung über ausserordentliche Massnahmen auf dem Gebiete des bürgerlichen Rechts, der bürgerlichen Rechtspflege und des Kostenrechts aus Anlass des totalen Krieges, of Sept. 27, 1944 (*RGBl*, I, 229). It is interesting that no restrictions were made as to criminal law.
37. Dr. Roland Freisler, *Etwas über Führertum in der Rechtspflege*. Schriften der Akademie für Deutsches Recht No. 1, Berlin, 1935.
38. Landgerichtsdirektori R. Töwe, in *Deutsche Richterzeitung* (Berlin, 1935), p. 225.
39. Amtsgerichtsdirektor Dr. Friedrich, in *Deutsches Recht* (Berlin, Leipzig, Wien, 1939), p. 344.
40. How labor courts had to adjust themselves to economic necessity may be seen in the wavering attitude toward breach of contract. According to the decree of December 22, 1936 (*RABl*, 1937, p. 13) the courts must back an employer who retains the book of a worker who leaves a job before expiration of contract. On March 15, 1937, the Stettin Labor Court ordered restitution of a book in such a case in order not to deprive agriculture of a worker.—*Monatshefte für NS Sozialpolitik* (Stuttgart und Berlin, 1937), p. 477. On September 21, 1938 the Federal Labor Court held that the employer had the right to withhold the book of a worker who deliberately committed certain acts in order to be dismissed.—*ARS*, XXXIV, 98.
41. Public law is the body of law governing relations between the state and the individual; private law governs relations between individuals.
42. Ernst Rudolf Huber, "Einheit und Gliederung des völkischen Rechts," *Zeitschrift für die gesamte Staatswissenschaft*, XCVIII (1938), 31 ff.
43. Wilhelm Ebel, *Arbeit und Arbeiter in der deutschen Rechtsgeschichte*. Göttinger Akademische Reden, 1939, Heft 8 (p. 30—not paged).
44. *Das Arbeitsverhältnis in der Ordnung der nationalen Arbeit*, Hamburg, 1935.
45. In German law the rules which dominate family life are separated from those dominating contractual property relations.
46. Decision of Jan. 19, 1938. *ARS*, XXXIII, 172.
47. May 20, 1936, *ARS*, XXVII, part 2, 93 ff.
48. Mar. 18, 1936, *ARS*, XXVI, 161.
49. Federal Labor Court, Mar. 23, 1935, *ARS*, XXIII, 170; Mar. 11, 1936, XXVI, 321; Jan. 16, 1937, XXX, 70.

50. *ARS*, XXXI, 181.
51. *ARS*, XXXII, 328.
52. *ARS*, XXXII, 316.
53. *ARS*, XXXIII, 195.
54. Reichsgerichtsrat Dr. Lersch, in *SP*, Jan. 15, 1940, pp. 40-41.
55. Decision of the Federal Labor Court of March 20, 1942, *Deutsche Bergwerks-Zeitung* (Düsseldorf), May 15, 1942.
56. July 13, 1935, *ARS*, XXIV, 93; Jan. 20, 1937, *ARS*, XXIX, 119, and others.
57. Jan. 24, 1934, *ARS*, XX, 119; March 18, 1936, *ARS*, XXVI, 242; Nov. 21, 1936; XXVIII, 308; Oct. 6, 1937, *ARS*, XXXII, 248; Nov. 10, 1937, *ARS*, XXXII, 333; May 17, 1939, *ARS*, XXXVI, 107.
58. August Danzer-Vanotti, in *SP*, Sept. 24, 1937, pp. 1138 ff.
59. Aganist this practice and the decisions of the Federal Labor Court: Wilhelm Herschel in *SP* May 24, 1934, pp. 632 ff. July 2, 1937, pp. 777 ff. Sept. 24, 1937, pp. 1142 ff.
60. *ARS*, XXVI, 107.
61. *ARS*, XXVI, 115.
62. Gesetz über Heimarbeit of Mar. 23, 1934, *RGBl*, I, 214, Sec. 20.
63. *RGBl*, I, 691.
64. One RTA, e.g., ordered a worker who had been employed 40 hours weekly because he wished to earn little and avoid paying alimony, to work 60 hours weekly without overtime pay (*Der Deutsche Volkswirt*, Berlin, August 12, 1938, p. 2256).
65. Up to September 1937, about 3,090 collective rules had been issued, while 3,900 collective agreements were still in existence in June, 1937, aside from those for public service.—Franz Seldte, "Aufgaben und Tätigkeit der Reichstreuhänder der Arbeit," *Zeitschrift der Akademie für deutsches Recht*, 1937, p. 613.
66. It would lead too far to describe the dualism of party and state (with the party claiming priority) which results in overlapping, disorderly and complicated organizations, and conflicting jurisdictions. Although the leading offices in party and state are usually in the same hands, the staffs are different. On important questions government and party leadership have issued orders of identical wording.—Gottfried Neesse, in *Verwaltungsarchiv*. XLIII (1938), 23.
67. *Ibid.*, p. 17.
68. Ernst Fraenkel, *The Dual State*, p. xiii.
69. Law of Feb. 10, 1936, *PrGS*, p. 21. The Prussian Oberverwaltungsgericht decided on May 2, 1935, that the Gestapo was immune from judicial control and that a person in protective custody could not appeal to a court or demand a trial.—*JW*, 1935, LXIV, pp. 2398-99. "Protective custody" is used to protect not the individual but the state. Its application was sanctioned by the decrees of Feb. 28, 1933 (*RGBl*, I, 83); Nov. 30, 1933; March 8, 1934, Feb. 25, 1935 (*PrGS*, 1933, p. 413; 1934, p. 143; 1935, p. 231).

Gestapo orders are frequently executed by the SS, the unofficial army for internal defense, consisting of about 250,000 trained men before the outbreak of the war. High officials of the Gestapo are officers in the SS. The latter runs the concentration camps, the notorious instruments of terror, working by methods of beating, torture, and humiliation. *Das Schwarze Korps*, official organ of the SS, publishes in every issue denunciation and exposures of persons who remain unco-ordinated. Inmates of concentration camps, besides Jews, include race defilers, political adversaries and political suspects, and a large percentage of persons unwilling to work, such as vagrants or workers who refuse to accept assigned jobs. All are held as long as the police think fit.

70. Hans Peter Ipsen, *Politik und Justiz*, pp. 171 ff.

71. *Zeitschrift für die gesamte Staatswissenschaft*, XCVIII, 200 ff.

72. "Der nationalsozialistische Rechtsstaat," in *Die Verwaltungsakademie*, I (Berlin, 1935), 6.

73. Ernst Fraenkel sums up the difference between a Rule of Law State (Rechtsstaat) and the Third Reich as follows: "In the Rechtsstaat, the courts control the executive branch of the government in the interest of legality. In the Third Reich the police power controls the courts in the interest of political expediency."—*Loc. cit.*, p. 40.

74. Hermann Reuss, in *JW* (1937), pp. 422-23.

75. The Act of Feb. 16, 1934, *RGBl*, I, 91, gives the Reich President the right to stop any criminal proceedings.

76. E.g., when the courts sided with the Protestant Church (law of June 26, 1935, *RGBl*, I, 774). When, by law of Dec. 13, 1934 (*RGBl*, I, 1235), claims arising from "illegal acts committed in connection with the National Revolution" were transferred to the Minister of Interior, pending suits were withdrawn from the courts.

77. The most drastic changes have occurred in criminal law, which is supposed to be based on the people's moral conception of right and wrong. The criminal law has been revolutionized by substituting the principle of "material" for that of "formal" justice. Practically, this has meant abolition of the principle *nulla poena sine lege* (no punishment without law). Courts were entitled to punish on the basis of analogy and according to the "sound feeling of the people" (Law of June 28, 1935, *RGBl*, I, 839). The government has compelled the judiciary to impose sentences according to its wishes by retroactive laws (e.g., in the Reichstag fire case). Punishment is inflicted not for the purpose of correction but as revenge or in order to eliminate "inferior" people. Brutality shall deter. Duration and severity of sentences have been increased and new penalties have been added, such as castration and denial of citizenship, generally accompanied by confiscation of property. Rights of accused have been curtailed and acquitted persons have been placed in the hands of the Gestapo for "education" in concentration camps. Special tribunals without possibility of appeal have been set up to handle selected categories of offenders. The most formidable is the People's Court (Volksgerichtshof) which deals with high treason and political activities directed against the regime (law of April 24, 1934, *RGBl*, I, 341). Severe penalties, including death, are imposed after secret proceedings in which all procedural rights are denied. Witnesses are anonymous. The People's Court is composed of two trained judges and three lay judges appointed by Hitler from among the SS and the party hierarchy on the basis of "special knowledge in defense against subversive activities," thus limiting substantially the influence of the learned judges. There is no appeal from

its verdicts on fact or on law.—Otto Kirchheimer, "Criminal Law in National Socialist Germany," *Studies in Philosophy and Social Science* (New York, 1939), pp. 444 ff.

78. Decision of Feb. 10, 1937, *ARS*, XXVIII, 315.

79. Federal Supreme Court, Feb. 17, 1939, *RGZ*, Vol. CLX, p. 193.

80. Decree of Dec. 2, 1936 (*DJ*, 1936, p. 1833). The party is effectively protected by the law of December 20, 1934, "against insidious attacks against state and party" (*RGBl*, I, 1269), which punishes even remarks "likely to undermine the confidence of the people in political leadership." Party affiliates also enjoy privileges. The Hitler Youth must be informed by the labor and district labor courts of all decisions concerning youth and of an importance beyond the particular case.—Order of the Reich Minister of Justice of May 24, 1939, *DJ*, 1939, p. 995.

81. *Hitler. Sozialismus wie ihn der Führer sieht.* Worte des Führers zu sozialen Fragen zusammengestellt von F. Meystre (München, 1935), p. 61.

82. Prosecutor Moser von Filseck at the German Juristentag, 1936, *Deutsche Rechtspflege* (May 25, 1936), p. 220.

83. *JW*, 1933, p. 1271.

84. Heinrich Müller, *Berufsbeamtentum und Nationalsozialismus*, 4th ed. (München, 1933), p. 53.

85. The supreme judge of the NSDAP, Reichsleiter Buch, *DJ*, 1937, p. 1048.

86. Minister Hans Frank at the Jurists' conference on Jan. 14, 1936.—*Deutsche Rechtspflege*, 1936, p. 8.

87. *Ibid.*, p. 9. Likewise, *DJ*, 1938, p. 1462.

88. *DJ*, 1934, p. 1333, and 1935, p. 241.

89. *Gesetz zur Wiederherstellung des Berufsbeamtentums*, Apr. 7, 1933, *RGBl*, I, 175, and ordinances. The law was superseded by the Civil Service Act (Deutsches Beamtengesetz of Jan. 26, 1937, *RGBl*, I, 39) which continued the provision for removal of unreliable judges (Sec. 71).

90. This was a violation of Article 104 of the Constitution, which provides that judges are appointed for life: "They may be removed from office, permanently or temporarily transferred to another position, or retired, only on authority of a judicial decision, and only upon grounds and by procedure fixed by law."

91. *RGBl*, I, 188.

92. *RGBl*, I, 1258, and Rechtsanwaltsordnung of Dec. 13, 1935 (*RGBl*, I, 1470). How the National Socialists interpret the honor of a lawyer was revealed in the suit about exclusion of a lawyer who, in 1931, corresponded with the pacifist, Wilhelm Foerster, and criticized National Socialism. He was expelled for high treason by decision of the honor court of the Chamber of Lawyers.—*JW*, 1935, p. 783. Judgment of Dec. 19, 1934.

93. There were few women in the profession. It had been opened to them only in the 1920's and training required from seven to eight years. The total number of women judges was 36 in 1933. The author remembers only one as chairman of a labor chamber. The number of independent women lawyers was 167, of employed lawyers, 84.—*Deutsche Juristen-Zeitung*, 1935, p. 1106.

94. Gesetz zur Aenderung der Vorschriften auf dem Gebiet des allgemeinen Beamten-Besoldungs- und Versorgungsrechts, *RGBl*, I, 433, Ch. II, sec. 3, No. 2.

95. In an article in the official journal, Secretary of State Freisler points out that selection must take into consideration effective activity in the World War, the fight for National Socialism, military service, and number of children.—*DJ*, 1939, p. 1353.

96. Various orders have stressed that officials of merit in the NSDAP, especially those who belonged to it before 1933 or have a low membership number, are to be given preference in promotions (e.g., Order of March 21, 1934, *DJ*, 1934, p. 403; Order of Aug. 23, 1935, *DJ*, 1935, p. 1254).

97. Secretary of State Freisler. In *DJ* (1935), p. 1685.

98. *DJ*, 1934, p. 1645. The degradation of justice was accelerated by a strong rejuvenescence of the body of judges; the younger age groups were more strongly National Socialist than the older generation. Applicants for bar and bench are carefully supervised during their training period and compelled to take part in "political instructions." Training was regulated in the Justizausbildungsordnung (Federal Regulations regarding the educational requirements for the legal profession and bench) of July 22, 1934 (*RGBl*, I, 727) and ordinances and codified on Jan. 4, 1939 (*RGBl*, I, 5). Before being admitted to the university, a young man must prove political reliability in the labor service and serve in the SA. The study of law includes lectures on race, national sociology, blood and soil, and politics. The displacement of a large number of old law professors has lowered the level of university teaching. University professors, too, are drilled in community camps (*Deutsches Recht* A, 1939, p. 1619). At the end of his studies the student must take a character test consisting of political questions. The first four terms are, as a young jurist said, to a large degree "wasted effort, wasted time and wasted money."—*Zeitschrift der Akademie für deutsches Recht*, 1939, p. 146. During the war the whole period was shortened to four terms.

Admission to probationary service which follows the first juridical examination after completion of university training, has been made a matter of discretion. If admitted, the Referendar swears loyalty to Hitler. Added to the training in courts and lawyers' offices are "working communities" (Arbeitsgemeinschaften) in which, under the leadership of a trustworthy National Socialist jurist, the Referendar is educated in the community spirit. Before the war, visits were made to the Navy, "the bleeding frontier," and other parts of the country.

Before admission to the second state examination, conformity is tested in a special camp of military character. Here students live in barracks, wear uniforms. Three platoons of 56 men each are recruited every two weeks. Thirty per cent of the time is dedicated to law, 15 per cent to political discussions, 35-40 per cent to military training, the rest to maintaining the camp.—Camp Commander Hildebrandt, in *DJ*, 1936, p. 1757, and Amtsgerichtsrat Friedrich, *ibid.*, p. 759. Discussions dealt with the reform of jurisprudence in National Socialist spirit. Although the six weeks in camp precede the oral examination, the referendars are not allowed to prepare for it in camp. Lectures in peace time emphasized such topics as race biology, encirclement of the Reich by enemies, the rise of the NSDAP, atrocity propaganda in foreign countries, the struggle of the German groups in Hungary, etc. Sports were military in character.

Certificates of conduct and political and sport tests were parts of the second examination.

While formerly the passing of this examination qualified the young jurist for bench and bar, now this privilege is granted only to loyal supporters.—Order of the Prussian Minister of Justice of November 20, 1933, *DJ*, p. 729. They must leave the profession unless admitted to a probationary period of one year in the courts in preparation for a post as judge or public prosecutor, or in an attorney's office.—Reichsrechtsanwaltsordnung of Feb. 21, 1936, *RGBl*, I, 107. During this year, they are paid. Admission to probation may be revoked without appeal. The period may be cut for "tested" persons. At the end of the year the Minister of Justice decides whether the assessor shall be admitted for another three years' service as a candidate for the profession of judge or prosecutor in the one branch, of advocate in the other. After eleven years the assessor finally ends his training. He does not yet know whether he will be definitely admitted. Referendars and assessors are expected to take part in party activities.—Decree of the Reich Minister of Justice of May 11, 1934, *DJ*, 1934, p. 632, and an appeal of the Party Chief of Officials of Justice of Jan. 30, 1937, *DJ*, 1937, p. 364.

The regime has revealed its evaluation of law training by appointing in 1933 the late Mr. Kerrl temporarily a court secretary, first National Socialist Minister of Justice of Prussia.

99. The SA periodical, *Der SA Mann*, writes: "Liberalistic objectivity was a dangerous poison. The old state did not differentiate whether it was a National Socialist who killed a Communist or vice versa."—Quoted in *DJ* (1938), p. 1733.

100. Nov. 26, 1935, *ARS*, XXVI, 314.

101. Labor Court, Hamburg, Aug. 23, 1935, *DJ*, p. 1771.

102. The task of law, jurisprudence, and the administration of law "is the maintenance and protection of the people against anti-social groups which desire to evade or who otherwise fail to fulfill all obligations required by the community," said Hitler in a Reichstag speech on January 30, 1937. *Deutsche Rechtspflege* (1937), p. 33. A broadcast from Germany in June, 1942, defined anti-social elements as "irresponsible, lazy, quarrelsome persons, annuity hunters, loath to do any kind of work, and the insurance sponger, or whoever tries to burden the community with his upkeep and that of his children; whoever is particularly uneconomical, uncontrolled," etc. Regional committees appointed to deal with these anti-social elements shall decide whether they are to be sent to a welfare institution, forced labor, or an educational camp of the Gestapo (*New York Times*, June 21, 1942). "Educational camp" is a euphemistic term for concentration camp.

103. They must sign a statement that the agreements were made of their free will and not under duress.

104. Oberlandesgericht, München, Dec. 8, 1937, *DJ*, 1938, p. 724.

105. The difference in the treatment of Jews and other state enemies is revealed in the fact that National Socialist lawyers were allowed to assist Communists but were ousted from the party when they accepted cases of Jewish clients.

106. Judgment of the Dortmund District Labor Court, July 25, 1933,

ARS, XIX, Part II, 3. As late as Oct. 7, 1936, the Federal Labor Court ruled that dismissals of Jews should not be extended beyond the letter of the law. "The institution should have . . . shown that in the present case special circumstances made it seem impossible to continue the employment relationship. It has advanced no such reasons. . . ."—*ARS*, XXVIII, 134.

107. *ARS*, XXIX, 290. Other decisions have justified dismissals with the argument that the employer would have lost the patronage of the party or would have been unable to take part in the "efficiency contest" of the DAF.—Labor Court, Saalfeld, Aug. 13, 1937, *JW*, 1937, p. 2850.

108. June 27, 1936, *JW*, 1936, p. 2529.

109. When, after 1938, because of the shortage of labor, Jews were called to work in an inferior status, special judges were assigned to deal with conflicts concerning Jewish workers. Their decisions were final.— Order of October 31, 1941, *RGBl*, I, 681. The policy of making Jews work, however, was replaced after a short time by one of complete extermination.

110. Federal Labor Court, Feb. 28, 1934, *ARS*, XX, 102; July 4, 1934, *ARS*, XXI, 191.

111. Jan. 12, 1935, *ARS*, XXIII, 107; July 4, 1934, *ARS*, XXI, 188; Mar. 21, 1934, *ARS*, XX, 241; Mar. 14, 1934, *ARS*, XX, 196.

112. Mar. 28, 1934, *ARS*, XX, 201; May 26, 1937, *ARS*, XXX, 127. Alfred Rosenberg describes the outcast position of nonconformists as follows: "He who is not devoted to the interests of the people, cannot claim their protection."—*DJ*, 1938, p. 360).

113. District Labor Court, Frankfurt a/Main, Decision of Nov. 27, 1933, *ARS*, XIX, Part II, 207.

114. Labor Court Osnabrück, July 30, 1935, *DJ*, 1936, p. 190.

115. Labor Court Marienwerder, Feb. 21, 1935, *DJ*, p. 787.

116. Oct. 27, 1937, *ARS*, XXXI, 229, and Labor Court Leipzig, March 24, 1936, *DJ*, p. 779; Labor Court Plauen, April 19, 1937, *DJ*, p. 1088.

117. Dec. 15, 1937, *ARS*, XXXI, 367.

118. Labor Court Karlsruhe, May 2, 1934, *JW*, 1935, p. 1299.

119. The District Labor Court Gleiwitz decided on Oct. 20, 1936 that the courts need not review the evaluation of a person's political character by the district leadership.—*Deutsche Rechtspflege*, 1936, p. 591. *Rechtsprechungsbeilage*.

120. Judgment of the Federal Labor Court, Apr. 14, 1937, *ARS*, XXX, 22.

121. Oberlandesgericht Hamburg, May 4, 1937. *Hanseatische Rechts- und Gerichtszeitschrift*, 1937, p. 216.

122. *DJ*, 1940, p. 461.

123. Judgment of the District Labor Court Gleiwitz, Aug. 17, 1933, *ARS*, XIX, Part II, p. 16.

124. Aug. 21, 1937, *ARS*, XXX, 297.

125. Amtliche Nachrichten des Reichsversicherungsamts, *RABl*, 1936, IV, 232.

126. Sec. 1715 a RVO entitled the Reichsversicherungsamt to give leading decisions without case.

127. *AOG*, Sec. 35 ff.; and Order of Mar. 28, 1934, *RGBl*, I, 255.

128. The chairman of the social honor court draws up a list of the

branches of industry from which he intends to appoint assessors. He transmits the list to the DAF, which nominates at least three leaders and three confidential men for each branch. Women are not excluded. If an assessor commits a gross breach of his official duties, he may be removed from office. Tenure has been prolonged indefinitely by decree of April 25, 1940.—*RABl*, p. 199.

129. Order of March 28, 1934, *RGBl*, I, 255.
130. Decree of the Führer and Chancellor of June 25, 1935, *RGBl*, I, 1096.
131. Sept. 30, 1935, *ARS*, XXV, 87.
132. Doubts of interpretation are to be settled in the labor courts.— Federal Social Honor Court, Apr. 16, 1935, *ARS*, XXIV, 43.
133. Social Honor Court Karlsruhe, Nov. 20, 1934. *ARS*, XXII, Part II, 89; Social Honor Court Mitteldeutschland, Dec. 17, 1934, *ibid.*, p. 139; Social Honor Court Sachsen, Dec. 18, 1934, *ibid.*, XXIII, Part II, 49; Dec. 12, 1935, *ibid.*, XXVI, 67.
134. Aug. 5, 1935, *ARS*, XXV, 159.
135. Mar. 22, 1937, *ARS*, XXX, 110.
136. The slight 1936 increase (to fifty-four) of employees against whom action had been taken was due to the fact that the RTA's prosecuted breaches of contract of farm labor in social honor courts, until the decree of Dec. 22, 1936 (*RGBl*, 1937, I, 13), authorized employers to retain work books and removed such cases from the courts.
137. The 95 cases of malicious abuse of authority in 1935 included 55 of abusive language, 16 of immoral advances toward women, 21 of manhandling.
138. Social Honor Court Sachsen, Dec. 15, 1934, *ARS*, XXIII, Pt. II, 53.
139. Federal Social Honor Court, Aug. 5, 1935, *ARS*, XXIV, 209.
140. Kurt Gusko, in *Monatshefte für N. S. Sozialpolitik*, 1935-36, p. 262.
141. One employer was punished in 1937 because he frequently failed to answer letters of the RTA.—*SP*, Jan. 15, 1938, p. 105.
142. Social Honor Court Ostpreussen, Mar. 11, 1935, *ARS*, XXIII, Part II, 239; June 18, 1935, *ibid.*, XXIV, 285.
143. See e.g., the article of a high official, Dr. Steinmann, in *RABl*, 1936, II, 415 ff.
144. Social Honor Court Brandenburg, July 24, 1935, *ARS*, XXV, Part II, 55.
145. Dec. 12, 1935, *ARS*, XXV, 267.
146. "In the National Socialist state, measures aiming at class struggle, such as the strike and lockout, are inconceivable. Although such measures are not expressly forbidden by the AOG, it follows from Sec. 1 . . ." (Social Honor Court Mitteldeutschland, Nov. 19, 1935, *ARS*, XXVI, Pt. II, 193). Needless to say that the Gestapo deals with strikes and attempts to strike in a very drastic manner. It is, of course, mere hypocrisy to classify the "measures" inflicted upon striking workers by the Gestapo, particularly confinement in a concentration camp, as a means of "education" rather than "punishment."
147. Of 117 fines imposed in 1936, 52 were less than 100 marks, 57 between 100 and 1,000 marks, and eight above 1,000 marks.—*SP*, Jan. 9, 1938, pp. 43 ff.

148. Apr. 16, 1935, *ARS*, XXIV, 43. On June 10, 1937, the Federal Social Honor Court reduced the sentence of an employer from permanent to temporary disqualification as leader on the grounds that he promised improvement. *ARS*, XXX, 179.

149. Of 204 cases brought into the courts in 1935, 57 related to factories, 45 to farms, 28 to handicraft shops, 20 to trade undertakings, 17 to hotels and restaurants.—*RABl*, 1936, II, 67. In 1936, of 189 actions against employers, 45 were in handicrafts, 37 in industry, 20 in retail trade, 2 in wholesale trade, 14 in trucking, 9 in restaurants and hotels.—*SP*, Jan. 9, 1938, pp. 43 ff.

150. *RABl*, 1940, V, 347.

151. In 34 cases the RTA withdrew the complaint; in 55, the chairman decided without a full court.

152. *Ehren- und Disziplinarordnung der DAF* of Jan. 11, 1936, newly published Aug. 1, 1939.—*Amtliches Nachrichtenblatt der Deutschen Arbeitsfront* of Aug. 30, 1939, p. 57. It should be noted, furthermore, that the special courts of the DAF may assume jurisdiction in cases of "unsocial behavior" even after the social honor court has passed on a case. "Double jeopardy" is not barred.

153. *JW*, 1935, p. 1282; *SP*, Jan. 10, 1935, pp. 52-53.

154. *RABl*, 1936, II, 57-58.

155. *SP*, Jan. 9, 1938, pp. 43 ff.

156. *Deutsche Sozialpolitik. Berichte der deutschen Arbeitsfront, Zentralbüro, Sozialamt*, June 1, 1938-Dec. 1, 1938 (Berlin, 1939), pp. 109 ff.

157. *RABl*, 1940, V, 347.

158. *RABl*, 1941, V, 311.

159. *RABl*, 1943, V, 471-72.

160. *Hamburger Fremdenblatt*, Nov. 22, 1944.

161. Some sections of the party as the Hitler Youth, Storm Troops, etc., have special courts besides, which decide about disobedience and other offenses of "unsoldierly behavior."

162. Major Walter Buch, *Wesen und Sinn der Parteigerichtsbarkeit*, Zeitschrift der Akademie für Deutsches Recht, 1936, p. 201.

163. Reichsleiter Walter Buch at the conference of the Reichspressestelle of the NSDAP.—*DJ*, 1936, p. 265; Fritz Mehnert, in *Der Schulungsbrief*, 1936, pp. 341 ff.

164. John Brown Mason, "The Judicial System of the Nazi Party," *The American Political Science Review*, Feb., 1944, p. 99.

165. *DJ*, 1937, p. 851.

166. Quoted by Hans Fabricius, *Organisatorischer Aufbau der NSDAP, Grundlagen, Aufbau und Wirtschaftsordnung des nationalsozialistischen Staates*, H. H. Lammers and Hans Pfundtner, ed., Berlin, 1939, I, Gruppe 1, No. 7, Pt. 12.

167. It is a matter of experience that the party courts collaborate with the Gestapo. Thus the defendant in a party court may be handed to the Gestapo, which makes use of evidence introduced in the party court.

168. Helmut Giesebrecht, *Das Verfahren vor den Ehrengerichten* (Berlin, 1938), pp. 149 ff.

169. Circulars of Apr. 19 and Apr. 24, 1940, *RABl*, I, 251-52.

170. *RABl*, I. 137.

171. Rechtsschutz-Ordnung der Deutschen Arbeitsfront, Siebert, *Das deutsche Arbeitsrecht, op. cit.*, D 121a.

172. *Der Schulungsbrief*, 1939, No. 5, p. 213.

173. Werner Hellwig, quoted from *Der Angriff* in *DJ*, 1936, p. 229. The Essen office settled 3,005 cases out of 10,133 outside the courts and submitted only 1,467 to the courts.—*DJ*, 1936, p. 158. The Berlin service in 1935 settled 17,264 cases as compared to 5,462 compromises in the courts. For 1936, the figures were 20,738 and 4,241 respectively.—Rohlfing, "Entwicklung und Sinn der Arbeitsgerichtsbarkeit," in *Zehn Jahre Arbeitsgericht, loc. cit.*, p. 12. *Der Schulungsbrief* claims that in 1938 40 per cent of all labor law cases were settled by the offices without courts (Dec. 31, 1938, p. 203). The offices, however, were consulted in many cases not belonging to labor law. A report of the Cologne office mentions a mother, threatened by her son, demanding he be sent to a workhouse.—*Arbeitertum*, Sept. 1, 1934, p. 27. It should be noted that the unions—to a certain extent—had exercised a similar function. Negotiations between the officers of the unions and employers in order to avoid labor disputes in the labor courts were a matter of everyday experience.

174. Gregor Ziemer in his colorful book on National Socialist education describes his reaction when an English friend who dismissed his maid was threatened with suit in the labor court: "I winced. I knew what it meant, for I had gone through it when I had dismissed a maid who objected to waiting on table when we had Jewish students present. I had reinstated her, too. I knew that at the labor court the judge would be in full Party uniform, so would be the lawyer for the girl, so would be our lawyer, if we could find one. As a foreigner, I would have no chance at all. . . ."— *Education for Death* (London, New York, 1941), p. 126.

NOTES TO APPENDIX I

1. Sec. 152, *GO*.
2. Sec. 153, *GO*.
3. Children in other than factory work were protected by an act of March 30, 1903 (*RGBl*, p. 113), the Kinderschutzgesetz. Children in agriculture and household work were not protected.
4. *Deutsches Handelsgesetzbuch* of May 10, 1897 (*RGBl*, p. 219).
5. Dec. 20, 1911, *RGBl*, p. 976.
6. Aug. 18, 1896 (*RGBl*, p. 195).
7. May 22, 1918, *RGBl*, p. 423.
8. June 26, 1916, *RGBl*, p. 635.
9. *RGBl*, p. 1333.

NOTES TO APPENDIX II

1. *RGBl*, p. 1303. It was sanctioned by the provisional Act of March 4, 1919. *RGBl*, p. 285.
2. **Art.** 159, 124, 165. The first paragraph of Art. 165 reads, "Wage earners and salaried employees are authorized to co-operate on equal terms with the employers in the regulation of wages and working conditions, as well as in the entire economic development of the productive forces.

The organization on both sides and the agreements between them are recognized." Discrimination against organized labor was outlawed by Sec. 81, 84 of the Works Council Act.

3. Verordnungen über Einstellung und Entlassung von Arbeitern und Angestellten während der Zeit der wirtschaftlichen Demobilmachung, Jan. 4, 1919, *RGBl*, p. 8; Jan. 24, 1919, *RGBl*, p. 100; Sept. 3, 1919, *RGBl*, p. 1500; Feb. 12, 1920, *RGBl*, p. 218.

4. Nov. 8, 1920, *RGBl*, p. 1901; Oct. 15, 1923, *RGBl*, I, 983.

5. Gesetz über die Beschäftigung Schwerbeschädigter of Apr. 6, 1920, *RGBl*, p. 458 and Jan. 12, 1923, *RGBl*, I, 57, and amendments.

6. Law of July 9, 1926, *RGBl*, I, 399.

7. Decrees of Nov. 23, 1918 (*RGBl*, p. 1334); Mar. 18, 1919 (*RGBl*, p. 315); Dec. 21, 1923 (*RGBl*, I, 1249); Apr. 14, 1927 (*RGBl*, I, 110), and others.

8. Verordnung über eine vorläufige Landarbeitsordnung of Jan. 24, 1919, *RGBl*, p. 111.

9. Act of June 27, 1923 (*RGBl*, I, 472, 730).

10. *RGBl*, p. 1456. Newly edited as decree of Mar. 1, 1928 (*RGBl*, I, 47).

11. Verordnung über Tarifverträge, Arbeiter- und Angestelltenausschüsse und Schlichtung von Arbeitsstreitigkeiten of Dec. 23, 1918 (*RGBl*, p. 1456).

12. The German unions were nationwide. Similar to state agencies, they were hierarchical organizations. The jurisdiction of their central authorities were very broad. Locals had very restricted competence and local officers were supervised by the central agencies.

13. On Jan. 1, 1925, 66.1 per cent of all workers were covered by collective agreements. "DieTarifverträge in Deutschen Reich," *35. Sonderheft zum Reichsarbeitsblatt*, p. 9.

14. Oct. 30, 1923, *RGBl*, I, 1043, and Ordinances of Dec. 29, 1923, *RGBl* (1924), I, 9.

15. Federal Supreme Court Decision, Mar. 7, 1922, *RGZ*, CIV, 171, and a few other decisions.

16. Frieda Wunderlich, *Labor Under German Democracy, Arbitration 1918-1933*, p. 60.

17. Judgment of Apr. 6, 1922, *RGZ*, CIV, 327. The use of the closed shop clause against members of another union had been barred by agreement of the three main trade union federations.

18. *RGBl*, I, 1249.
19. *RGBl*, I, 517 (523).
20. *RGBl*, I, 699 (726).
21. *RGBl*, I, 425 (428-29).
22. *RGBl*, I, 433.
23. *RGBl*, p. 147.

NOTES TO APPENDIX III

1. *Statistisches Jahrbuch für das Deutsche Reich*, 1932, pp. 555 ff.
2. *Jahrbuch der Berufsverbände in Deutschen Reich*, 1930, *52. Sonderheft zum Reichsarbeitsblatt*, p. 29.

BIBLIOGRAPHY

I. THE PRE-HITLER PERIOD

Books and Articles

Aus der Praxis des Gewerbegerichts Berlin. Ed. by Max v. Schulz, Reinhold Schalhorn, Ludwig Schultz. Berlin, 1913.
Bahr, Richard. *Gewerbegericht, Kaufmannsgericht, Einigungsamt.* Leipzig, 1905.
Baum, Georg. *Gerechtigkeit und Berufsinteresse im Arbeitsgerichtsprozess.* Berlin, 1928.
———. *Kollektivismus und Individualismus im Arbeitsgerichtsprozess.* Berlin, 1931.
Burkhardt, Erich, Dersch, Hermann, and others. *Zehn Jahre Arbeitsgericht. Wichtige Fragen aus dem Arbeitsrecht. Eine Festgabe zur Zehnjährigen Wiederkehr der Einführung der Arbeitsgerichte in Deutschland.* Leipzig and Berlin, 1937.
Davis, Horace B. "The German Labor Courts," *Political Science Quarterly*, September, 1929.
Dersch, Hermann, and Volkmar, Erich. *Arbeitsgerichtsgesetz.* 2nd ed., Mannheim, Berlin, Leipzig, 1927.
Felten, Heinz. "Die Stellung der Laienrichter bei den Arbeitsgerichtsbehörden und die sozialrechtliche Bedeutung des Arbeitsgerichtswesens," *Sozialrechtliches Jahrbuch.* Ed. by Theodor Brauer and others. Mannheim, Berlin, Leipzig, 1932-33. Vols. II and IV.
Fraenkel, Ernst. "Rechtsprechung und Gewerkschaften," *Internationales Handwörterbuch des Gewerkschaftswesens.* Berlin, 1932. Vol. II.
———. *Zur Soziologie der Klassenjustiz.* Berlin, 1927.
Herzog, Herbert. *Die Vertretung der Parteien vor den Arbeitsgerichten im deutschen Reiche und im übrigen Europa.* Berlin, 1934.
Jastrow, I. *Sozialpolitik und Verwaltungswissenschaft.* Berlin, 1902. Vol. I.
Kahn Freund, Otto. *Das soziale Ideal des Reichsarbeitsgerichts.* Berlin, 1932.

Kaskel, Walter. *Die Arbeitsgerichtsbarkeit.* Arbeitsrechtliche Seminarvorträge. Berlin, 1929.
Kny, Lothar. *Die Arbeitsgerichtsbehörden.* Berlin, 1928.
Lautenschlager, Ernst. "Die Rechtsprechung im Gewerbegericht," *Jahrbuch für Gesetzgebung, Verwaltung, und Volkswirtschaft im deutschen Reich,* Vol. XVII. Leipzig, 1893.
Stieda, Wilhelm. "Das Reichsgesetz betreffend die Gewerbegerichte, vom 29. Juli 1890," *Jahrbücher für Nationalökonomie und Statistik.* Vol. LVII. Jena, 1891.
Sumner, Helen L. *Industrial Courts in France, Germany, and Switzerland.* United States Department of Commerce and Labor, Bull. No. 98 of the Bureau of Labor. Vol. XXIV. Washington, D. C., 1912.
Wunderlich, Frieda. *Labor under German Democracy. Arbitration 1918-1933.* Social Research Supplement, No. 2. New York, 1940.

Periodicals and Official Documents

Afa, *Angestelltenbewegung.* Berlin, 1921-25, 1925-28, 1928-31.
Die Arbeit. Zeitschrift für Gewerkschaftskunde, Politik und Wirtschaftskunde. Berlin.
Der Arbeitgeber. Zeitschrift der Vereinigung Deutscher Arbeitgeberverbände. Berlin.
Arbeitsrecht. Stuttgart.
Das Arbeitsgericht (formerly *Gewerbe- und Kaufmannsgericht*). Berlin.
Arbeitsrechts-Praxis. Berlin Verlagsgesellschaft des ADGB. 1928-32.
Blätter für Soziale Praxis. Frankfurt a.M., 1893-95. Merged in *Soziale Praxis,* 1895.
Deutsche Juristen-Zeitung. Berlin. Since 1937, absorbed by *Zeitschrift der Akademie für deutsches Recht.*
Deutsche Richterzeitung. Leipzig, Berlin. Since 1936, *Deutsche Rechtspflege.*
Entscheidungen des Reichsarbeitsgerichts und der Landesarbeitsgerichte. Ed. by Hermann Dersch and others. Mannheim, Berlin, Leipzig. Since 1934, called *Arbeitsrechtssammlung.*
Entscheidungen des Reichsgerichts in Zivilsachen. Berlin.
Geschäftsbericht der Vereinigung der deutschen Arbeitgeberverbände. Berlin.
Gewerkschafts-Zeitung. Organ des Allgemeinen Deutschen Gewerkschaftsbundes. Berlin. Until 1919, *Correspondenzblatt der General Kommission der Gewerkschaften Deutschlands,* and from 1920 to 1923 *Korrespondenzblatt des Allgemeinen Deutschen Gewerkschaftsbundes.*
Jahrbuch des Allgemeinen deutschen Gewerkschaftsbundes. Berlin, 1923-32.

Jahrbuch der Berufsverbände im deutschen Reich, 1930. 52 Sonderheft zum *Reichsarbeitsblatt.* Berlin.
Juristische Wochenschrift. Ed. Deutscher Anwaltsverein. Leipzig and Berlin. Since April, 1939, united with *Deutsches Recht A.*
Neue Zeitschrift für Arbeitsrecht. Mannheim, Berlin, Leipzig.
Protokoll der Verhandlungen des 11. Kongresses der Gewerkschaften Deutschlands, Leipzig, 1922. Berlin, 1922.
Protokoll der Verhandlungen des 14. Kongresses der Gewerkschaften Deutschlands. Frankfurt a.M., 1931. Berlin, 1931.
Rechenschaftsbericht des deutschnationalen Handlungsgehilfenverbandes. Hamburg.
Regierungsentwurf eines Arbeitsgerichtsgesetzes nebst Begründung. 28. Sonderheft zum *Reichsarbeitsblatt.* Berlin, 1925.
Reichsarbeitsblatt. Berlin.
Reichsgesetzblatt. Berlin.
Soziale Praxis. Berlin.
Sozialpolitisches Zentralblatt. Berlin, 1892-95. Later, *Soziale Praxis.*
Verhandlungen des 32. deutschen Juristentages. Berlin, Leipzig, 1922.
Vierteljahrshefte zur Statistik des deutschen Reichs. Berlin.
Zentralblatt der Christlichen Gewerkschaften Deutschlands. Berlin.

II. THE PERIOD OF NATIONAL SOCIALISM

Books and Articles

Burkhardt, Erich, Dersch, Hermann, and others. *Zehn Jahre Arbeitsgericht.* (See this bibliography, Part I.)
Cole, Taylor, "National Socialism and the German Labor Courts," *The Journal of Politics,* May, 1941.
Dietrich, Otto. *A Revolution of Thought.* Berlin, 1939.
Fraenkel, Ernst. *The Dual State.* New York, London, 1941.
Freisler, Roland. *Etwas über Führertum in der Rechtspflege.* Schriften der Akademie für deutsches Recht, No. 1. Berlin, 1935.
Giesebrecht, Helmut. *Das Verfahren vor den Ehrengerichten.* Berlin, 1938.
Heneman, Harlow J. "German Social Honor Courts," *Michigan Law Review,* March, 1939.
Hitler. Sozialismus wie ihn der Führer sieht. Worte des Führers zu sozialen Fragen. Zusammengestellt von F. Meystre. München, 1935.
Ipsen, Hans Peter. *Politik und Justiz.* Hamburg, 1937.
Jahrbuch der nationalsozialistischen Wirtschaft. Ed. Otto Mönkmeier. München, 1937.

BIBLIOGRAPHY

Kirchheimer, Otto. "Criminal Law in National Socialist Germany." *Studies in Philosophy and Social Science*. New York, 1939.
Koellreutter, Otto. *Der nationalsozialistische Rechtsstaat*. Die Verwaltungsakademie. Berlin, 1935.
Labour Courts. International Labour Office, Studies and Reports, Series A, No. 40. Geneva, 1938.
Loewenstein, Karl. *Hitler's Germany*. New York, 1939.
―――. "Law in the Third Reich," *Yale Law Review*, March, 1936.
SA Geist im Betrieb: Die Kampfschrift der obersten SA Führung. München, 1938.
Shartel, Burke, and Wolff, Hans Julius. "Civil Justice in Germany," *Michigan Law Review*, April, 1944.
Siebert, Wolfgang. *Das Arbeitsverhältnis in der Ordnung der Nationalen Arbeit*. Hamburg, 1935.
―――. *Das deutsche Arbeitsrecht*. Hamburg, 1938.
Der Sinn des Gesetzes zur Ordnung der nationalen Arbeit. Ed. Reichsarbeitsministerium. Berlin, 1934.
Wolf, Erik. *Richtiges Recht im nationalsozialistischen Staat*. Freiburger Universitätsreden No. 13.

Periodicals and Official Documents

Arbeitertum. Amtliches Organ der Deutschen Arbeitsfront einschliesslich NS Gemeinschaft Kraft durch Freude. Berlin.
Der Aufbau. Alleiniges amtliches Organ des Amtes für Handel und Handwerk der NSDAP und der DAF für die Reichsarbeitsgemeinschaften 17 und 18. Berlin.
Deutsche Justiz, Rechtspflege und Rechtspolitik. Amtliches Blatt der deutschen Rechtspflege. Berlin. Formerly, *Justizministerialblatt für die preussische Gesetzgebung und Rechtspflege*.
Deutsche Rechtspflege. Organ des deutschen Rechtsdienstes. United in April, 1939, with *Deutsches Recht B*.
Deutsches Recht. Zentralorgan des nationalsozialistischen Rechtswahrerbundes. Berlin, Leipzig, Wien.
Deutsche Sozialpolitik. Bericht der deutschen Arbeitsfront. Zentralbüro Sozialamt, Jan. 1-Dec. 31, 1938. Berlin.
Informationsdienst Mitteilungsblatt der NSBO. Pressestelle. 1933.
Monatshefte für NS Sozialpolitik. Stuttgart and Berlin.
Nationalsozialistisches Jahrbuch. München.
Reichsarbeitsblatt. Berlin.
Reichsgesetzblatt. Berlin.
Der Schulungsbrief. Das zentrale Monatsblatt der NSDAP und DAF. Berlin.
Soziale Praxis. Berlin.
Vierteljahrshefte zur Statistik des deutschen Reichs. Berlin.
Zeitschrift der Akademie für deutsches Recht. München and Berlin.

INDEX

Abandonment of the claim, industrial and commercial courts, 38, 47; labor courts, 73, 94
Absolutism, 13, 14, 17
Academy of German Law, 148, 223, 224
Academy of Labor, 91, 213
Accident, industrial, 4, 214
ADGB, 71, 89, 127, 132, 138, 200, 211-12, 213-14, 220, 221, 238
Administration of justice, 15, 60, 62, 107, 129, 130, 154, 155
Administrative courts, 3, 4, 5-6, 42, 78, 214
Administrative disputes, 8, 71
Admission of the claim, industrial and commercial courts, 38, 47; labor courts, 73, 74, 76, 94
Afa League, 50, 89, 90, 130, 200, 212, 220, 238
AGG. *See* Labor Court Act
Agreement for expert opinions in arbitration, 82
Agricultural Labor Decree, Federal. *See* Provisional Agricultural Labor Decree, Federal
Agricultural workers, 22, 31, 37, 40, 42, 45, 49, 84, 119, 128, 145, 176, 177, 189, 190, 225, 233; court chambers for, 31, 86; protection of, 192
Allgemeiner deutscher Gewerkschaftsbund. *See* ADGB
Allgemeiner freier Angestelltenbund. *See* Afa League
Allocation of labor, 142, 145ff., 159, 160
Amtsgericht. *See* Ordinary local court
Anthes, Hans-Georg, 115, 119, 218, 219
AOG. *See* National Socialist Labor Act
Appeal, ordinary court of, 10, 21, 28, 29, 37, 40, 214; to district labor court, 64, 75ff., 96, 99, 100, 110, 125, 155, 214; to labor courts, 104. *See also,* Commercial courts; Industrial courts; Labor courts, People's Court
Appeal for review, 76-77, 99, 100, 102, 103, 110, 155, 158; direct appeal for review, 77, 102, 103
Appointment of assessors to the labor courts. *See* Assessors, appointment
Apprentices, 23, 26, 29, 45, 59, 65, 66, 67, 79, 86, 104, 158, 195
Arbeitsfront. *See* German Labor Front
Arbeitsgerichte. *See* Labor courts
Arbeitsgerichtsgesetz, AGG. *See* Labor Court Act, Federal
Arbeitsnachweisgesetz, 1922. *See* Placement Service Act, Federal, of 1922
Arbeitsvermittlung und Arbeitslosenversicherung, Gesetz, 1927. *See* Placement and Unemployment Insurance Act, Federal, 1927
Arbitral bodies, 45, 79ff., 131ff., 156; arbitral tribunals, 79ff., 121, 131ff., 156, 215; conciliation authorities, 80, 81, 132, 156; expert opinion bodies, 80, 82, 132, 156
Arbitration, 6, 26, 31, 114, 126, 159, 182, 191; separated from adjudication, 43-44, 71
Arbitration award, 80, 122, 195-96; dispute about its legality, 6, 109, 114, 122, 196
Arbitration bodies, 45, 80, 215
Arbitration decrees, 43, 111, 138, 195, 211; ordinances to the, 126, 219, 236
ARS. *See* Entscheidungen des Reichsarbeitsgerichts und der Landesarbeitsgerichte
Assessors, appointment, 76, 77, 126ff., 154, 155, 225; appraisal, 107, 217; compensation, 213; district labor courts, 63-64, 88ff., 154; Federal Labor Court, 64, 88, 91, 154, 155, 213, 214; German Labor Front courts, 177; industrial and commercial courts, 25, 26, 27, 31, 35, 37, 41, 43, 85, 206; labor courts, 60ff., 74, 83, 85, 86, 88ff., 213; mining courts, 30; NSDAP courts, 180; social honor

241

courts, 173, 232-33; statistics, 88ff.; trade union affiliation, 86, 89ff.; training, 63, 91, 130, 213; under National Socialism, 141, 154, 155, 184
Assessors' committees, 63, 64, 131, 155
Association of German Municipalities, 126
Association of industrial and commercial courts, 36-37, 92, 209
Association of industrial courts, 92, 209
Association of labor courts, 91-92
Association of Women Commercial and Office Employees, 90
Auxiliary Service Act, Federal, 31, 190, 208, 210

Bahr, Richard, 23, 205
Baum, Georg, 219
Beamten- Besoldungs- und Versorgungsrecht. *See* Civil service law
Bendix, Ludwig, 113, 218, 219
Berggewerbegerichte. *See* Mining Courts
Berlin labor courts, 105
Beschäftigung Schwerbeschädigter. *See* Disabled men
Beschlussverfahren. *See* Summary procedure
Betriebsobmann. *See* German Labor Front, shop steward
Betriebsordnung. *See* Shop rules
Betriebsrat. *See* Works Council
Betriebsrätegesetz, BRG *See* Works Council Act, Federal
Block steward. *See* German Labor Front
Bona fide trade unions, 12, 128, 192. *See also* Trade unions
Breach of contract, 68, 70, 146, 159, 197, 226, 233
BRG. *See* Works Council Act, Federal
Buch, Walter, 166, 180, 229, 234
Bureau for Estate Organization, 139, 140
Bürgerliches Gesetzbuch. *See* Civil Code, Federal
Burkhardt, Erich, 226
Business managers, 62

Carta del lavoro, 119
Cell steward. *See* German Labor Front

Chairmen, commercial courts, 30; district labor courts, 63, 64, 87, 101; German Labor Front courts, 177; Federal Labor Court, 87; guild committees, 66; industrial courts, 25, 26, 28, 36; labor court chambers, 43, 63; labor courts, 60, 61, 66, 74, 83ff., 108; under National Socialism, 154, 155, 157; NSDAP courts, 180; social honor courts, 173; summary procedure, 78
Chambers of commerce, 39, 128; district labor courts, 63, 64, 88, 89, 216, 225; handicraft, 39, 128; industrial courts, 25, 45; labor courts, 60-61, 83ff., 105, 225; lawyers, 229; Leipzig Agreement, 141, 148. *See also* Territory of courts and chambers
Child protection, 189, 190, 235
Christian Salaried Employees' Federation. *See* Gedag
Christian trade unions, 35, 52, 89, 92, 128, 194, 200, 201, 220
Christian workmen and salaried employees. *See* DGB
Civil Code, Federal, 11, 18, 21, 111-12, 115, 116, 131, 160, 190, 205
Civil servants, 5, 61, 65-66, 160, 166-67, 172, 177, 189
Civil service law, 5, 166-67, 229
Closed shop, 180, 194, 196
Closing-Down Order, Federal, of 1920, 191-92, 236
Code of Civil Procedure, Federal, 10, 13, 16, 17, 18, 65, 72, 76, 79, 131, 197, 205, 214
Code of Criminal Procedure, Federal, 173
Code for Public Enterprises, 222
Coke, Lord, 13
Collective Agreement Decree, Federal, of 1918, 112, 138, 192-93, 236; amendments, 196-97
Collective agreements, before 1918, 27, 190; after 1918, 6, 27, 28, 47, 53, 59, 66ff., 71, 75ff., 79ff., 112ff., 121, 122, 127, 131, 144, 145, 156, 191, 192, 222, 236; achieved by conclusion, 114, 192ff.; by extension, 80, 193, 195, 215; by imposition by compulsory arbitration award, 6, 195; complaints of employers against, 196, 197; dis-

INDEX 243

putes about, 28, 66ff., 96, 101; emergency decrees interfering with, 197; guaranteed by the Joint Agreement of 1918, 193; principles of conclusion by economic associations of employers and employees only, 192 ff.; non-deviation from the agreed stipulations, 117-18, 192, 195, 197; types of regulations, normative, 194-95; obligatory, 194-95; works councils' activity, 198-99; under National Socialism, 143, 159, 222, 227

Collective bargaining before 1914, 189; promoted by military authorities, 190; sanctioned by constitution, 191

Collective disputes, 28, 31, 34, 68, 93, 96, 118ff., 131, 156, 182ff., 190. *See also* strikes

Collective rules, 143 ff, 156, 159, 160, 163, 176, 222, 223, 227

Commercial Code, Federal, 21, 190

Commercial Court Act, Federal, 30, 41ff.

Commercial courts, 30 ff, 41ff., 59, 208; administrative functions, 30, 37, 71, 208; appeal, 31, 47; appraisal, 35ff.; conciliation functions, 30, 37, 208; jurisdiction, 30, 31, 40, 43, 44, 211; organization, 30; reorganization, 43ff.; statistics, 32ff., 36, 46ff.; territory, 40, 84

Commercial employees. *See* Employees, commercial

Commissioner General of Manpower, 146, 182

Communal authorities in charge of labor disputes, 23, 24

Communist unions, 127, 201

Communists, 56, 168, 170, 185

Community of risks. *See* Works community

Company unions, 118-19, 193

Competitive clause, 30, 41, 48, 208

Complaint objects. *See* Objects of complaint

Complaints, against guild committees' decisions, 104; in summary procedure, 78, 101ff.; judgment complaints, 99; revision complaints, 78-79, 102, 103

Complaints on questions of law, 78-79, 100, 101

Concentration camps, 168, 227-28, 231

Conciliation authorities of the Arbitration Decree, 42ff., 198

Conciliation committees, during the First World War, 31, 210; of 1918, 41ff., 183, 211

Conciliation functions of industrial and commercial courts, 28, 30, 43, 207. *See also* Settlement by voluntary agreement

Confederation of Wage Earners, Salaried Employees and Civil servants. *See* Ring

Confidential council, Confidential men, 143-44, 146, 148, 155, 159, 174, 176, 178, 183, 184, 222-23

Conflicts between associations and their members, 69

Conflicts between employers and employees, 66ff., 96, 101, 102, 103, 113, 156, 183, 214; individual, 42, 79; of rights and interests, 43-44, 126, 183

Conflicts between fellow workers, 66, 67, 80, 96, 102, 103, 156

Conflicts between parties to collective agreements, 66ff., 79, 96, 101, 102, 103, 113, 156; litigation concerning the existence of a collective agreement, 67; litigation concerning the fulfillment of obligations, 67. *See also* tort actions

Conflicts out of works council relations, 66, 69, 70, 97

Conseils de prud'hommes, 22

Constitution. *See* Weimar Constitution

Constitution, of the district labor courts, 63, 64; Federal Labor Court, 64; labor courts, 60ff.

Contempt-of-court rules, 68

Contra bonos mores, 208

Contract law. *See* Labor contract

Contractors, 65, 124, 179, 220

Counsel, 8 ff., 12, 27, 55, 72, 83, 121ff., 174. *See also* Lawyers; Poor law council; Trade unions and the labor courts

Court and procedure, 12ff.; Anglo-Saxon concept of, 3, 7ff.; German concept of, 3, 4, 5ff., 12ff.

Court Fees Act, Federal. *See* Fees

244 GERMAN LABOR COURTS

Court of appeal. *See* Provincial court of appeal
Court system, 206
Criminal Code, Federal, 175, 189, 228-29
Criminal courts, 70, 71, 181, 182
Criminal law, 228-29

DAF. *See* German Labor Front
Danzer-Vanotti, August, 162, 227
Daeschner, Reichstreuhänder der Arbeit, 147
Declaratory judgment, 66ff., 131, 197
Dersch, Hermann, 214
Deutsche Arbeitsfront, DAF. *See* German Labor Front
Deutscher Gewerkschaftsbund. *See* DGB
Deutscher Städtetag. *See* Association of German Municipalities
Deutsches Beamtengesetz. *See* Civil service law
Deutsches Handelsgesetzbuch. *See* Commercial Code, Federal
Deutschnationaler Handlungsgehilfenverband. *See* DHV
DGB, 51, 89, 131, 200
DHV, 86, 89, 90, 129, 130, 132, 201, 216, 217, 220
Dietrich, Otto, 151, 224
Disabled men, 115, 192, 236
Dismissal, 27, 42, 44, 49, 70, 72, 73, 74 ff., 80, 85, 96, 101, 111, 113, 114, 160, 161, 176, 184-85, 192, 198, 206-7, 210-11, 218, 223, 224, 235; of assessors, 62, 213; of disabled men, 192; of former trade union officials, 170; of judges, 166, 167, 229; of salaried employees, 192; of war veterans, 191; of works council members, 62, 70, 97, 113, 198, 213; under National Socialism, 143, 168ff., 173, 222
District labor courts. *See* Labor courts, district
Division of power, 151
Domestic servants, 21, 40, 190, 210; chambers, 86, 105; restriction of organization, 189ff.
Dualism of party and state, 227
Duration of litigation, industrial and commercial courts, 33, 38, 48, 209; labor courts, 92-93, 95, 98 ff, 107-8, 217
Duty Year, 146

Ebel, Wilhelm, 160, 226
Ebert, Staatsanwaltschaftsrat, 167, 230
Egloff, Helmut, 147, 223
Ehren-und Disziplinarordnung der DAF. *See* German Labor Front, code of honor
Elections, industrial courts, 35, 41, 208-9. *See also* Assessors, appointment
Elite guard (SS), 165-66, 172, 177, 221, 227-28
Emergency Decrees, Federal, 72-73, 197, 214
Employees, assessors in labor courts, 61-62; commercial, 30, 40, 41, 65, 86, 105, 131, 190, 209, 211; public, 26, 40, 62, 65, 131-32, 155, 189, 197; salaried, 30, 40, 65, 79-80, 84-85, 91, 93, 105, 109, 111, 121-22, 130, 132, 150, 192, 224, 236
Employers, 65, 69, 113-14, 124, 147ff., 183; assessors in industrial and commercial courts, 35, 37; assessors in labor courts, 60ff., 155; attitude toward conciliation committees, 42; toward industrial courts, 34, 36, 37; toward labor courts, 109
Employers associations, 12, 41, 50, 54, 60, 64, 65, 68, 72, 98, 113ff., 120ff., 137, 139, 154, 191ff., 219
Employment offices, 67, 142, 146-47, 159, 184-85, 192, 195
Enemies of the state, 168ff., 231
Enabling Act, Federal, of 1933, 152
Enforcement of decisions, 28, 66, 75, 81, 174
Enterprise communities. *See* German Labor Front
Entscheidungen des Reichsarbeitsgerichts und der Landesarbeitsgerichte, ARS, 167, 171, 180, 201, 203-5, 211, 219-23, 228; RAG, 94, 141-3, 145-7, 214
Equality before the law, 167ff.
Equity, 11
Estoppel doctrine, 11

INDEX

Evidence, 8, 12, 17
Exclusion of Labor Court jurisdiction, 79ff., 131ff.
Expert opinion bodies, 80, 82

Fabricius, Hans, 234
Fachämter. *See* German Labor Front, Trade offices
Factory courts, 22
Federal Industrial Code. *See* Industrial Code
Federal Institute for Placement and Unemployment Insurance. *See* Institute for Placement and Unemployment Insurance, Federal
Federal Labor Court. *See* Labor Court, Federal
Federal Ministry of Economics. *See* Ministry of Economics, Federal
Federal Ministry of the Interior. *See* Ministry of the Interior, Federal
Federal Ministry of Justice. *See* Ministry of Justice, Federal
Federal Ministry of Labor. *See* Ministry of Labor, Federal
Federal Social Honor Court. *See* Social Honor Court, Federal
Federal State and Municipal employees. *See* Employees, public
Federal Supreme Court. *See* Supreme Court, Federal
Federal Supreme Court for Social Insurance. *See* Supreme Court for Social Insurance, Federal
Federal War Pension Act. *See* War Pension Act, Federal
Federation of employers associations, 50, 52, 191, 212
Federation of Executive Employees. *See* Vela
Federation of National Socialist German Jurists, 140
Fees, 21, 26, 38, 53, 55, 74, 76, 79, 212, 214-15
Felten, Heinz, 109, 130, 213, 216-17, 220
Fischer, Ludwig, 224
Fiscus, 5
Flatow, Georg, 90, 212, 217
Foerster, Wilhelm, 229

Follower (employee), 138, 172
Forfeiture clause, 162
Fraenkel, Ernst, 3ff., 51, 130, 164, 212, 219, 220, 227, 228
Frank, Hans, 151, 166, 224, 229
Free trade unions (socialist), 35, 50ff., 89, 92, 114, 126, 194, 200
Freedom of association, 69, 138, 156, 189, 190-91, 211, 235-36
Freedom of opinion, 213
Freisler, Roland, 153, 159, 166, 167, 224-25, 226, 229, 230
Friedrich Wilhelm (the Grand Elector), 13
Friedrich, Judge, 159, 226, 230
Führer principle, 151ff., 158-59, 163, 167, 171, 224

GDA, 89, 130, 200, 220
Gedag, 89, 200, 220
General Federation of Free Trade Unions. *See* ADGB
General Federation of Free Trade Unions of Salaried Employees. *See* Afa League
Generalbevollmächtigter für den Arbeitseinsatz. *See* Commissioner General for Manpower
Gericht. *See* Courts
Gerichtskostengesetz. *See* Fees
German confederation of trade unions. *See* DGB
German Labor Front, 138 ff., 149, 183, 220-21; authorization of lawyers, 157; block steward, 142; cell steward, 142; code of honor, 177; collection of labor court decisions, 172; courts, 177, 180, 181, 234; dues, 141, 222; enterprise communities, 140, 149, 184; legal advisory offices, 141-42, 157-58, 184, 222, 235; local stewards, 142; membership, 140, 142, 170, 171; nomination of assessors, 155, 184, 233; organization for Germans abroad, 141, 222; shop stewards, 141, 142, 149, 171, 184, 222; strength through joy, 141, 142; trade offices, 140, 184; and trade unions, 220-21
German National Trade Union of Commercial Employees. *See* DHV
Gesamtverband der Christlichen Ge-

werkschaften. See Christian trade unions
Gesamtverband Deutscher Angestelltengewerkschaften. See Gedag
Gesetz über den vaterländischen Hilfsdienst. See Auxiliary Service Act, Federal
Gesetz zur Ordnung der nationalen Arbeit, AOG. See National Socialist Labor Act
Gestapo, 149, 164, 165, 185, 227-28, 231, 233, 234
Gewerbegericht, Das (periodical), 209
Gewerbe-und Kaufmannsgericht, Das (periodical), 37, 92, 209
Gewerbegerichte. See Industrial Courts
Gewerbegerichtsgesetz, GGG. See Industrial Court Act, Federal
Gewerbeordnung, GO. See Industrial Code
Gewerkschaftsbund, Deutscher. See DGB
Gewerkschaftsbund der Angestellten. See GDA
Gewerkschaftsring Deutscher Arbeiter-, Angestellten- und Beamtenverbände. See Ring
GGG. See Industrial Court Act, Federal
Giesebrecht, Helmut, 234
GO. See Industrial Code
Goebbels, 147, 158
Goering, Hermann, 147, 223
Goerrig, Franz, 223
Guild arbitral courts, 23, 24, 29, 31, 37, 40, 45, 59, 84
Guild committees, 29, 45, 66, 104, 158, 215
Guilds, 23, 59, 66
Gürtner, Franz, 152, 224
Gusko, Kurt, 175, 233
Gütestelle. See Conciliation authorities

Handelsgesetzbuch. See Commercial Code, Federal
Heimarbeitsgesetz, 1911, 1934. See Home workers
Hellwig, Werner, 235
Herschel, Wilhelm, 92, 227
Herzog, Herbert, 219

Hildebrandt, Camp Commander, 230
Hirsch-Duncker trade unions (liberal), 89, 194, 200, 209, 220
Hitler, Adolf, 13, 140, 152, 163, 165 ff., 224, 228, 230, 231
Hitler Youth, 170, 221, 228, 234
Home workers, 22, 28, 65, 139, 148, 163, 190, 192, 227
Hours of work, 85, 191, 192, 196, 216
Huber, Ernst Rudolf, 160, 164, 222, 226, 228
Hugenberg, Alfred, 225

Illinger, Ludwig, 172
Industrial Code, Federal Industrial Code, 21, 23-24, 138, 189-90; Prussian Industrial Code of 1845, 22, 205
Industrial Court Act, Federal, 24, 41ff., 54, 121, 205, 206; amendment of 1901, 25, 35, 206; amendment of 1922, 41ff.
Industrial courts, *prior to 1891*, courts of the Industrial Code, 23, 205; guild courts, 23, 24; Prussian courts, 22, 23, 205; Rhenish courts, 22, 23, 24, 205; Saxon courts, 23, 205; *after 1891*, 25ff., 59; administrative functions, 29, 37, 71, 207; appeal, 28, 36, 41; appraisal, 35 ff.; chambers, 25, 206; conciliation functions, 28, 34, 37, 207; costs, 206; elections, 26, 35, 208, 209; jurisdiction, 26-27, 40, 41, 43, 44; organization, 25ff.; procedure, 27, 28; reorganization, 43ff.; statistics, 32, 34, 36, 46ff., 208-9; territory, 40, 45, 84
Injunctions, 68, 69, 77
Innungen. See Guilds
Innungsausschüsse. See Guild committees
Innungschiedsgerichte. See Guild arbitral courts
Insidious attack against state and party, Federal Act against, 229
Invalidity and old age insurance, 71
Inventions, 67, 70
Ipsen, Hans Peter, 164, 228
Israel, Gertrud, 129, 220

Jastrow, Ignaz, 21, 39, 54, 205, 207, 209, 210, 213, 217

INDEX

Jehovah's witnesses, 168
Jews, 149, 166, 168ff., 185, 228, 231, 232
Joint Agreement of the Federation of Employers Organizations and Trade Unions, November 1918, 191, 193
Jonas, Martin, 226
Judges, in district labor courts, 63-64, 87; in Federal Labor Court, 64, 87; in German Labor Front courts, 177; in industrial courts, 25, 28; in labor courts, 60, 62, 87; in NSDAP courts, 180; in social honor courts, 173-74; independence of, 17, 41, 165ff., 229; judges as civil servants, 14, 15, 166; labor's attitude toward, 50-51; learned and lay judges, 8, 10ff., 39, 60, 64, 92; People's Court, 228; position in the legal system, 12, 13ff.; separation of bench and bar, 13; under National Socialism, 153, 165ff., 185-86, 229. *See also* Chairmen, Assessors
Judgments, commercial courts, 33, 47; industrial courts, 33, 38, 47; labor courts, 94ff.; district labor courts 99-100; Federal Labor Court, 102
Judgments by default, industrial and commercial courts, 38, 47, 73, 76; labor courts, 94, 101
Jurisdiction, of courts in general, 4, 6; of comercial courts, 30-31, 45; of guild arbitral courts, 29; of industrial courts, 26-27, 40, 41, 43, 45; of labor courts, 65ff., 120, 156, 163, 172ff., 181ff.
Jury trial, 7, 8, 11
Justice, National Socialist conception of, 151ff.
"Justizlose Hoheitsakte," 164
Justizverwaltung. *See* Administration of justice

Kahn Freund, Otto, 53-54, 119, 212, 217-19
Karger, Walter von, 130, 220
Kaskel, Walter, 51, 212
Kaufmannsgericht. *See* Commercial court
Kaufmannsgerichtsgesetz, KGG. *See* Commercial Court Act, Federal

Kerrl, Hans, 231
KGG. *See* Commercial Court Act, Federal
Kinderschutzgesetz. *See* Child protection
Kirchheimer, Otto, 229
Kleeis, Friedrich, 127, 220
Knappschaftsgesetz. *See* Miners' Insurance Act, Federal
Koellreuter, Otto, 164, 228
Kraft durch Freude. *See* German Labor Front, strength through joy
Kreis-und Ortsgerichte der NSDAP. *See* NSDAP courts

Labor contract, German civil law, 5, 8, 21, 22, 23, 27, 44, 52, 66, 67, 79, 117, 189ff., 211; National Socialist law, 137ff., 160ff., 172ff., 181, 183. *See also* Labor law
Labor Court, Federal, 59-60, 64, 79, 84; contested decisions, 113ff., 127-28, 162, 216; organization, 64, 72; procedure, 76ff., 110-11; statistics, 102-3; under National Socialism, 155, 157
Labor Court Act, 1926, Federal, 7, 13, 16, 18, 30, 59ff., 131; 1934 amendment, 151, 154ff.; 1935 amendment, 157; bills, 55-56
Labor courts, 59ff., 154; appeal, 75-76, 107; appraisal, 106ff.; authorities, 59ff.; chambers, 43, 45, 47, 49, 59, 60, 84ff., 216; character of, 15, 16; competition with social honor courts, 175, 181-82; constitution, 15, 50-51, 60ff., 154-55; decrease in cases, 182, 184-85, 235; jurisdiction, 65ff., 156, 163; organization, 60ff.; procedure, 71ff., 112, 153, 156ff.; reform discussion, 47, 49ff., 158, 159; self-government, 154-55; statistics, 84ff., 92ff.; territory, 60, 83ff., 215-16; under National Socialism, 151ff.
—District, 59, 60, 63-64; chairmen, 63, 64, 87, 101; chambers, 63; organization, 63-64, 213-14, 216; procedure, 76-77; statistics, 87-89, 99ff.; territory, 84, 215-16; under National Socialism, 155
Labor law, 40, 110ff.; before 1918,

189ff.; Committee for the Creation of Unified Labor Law, 40, 55; courses in, 51, 52, 63, 212, 213; after 1918, 112 ff, 191 ff. See also Labor contract
Labor relations under National Socialism, 166ff.
Labor service, 146, 177, 223
Lammers, Hans Heinrich, 234
Landarbeitsordnung, Verordnung über eine vorläufige. See Provisional Agricultural Labor Decree, Federal
Landesarbeitsgericht. See Labor courts, district
Landgericht. See Ordinary district court
Landsberger, M., 209, 211
Lautenschlager, Ernst, 106, 109, 206, 217
Law merchant, 18
Lawyers, industrial courts, 27; under National Socialism, 157-58, 231; admission, 12, 13, 27 49, 52ff., 71ff., 110, 120ff., 157-58, 226
Lawyers Code, Federal, of 1935, 229; of 1936, 166, 229
Lawyers fees, 72-73, 74, 76
Laymen in German courts, 8, 10ff, 49, 60. See also Assessors, Judges
Leaving certificate, 31, 208
Legal advisory offices of the German Labor Front. See German Labor Front
Legal advisory offices of the NSDAP. See NSDAP
Lersch, Dr., 227
Ley, Robert, 139ff., 147, 220
Luppe, Hermann, 51, 212

Mandatory, summary and small cases, 22, 205
Marine offices, 30, 70, 156, 208, 214
Mason, John Brown, 180, 234
Mehnert, Fritz, 234
Meystre, Fritz, 165, 229
Michel, Max, 129, 220
Military courts, 177
Miners' Insurance Act, Federal, 128, 220
Mining courts, 24, 29-30, 40, 45, 59, 85, 86, 207, 208

Mining laws, 21, 190
Ministry of Commerce and Industry, Prussian, 60, 128, 212
Ministry of Economics, Federal, 139, 140, 153, 157
Ministry of the Interior, Federal, 228
Ministry of Justice, Federal, 64, 153 ff, 157, 225, 231
Ministry of Justice, Prussian, 128, 174, 212, 231
Ministry of Labor, Federal, 40, 55, 60, 64, 77, 139, 140, 153, 154, 157, 174, 176, 183-84, 215
Ministry of Labor and Public Welfare, 15, 60
Ministry of Transportation, Federal, 140
Mobility of labor, 145
Mönckmeier, Otto, 223
Montesquieu, 17
Moser von Filseck, 165, 229
Müller, Heinrich, 166, 229
Multiplicity of jurisdictions, 181-82

National Chamber of Culture, 140, 155, 157
National Economic Council. See Provisional National Economic Council
National Socialist German Workers Party. See NSDAP
National Socialist Labor Act, 138ff., 147ff., 172, 221, 222
Nationalsozialistische Deutsche Arbeiterpartei. See NSDAP
Nationalsozialistische Betriebszellenorganisation. See NSBO
Natural law, 17
Neesse, Gottfried, 227
Neumann, Franz, 119, 218
Nipperdey, Hans Carl, 163
Non-militant unions, 119, 127-28, 153, 193, 200, 220, 225
Nörpel, Clemens, 53, 71, 121, 123, 132, 212, 214, 219, 220
Northwestern iron and steel industry, law suit in the, 6, 96, 122, 196
NSBO, 154, 225
NSDAP, 5, 138, 163, 165, 170, 171, 213, 228, 230; committees for investigation and arbitration, 180; courts,

INDEX 249

180ff., 234; legal advisory offices, 222; philosophy, 151ff., 160
Nulla poena sine lege, 228

Oberlandesgericht. *See* Provincial court of appeal
Oberstes Parteigericht der NSDAP. *See* NSDAP courts
Objects of complaint, industrial and commercial courts, 27, 48-49, 206, 207, 208; labor court system, 96, 101ff.
Offenses against social honor, 172ff.
Ordinary courts, 3, 45, 55, 59, 65, 70, 72, 83-84, 92, 112, 169, 181, 182, 214, 215; jurisdiction in labor conflicts, 30-31
Ordinary district court, 28, 45, 60, 63, 84, 215
Ordinary local court, 45, 60, 84, 93, 215
Ordinary procedure, 153, 156, 157
Ordnung der nationalen Arbeit, Gesetz zur. *See* National Socialist Labor Act.
Ortsobmann. *See* German Labor Front, local steward

Pachteinigungsämter. *See* Tenant protection courts
People's Court, 228-29
Penalties for offenses against social honor. *See* Social honor courts
Pfundtner, Hans, 234
Placement and Unemployment Insurance Act, Federal, of 1927, 126, 219; Institute, Federal, 152
Placement Service Act, Federal, of 1922, 126, 219
Plenipotentiary for the Total War Effort, 147
Political justice, 163ff., 185-86
Poor law counsel, 21, 55, 72, 73, 98, 125, 158, 226
Potthoff, Heinz, 51, 66, 212, 216
Precedents, 11, 12, 15, 18, 110-11, 123
Prenner, Hans, 210
Prerogative state, characteristics, 164ff.; abolishment of equality before the law, 167ff.; abolishment of the objectivity, impartiality and independence of the judge, 165ff.; removal of the political sphere from the jurisdiction of law, 164ff.
Presiding committee of the district court, 194
Prestige of the worker, 149, 150
Probivirial courts. *See* Conseils de prud'hommes
Procedure, arbitral bodies, 81; civil procedure, 8ff., 17, 27, 39, 72-73, 76, 79, 108, 153, 209; industrial courts, 27-28
Procedure of German courts, 9ff., 13
Procedure of the labor court authorities, 15-16, 71ff., 108, 156-57; district labor courts, 72, 76-77; Federal Labor Court, 76ff., 110-11. *See also* Summary procedure
Procedure, summary. *See* Summary procedure
Proclamation of the German government of November 12, 1918, 191, 235
Protective custody, 227
Protective legislation, 189 ff, 191ff.
Provincial court of appeal, 214
Provisional Agricultural Labor Decree, Federal, 42, 192, 211, 236
Provisional labor courts, 43ff., 45, 47
Provisional National Economic Council, 42, 45, 56, 71, 128
Prussian courts, 22, 23, 205
Prussian Industrial Code. *See* Industrial Code
Prussian Ministry of Commerce and Industry. *See* Ministry of Commerce and Industry, Prussian
Prussian Ministry of Justice. *See* Ministry of Justice, Prussian
Public law, 5ff., 65, 68, 78, 114, 160, 226

Radbruch, Gustav, 51-52, 212
RAG collection of court decisions. *See* Entscheidungen des Reichsarbeitsgerichts und der Landesarbeitsgerichte, RAG
Railway, chambers, 45, 49, 86; workers, 40, 78, 189, 190
Rechtsanwaltsordnung. *See* Lawyers' Code, Federal

250 GERMAN LABOR COURTS

Rechtsbeschwerde. *See* Complaints on questions of law
Rechtsbetreuungsstellen der NSDAP. *See* NSDAP, legal advisory offices
Rechtsstellen der Deutschen Arbeitsfront. *See* German Labor Front, legal advisory offices
Referendar, 124-25, 219, 230-31
Reformatio in peius as National Socialist principle, 174
Reich Agrarian League, 154
Reich Food Estate, 140, 155
Reich Trustee of Labor, 139ff., 143ff., 156, 173ff., 178, 183-84, 221, 227
Reichsarbeitsgericht. *See* Labor Court, Federal
Reichsbesoldungsordnung, Abänderung, 1937, 231
Reichsbetriebsgemeinschaften. *See* German Labor Front
Reichsehrengerichtshof. *See* Social Honor Court, Federal
Reichsgericht. *See* Supreme Court, Federal
Reichsknappschaftsgesetz. *See* Miners' Insurance Act, Federal
Reichslandbund. *See* Reich Agrarian League
Reichsnährstand. *See* Reich Food Estate
Reichstag, 24, 55, 56, 62, 69, 71, 120, 121, 125, 152, 224, 231
Reichstag fire, 228
Reichstreuhänder der Arbeit, RTA. *See* Reich Trustee of Labor
Reichsversicherungsamt. *See* Supreme Court for Social Insurance, Federal
Reichsversicherungsordnung RVO. *See* Social Insurance Code, Federal
Reichsversorgungsgesetz. *See* War Pension Act, Federal
Reichswirtschaftsrat, Vorläufiger. *See* Provisional National Economic Council
Renunciation of the claim. *See* Abandonment of the claim
Representation in Labor Courts, 52ff, 98, 121ff., 157-58. *See also* Counsel; Lawyers' admission; Poor law counsel; Trade unions and the labor courts

Reuss, Hermann, 165, 228
Rhenish courts, 22, 23, 24, 205
Richelieu, 13
Ring, 89, 200
Roesner, Ernst, 217
Rohlfing, Theodor, 217, 235
Roll calls, 148
Rosenberg, Alfred, 232
RTA. *See* Reich Trustee of Labor
RVO. *See* Social Insurance Code
RWR. *See* Provisional National Economic Council

SA. *See* Storm troops
Salaried employees. *See* Employees, salaried
Salary Act, Federal, amendment of 1937, 221
Sauckel, Fritz, 146
Saxon courts, 23, 205
Schiedsgerichte, *See* Arbitral bodies; arbitral tribunals
Schiedsgutachtenvertrag. *See* Agreement for expert opinions in arbitration
Schleicher, M., 132, 220
Schlichtungswesen. *See* Arbitration
Schmitt, Carl, 225
Schönberg, Gustav, 205
Schools for Economics and Administration, 213
Seamen, 66, 70, 156
Seamen's Code, Federal, 208, 214
Seemannsämter. *See* Marine offices
Seemannsordnung. *See* Seamen's Code, Federal
Seldte, Franz, 227
Self-government of the German Courts, 154-55
Senates of the Federal Labor Court, 64, 214
Settlement by voluntary agreement, 15-16, 92, 94; district labor courts and Federal Labor Court, 76, 100ff.; guild courts, 104; industrial and commercial courts, 27, 28, 38, 47; labor courts, 73-74, 92, 94, 108-9, 184, 217
Shop rules, 70, 143ff., 163, 176, 223
Shop steward. *See* German Labor Front

INDEX 251

Shop troops, 148
Siebert, Wolfgang, 160, 222, 226, 235
Simson, Gerhard, 217
Sinzheimer, Hugo, 51, 52, 211-12
Social Honor Court, Federal, 168, 173ff.
Social honor courts, 143, 146, 169, 172ff., 181-82, 225, 233; appraisal, 176-77; decisions, 168, 175ff., 233-34; organization, 173; penalties for offenses against social honor, 173, 176, 179, 233-34; procedure, 173-74; statistics, 176ff., 234; termination of cases, 179
Social insurance, 4, 71, 78, 189, 192, 214
Social Insurance Code, Federal, 206, 214
Social insurance courts, 4, 71, 111, 141, 189, 206, 214
Soziale Ehrengerichte. *See* Social honor courts
Soziale Praxis (SP), 209
Sports, 148, 149, 223-24, 230
Sprungrevision. *See* Appeal for review, direct
SS. *See* Elite guard
Staatspolizei, geheime. *See* Gestapo
Städtetag. *See* Association of German Municipalities
State courts, 45, 206
Statistics, 1901-1918, 32ff., 38; 1919-1927, 45ff.; 1927-1939, 87-89, 92ff., 94ff.; Social honor courts, 176ff., 234
Steelhelmet self-help, 154, 225
Stehr, Konrad, 123, 219
Steinmann, 233
Stieda, Wilhelm, 207
Storm troops (SA), 165, 180, 181, 221, 230, 231, 234
Strafgesetzbuch. *See* Criminal Code, Federal
Strafprozessordnung. *See* Code of Criminal Procedure, Federal
Strength through joy. *See* German Labor Front
Strike, 26, 35, 69, 115ff., 156, 160, 176, 189, 233. *See also* Collective disputes
Summary procedure, 42, 65, 66, 69-70, 72, 77ff., 97, 98ff., 156

Supreme Court, Federal, 55, 60, 64, 76-77, 111, 114-15, 153, 165, 169-70, 196, 206, 214, 218, 229, 232, 236
Supreme Court for Social Insurance, Federal, 111, 114, 171, 232
Syrup, Friedrich, 152

Tarifordnung. *See* Collective rules
Tarifverträge, Arbeiter- und Angestelltenausschüsse und Schlichtung von Arbeitsstreitigkeiten, Verordnung über. *See* Collective Agreement Decree
Technical employees, 26, 65, 105, 210
Tenant protection courts, 51
Territory of courts and chambers, 83ff., 215
Thierack, Otto Georg, 152
Töwe, 159, 226
Tort action, 5, 8, 44, 59, 66ff., 96, 101-2
Trade offices. *See* German Labor Front
Trade union League of Salaried Employees *See* GDA
Trade unions, 12, 26, 27, 30, 31, 69, 89, 106, 108, 113, 114, 153, 236; after 1918, 41, 50, 191ff., 200-1; before 1918, 189, 190; definition, 193; under National Socialism, 137-38, 149, 153-54, 156, 220-21
Trade unions and the labor courts, 50ff., 60, 64, 65, 69, 89ff., 120ff.; agreed arbitral bodies, 121, 132-33; appointment of assessors, 60, 62, 126ff., attitude toward chambers, 85; toward conciliation committees, 41; toward industrial and commercial courts, 34; toward Federal Labor Court, 115, 118ff.; representation in courts, 12, 52-53, 55, 71, 83-84, 98, 121ff., 130
Trade unions and works councils, 197ff.
Training for bench and bar, 230-31
Trustee of Labor. *See* Reich Trustee of Labor.

Umbreit, Paul, 51, 212
Unemployment insurance, 4, 71, 192, 218

Union of Salaried Employees. See ZdA

Vacation right, 114, 159, 161-62, 218
Value of object of litigation, district labor courts, 99; Federal Labor Court, 102; industrial and commercial courts, 34, 48; labor courts, 92, 95
Vaterländischer Hilfsdienst. See Auxiliary Service Act, Federal
Vela, 201
Verband Deutscher Arbeitsgerichte. See Association of Labor Courts
Verband Deutscher Gewerbegerichte. See Association of Industrial Courts
Verband weiblicher Handels- und Büroangestellten. See Association of Women Comercial and Office Employees
Vereinigung der Arbeitgeberverbände. See Federation of Employers Associations.
Vereinigung der Gewerbe- und Kaufmannsgerichte. See Association of Industrial and Commercial Courts
Vereinigung leitender Angestellten. See Vela
Vertrauensmann. See Confidential men
Vertrauensrat. See Confidential council
Volksgerichtshof. See People's Court
Vorläufige Landarbeitsordnung, Verordnung über eine. See Provisional Agricultural Labor Decree
Vorläufiger Reichswirtschaftsrat, RWR. See Provisional National Economic Council

Wage disputes, 49
Wage regulation, 145, 163, 227
Waivers of wages, 113, 117-18, 162-63
War Pension Act, Federal, 42, 211
War veterans, 42, 49, 191, 236

Weimar Constitution, 53, 78, 138, 177, 191, 193, 213, 229
Wettbewerbsklausel. See Competitive clause
Withdrawal of complaint, industrial and commercial courts, 38, 47; labor courts, 73, 74, 76, 94, 98, 100, 184
Witnesses, 8ff., 16, 73, 81, 165, 228
Wölbling, Paul, 50, 55, 211, 213
Women, 26, 37, 41; assessors, 90, 91, 180, 233; dismissal, 171; in the legal profession, 166, 229; sex relations, 175
Workbook, 145-46, 223, 226
Workers' committees, 31, 190
Workmen's compensation, 4, 141, 214
Works community, Federal Labor Court and Federal Supreme Court decisions, 115ff., 218; National Socialist, 138, 160, 170, 172, 175, 183. See also Labor contract, National Socialist law
Works council, 41ff., 49, 54, 62, 65, 66, 69-70, 72, 73, 75ff., 90, 97, 113, 143, 144, 156, 159, 182, 189, 191, 197-98, 210-11
Works Council Act, Federal, 41ff., 49, 69-70, 75, 78, 115, 116, 138, 189, 192, 197, 236
Works representation. See Works Council
Works rules. See Shop rules
Wunderlich, Frieda, 44, 211, 217, 236

Yellow dog contract, 211
Yellow unions. See Company unions; Non-militant unions
Youth protection, 148

ZdA, 90, 216
Zentralverband der Angestellten. See ZdA
Ziemer, Gregor, 235
Zivilprozessordnung, ZPO. See Code of Civil Procedure, Federal

www.ingramcontent.com/pod-product-compliance
Lightning Source LLC
Chambersburg PA
CBHW021358290426
44108CB00010B/299